Also by or translated by Royall Tyler

JAPANESE TALES

FRENCH FOLKTALES

JAPANESE NŌ DRAMAS

THE MIRACLES OF THE KASUGA DEITY

THE TALE OF GENJI

MISTRESS ORIKU: STORIES FROM A TOKYO TEAHOUSE

THE GLASS SLIPPER AND OTHER STORIES

THE ISE STORIES (with Joshua Mostow)

FLOWERS OF GRASS

THE TALE OF THE HEIKE

BEFORE *HEIKE* AND AFTER: *HŌGEN, HEIJI, JŌKYŪKI*

TO HALLOW GENJI: A TRIBUTE TO NOH

A READING OF THE TALE OF GENJI

A GREAT VALLEY UNDER THE STARS

UNDER CURROCKBILLY

FOURTEENTH-CENTURY VOICES I

   TAKEMUKI-GA-KI

Fourteenth-Century Voices II

FROM *BAISHŌRON* TO *NANTAIHEIKI*

From *BAISHŌRON* to *NANTAIHEIKI*

Royall Tyler

with

Thomas D. Conlan
and
Shuzo Uyenaka

BLUE-TONGUE BOOKS
Charley's Forest NSW Australia

CONTENTS

This life is like a dream. Grant me, I humbly beg, aspiration to enlightenment and a happy rebirth. I long more and more I long to withdraw from the world. Vouchsafe true aspiration and turn my karma in this life to fortunate rebirth in the next. Confer upon Tadayoshi my present karma and keep him from harm.

> Prayer by Ashikaga Takauji,
> Kenmu 3.8.17 [1336].

How have you been since you went down from Kyoto? I worry, you know. Here, on 5.22, Akiie, the governor of Mutsu, was killed in Izumi, between Tennōji and Sakai. His head was presented for inspection. Miraculously, Hachiman and Sumiyoshi appeared, plainly visible, in the midst of the battle, and a good half-dozen ships lay burned out and sunk. Such was the gods' will. It filled me with hope for the future.

> Uesugi Kiyoko, mother of
> Takauji and Tadayoshi,
> in a letter to one of them,
> Engen 3.5.27 [1338].

Notes overleaf

(1) Takauji's prayer: *Dainihon Shiryō*, series 6, vol. 3, *hoi*, p. 3. Although not to be taken literally, it expresses a pious medieval ideal. For a brief discussion, see Thomas D. Conlan, *State of War*, Center for Japanese Studies, University of Michigan, 2003, pp. 183-184.

(2) Uesugi Kiyoko's letter: *Nanbokuchō ibun*, Kantō-hen, vol. 1, no. 835 ("Uesugi Kiyoko shōsoku"), Tōkyōdō Shuppan, 2007, pp. 300-1. The recipient must have been one of her sons, probably Tadayoshi. Full text and translation at :

http://komonjo.princeton.edu/shoguns-mother/

The battle, *Ishizu no tatakai* (Engen 3.5.22), was fought on the shore at Izumi Sakai between Kitabatake Akiie and Takauji's chief lieutenant, Kō no Moronao.

FOREWORD

This book is a product of the friendship between me and Royall Tyler that began years back, on September 26, 2010, when, while translating *The Tale of the Heike,* he contacted me with a question about the caltrop (*hishi*), a rare weapon. Royall and I then became regular correspondents on topics ranging from medieval Japan to blue-tongue skinks.

I mentioned to Royall that I would be keen to see *Baishōron* translated. We then discovered that Dr. Shuzo Uyenaka was willing to make his translation of this text available to us to republish. When it was clear that there would be more space in the book, Royall and I both considered other texts and, bit by bit, the book became what it is now, concentrating on eye-witness accounts.

It will be apparent to the reader that these accounts are by supporters of the Northern Court and the Ashikaga. We found no eye-witness prose accounts of the Southern Court, the line through which the imperial succession is formally traced. So, in this book the famous figures of the Southern Court appear as enemies and rebels.

While the texts are quite varied, they are all poignant when set against the history of the time. For example, the writer of *Baishōron* finished his account with praise of Ashikaga Takauji and Tadayoshi, just as the brothers challenged each other in a struggle that left Tadayoshi dead and nearly destroyed the Northern Court and the Ashikaga. Nijō Yoshimoto's account of his trip to Mino includes the expected poems on famous sights, but, unusually for a travel diary, it also includes descriptions of his illness, the miserable accommodations and bad weather at Mino, and his fear. We see Takauji arrive at the camp through his eyes. In *Gen'ishū* one of Takauji's supporters, a warrior from the east, tells the story of the destructive battle thanks to which Takauji barely reconquered the capital in 1355. The two pieces by Imagawa Ryōshun, when set side by side, show the mature man travelling to Kyushu to quell the enemies of the Ashikaga, then the old man reflecting that he should instead have retired to his province to write poetry and not served so well that he came to be seen as a threat. While not first-person accounts, two short passages from *Taiheiki* are included to fill in some gaps in the story, such as the kidnapping of the reigning and retired Northern Court emperors by the temporarily resurgent Southern forces.

I was particularly interested in *Baishōron*, which I read as a graduate student, so I took on the task of updating the annotations and writing the introduction for it. Otherwise, the translations, introductions, and annotations are Royall's. But *Fourteenth Century Voices* is a joint effort in that it would not exist without our collaboration. In presenting it we hope to bring to life for interested readers the experiences of people who lived through a time when everything we think we know about Japan was in doubt.

Thomas D. Conlan
Princeton University

PREFACE

Taiheiki deserves a few more words than its bare mention in the preface to *Fourteenth-Century Voices I*. The forty *kan* of this vast, anonymous work (several volumes in any modern edition) dominates knowledge of fourteenth-century history. Perhaps one day someone will translate it all. For the moment, the translator of documents like these may feel acutely aware of *not* doing so.

However, that is not to question these documents' value. For one thing, the chronological accuracy of *Taiheiki* is not beyond dispute. Tom Conlan discusses that issue, with examples, in his introduction to *Baishōron* and pronounces *Baishōron*, for what it covers, more reliable. He also mentions a detectable anti-Northern Court bias. In *Nantaiheiki*, Imagawa Ryōshun castigates *Taiheiki* for its mistakes and omissions and reports this remark by Ashikaga Tadayoshi: "As far as I can see, [*Taiheiki*] contains an extraordinary number of errors...,It cannot be allowed to circulate." None of the passages to which Ryōshun personally objected, on behalf of the Imagawa line, survives in extant texts. Still, as a chronicle *Taiheiki* is imperfect. How could it be otherwise?

Moreover, one need not read much of *Taiheiki* to notice that its narrative is often colorful, ornamented, even theatrical in character. That does not necessarily indicate factual error, but one notes many possible concessions to the temptation to embroider for dramatic effect. Saionji Kinmune's death (translated in *Voices I*) may not have occurred precisely as described, and one need not take literally this doleful touch, after his grieving wife's return home: "From an old branch, an owl cried eerily into a desolate dawn." Perhaps Cloistered Emperor Kōgon really was knocked off a bridge into a river, in *Voices II*, by ruffians who renounced the world when they discovered who the poor old monk had been, and who vowed thereafter to serve him hand and foot; but perhaps not. The two *Taiheiki* passages about Kōgon included here serve their purpose, which is to illustrate the fate of a representative figure already prominent in *Voices I*. However, one may take some of the omniscient narrator's details with a grain of salt.

Seen from this perspective, the principal documents translated here and in *Voices I* assume fresh significance. As a personal record, *Takemuki-ga-ki* is poles apart from *Taiheiki*, and some key passages in *Baishōron* are clearly by an eyewitness. Nijō Yoshimoto's miseries in *Ojima no kuchizusami*, and his determined optimism about the future, are personally revealing; the *Gen'ishū* account of the battle of Tōji rings true; and *Michiyukiburi* conveys a strong impression of Ryōshun the man. As for *Nantaiheiki*, surely nothing else written by a fourteenth-century warrior approaches it in personal power.

Of Pine and Plum:

BAISHŌRON

Translated by Shuzo Uyenaka

Introduced and annotated by Thomas Conlan

INTRODUCTION

Among written accounts of medieval Japanese warfare, *Baishōron* remains relatively obscure.[1] *Taiheiki*, the more popular and far larger chronicle of the age, overshadowed it for centuries.[2] While *Taiheiki* recounts a generation of warfare in forty chapters and over a thousand pages, *Baishōron,* just over a tenth as long, covers six years in detail.

Baishōron's survival is remarkable, since the work was ideologically obsolescent when it was written. It recounts the glory of the Ashikaga brothers Takauji, the first shogun, and Tadayoshi. These two founded a warrior government and worked together until 1350, when they became embroiled in a mortal struggle known as the Kannō no jōran (the Kannō Anarchy, 1350-52). This conflict resulted in Tadayoshi's death and the near destruction of the Ashikaga regime. By presenting an early justification of Ashikaga rule, *Baishōron* is critical to under-standing why Takauji and Tadayoshi succeeded so well between 1333 until 1350. The only comparable surviving monuments to their authority consists of two remarkable portraits, one of Takauji and one Tadayoshi, likewise executed before 1350.[3]

The earliest reference to *Baishōron* dates from 1420,[4] and the oldest manuscripts of it date from the time of the Ōnin War (1467-77).

---

[1] Ogawa Makoto found 20 variants among 23 surviving texts, the vast majority copied during the Tokugawa period (1600-1868) but some early ones dating from the fifteenth century (Ogawa Makoto, *"Baishōron* shohon no kenkyū hosetsu" *Kokugakuin zasshi* vol. 80 no. 11 [1966]: 181-98).

[2] Hyōdō Hiromi, *Taiheiki "yomi" no kanōsei* (Kōdansha, 1995), particularly pp. 178–79, and Wakao Masaki, *"Taiheiki yomi" no jidai* (Heibonsha, 1999) discuss the significance of this work in the early modern era.

[3] Yonekura Michio, *Minamoto Yoritomo zō* (Heibonsha, 1995). Yonekura has shown that Tadayoshi's portrait was long mistaken for Minamoto Yoritomo's, while Takauji's was thought to have been Taira no Shigemori's. A third, of the second shogun, Yoshiakira, was later added to this collection.

[4] A catalog dating from Ōei 27.11.13 (1420) shows that Prince Sadafusa owned *Baishōron* along with texts such as *Heike, Hōgen monogatari, Heiji monogatari, Jōkyū*

However, the work attracted little attention until it was copied again in the seventeenth century.[5] Late in that century, scholars became interested in *Taiheiki* and published a comparative analysis of its variant texts, entitled *Sankō Taiheiki*. The *Sankō Taiheiki* compilers dismissed *Baishōron* as being riddled with errors and characterized it as unreliable because it repeatedly contradicted *Taiheiki*.[6]

Japanese historians more rigorously debated the reliability of sources during the Meiji era (1868-1912), while the state promoted the compilation of *Dainihon shiryō*, a voluminous chronological compendium of historical sources. The process of compiling this work revealed the inaccuracies of *Taiheiki*, which Suga Masatomo argued was filled with errors and omissions. In so doing he relied on fourteenth century documents and on *Baishōron*, which he introduced to a scholarly audience in 1890.[7] His work, expanded in 1894, remained for decades the definitive study of *Baishōron*.[8]

---

monogatari, and *Taiheiki*. See Kunaichō Shoryōbu hen, *Kanmon nikki shihai monjo; Kanmon nikki bekki* (Tenri: Yōtokusha, 1965), doc. 149, Ōei 27.11.13 Monogatari mokuroku, pp. 219-21 (273-74). This was first noted by Ichizawa Tetsu, "*Baishōron* ni okeru Kenmu sannen Ashikaga Takauji seisō no ichi—mō hitotsu no Tadarahama kassen Minatogawa kassen," *Kōbe daigaku shigaku nenpō* 16 (2001): 104-24.

[5] A 1466 (Kanshō 7) copy of the latter half of *Baishōron* is the oldest datable version, while the *Kyōdaibon*, copied in the sixth month of Bunmei 2 (1470), is the oldest verifiable complete text. See Yashiro et al., eds., "Kaidai," *Baishōron*, p. 17 for the date of the *Kyōdaibon*. The Tenri version's earlier date of 1442 appears to have been written in later. For the most detailed analysis, see Takahashi Sadaichi, "Kyōdaibon Baishōron kaisetsu,"*Kokugo kokubun*, vol. 33, no. 8, pp. 1-6.

[6] They nevertheless included it because of its references to the Southern Court. See *Sankō Taiheiki*, p. 2 and Kama Kisaburō, "*Taiheiki* to shijitsu tsukete *Kanshōbon Baishōron* no koto," *Kokubungaku* 11-2 (2.1966): 52-59, p. 59. Kama mentions that the 1466 manuscript of *Baishōron* was not discovered until after this work was compiled.

[7] Suga Masatomo, "Taiheki no byōmō iro ōki koto o bensu," *Shigaku zasshi* 1, no. 3, p. 28-34 (1890) and no. 4, pp. 38-46 (1890). Suga first quoted *Baishōron* on pp. 33-34. His work was overshadowed by the more famous critique of *Taiheiki*, the following year, by Kume Kunitake of the Tōkyō Daigaku Shiryō Hensanjo. Kume famously described *Taiheiki* as "worthless" as a historical source. (Kume Kunitake "Taiheiki wa shigaku ni eki nashi." *Shigaku zasshi* 2 no. 17, 18, 20, 22 [1891].) For an overview of the work's shortcomings see Conlan, *From Sovereign to Symbol* (New York: Oxford University Press, 2011), pp. 9-13.

[8] Suga Masatomo, "*Baishōron* kō," *Shigaku zasshi* 1, no. 4 (1890): 61-65 and vol. 5 no. 1 (1894): 44-48.

Ultimately, the *Dainihon shiryō* compilers decided to begin their compilation of post-Genkō [1331-333] sources with a quotation from *Taiheiki*.[9] The much shorter *Baishōron* first appears on p. 61 of this volume[10] and is used most prominently as a major source for the battles of Tadarahama and Minatogawa, the decisive encounters of 1336.[11]

Distinctive Features of the Text

The *Baishōron* author has remained anonymous, but analysis of the text provides ample clues to his identity. First, and most remarkably, the *Baishōron* account of the battles of Tadarahama and Minatogawa seems to come from an eyewitness.[12] Unlike the formulaic description of battles in most literary accounts of warfare, the *Baishōron* accounts of Tadarahama and Minatogawa describe the coloring of armor or horses in a way consistent with how an actual observer would have noted them.[13] Details like the sunlight on the eve of battle, a sudden dust storm impacting the battle, or for that matter, the fact that the billowing cape (*horo*) of one warrior prevented his armor from being recognized suggests a careful narrator who recounted what he actually saw. This is a rare account of medieval Japanese warfare by a participant.[14]

The next notable element of the text is its accuracy with respect to place and chronology. In comparison with *Taiheiki*, *Baishōron* provides remarkably precise dates for major events, as well as a

---

[9] The prominence accorded *Taiheiki* is surprising, since scholars such as Suga and Kume had questioned its accuracy. Miura Shūkō and Tanaka Yoshinari admitted that *Taiheiki* contained errors but still felt that it was essential for study of the age. For an overview of Miura's arguments, see Mori Shigeaki, *Taiheiki no gunzō* (Kadokawa, 1991), p. 306.

[10] *Dainihon shiryō* (hereafter DNSR) Series 6 no. 1 (1901), pp. 1 and 61.

[11] DNSR 6.3 (1903), pp. 133-139-46 for Tadarahama and pp. 409-15, 452 for Minatogawa.

[12] Fujimoto Masayuki first made this important observation in his *Yoroi o matou hitobito* (Yoshikawa Kōbunkan, 2000), pp. 179-83.

[13] Fujimoto, *ibid.*, pp. 181-83.

[14] The only comparable work is the Mongol invasion scrolls (*Mōko shūrai ekotoba*), which consist of Takezaki Suenaga's narrative of battle.

chronology consistent with actual geographical movement. For example, *Baishōron* correctly shows that Takauji first rebelled on Genkō 3.4.27 (1333) at Shinomura.[15] *Taiheiki,* by contrast, contains significant errors, most notably the notion that he switched sides on Genkō 3.5.7.[16] Likewise, the *Baishōron* narrative matches other documents, and is geographically and temporally possible. An example is Takauji's advance from Kamakura late in 1335.[17] Its chronology for the battle of Minatogawa, too, can be verified.[18] Finally, *Baishōron* correctly shows that Kenshun brought an edict from the Jimyōin emperor (Kōgon) legitimating Takauji's rebellion midway through the second month of 1336. This is confirmed by a letter written by Takauji on Kenmu 3.2.15 (1336) and a mobilization order dating from two days later.[19] *Taiheiki* claims that this edict was not issued until nearly ten weeks later, on Kenmu 3.5.1.[20]

Taiheiki exaggerates the size of armies and provides no consistency at all with respect to numbers.[21] *Baishōron,* too, mentions impossibly large numbers, but these are invariably reported as hearsay, not as

---

[15] Takeuchi Rizō, comp., *Kamakura ibun* (hereafter KI) (42 vols., Tōkyōdō Shuppan, 1971-91), vol. 41, docs. 32109-14, pp. 243-44 for Takauji's mobilization orders of 1333 (Genkō 3).4.27.

[16] Washio Junkei, ed. *Taiheiki (Seigen-in bon)* (Tōkō Shoin, 1936), maki 9, "Gogatsu nanoka kassen no koto onajiku Rokuhara ochiru koto," particularly pp. 212-18. Similar variation appears in the *Kandabon* version. See *Taiheiki (Kandabon)* (Kokusho Kankōkai, 1907), maki 9, "Gogatsu nanoka miyako kassen no koto," pp. 90-110 (hereafter *Kandabon Taiheiki*).

[17] Comparison of the *Baishōron* narrative with the petition of Nomoto Tomoyuki reveals the narrative's fundamental accuracy. For the Nomoto document, see Conlan, *State of War: The Violent Order of Fourteenth Century Japan* (Ann Arbor: Center for Japanese Studies, 2003), pp. 12-47. For further analysis, see Takeda Masanori, "'Taiheiki' Hakone Takenoshita kassen kō: *Taiheiki* to *Baishōron*," *Ibarajō kokubun* 6 (3.1994). Takeda showed the impossibility of the *Taiheiki* account and the fundamental accuracy of *Baishōron*.

[18] Compare the narrative with Seno Seiichirō, comp., *Nanbokuchō ibun Kyushu hen* (hereafter NBIK), (7 vols. Tōkyōdō Shuppan, 1980-92), vol. 1, doc. 616, 5.25.1336 Ashikaga Takauji kakikudashi an, p. 193.

[19] *NBIK* vol. 1, doc. 417, 2.15 Ashikaga Takauji shojō an, p. 144 and doc. 418, Kenmu 3.2.17 (1336) Ashikaga Takauji gunzei saisokujō, p. 145.

[20] See *Kandabon Taiheiki*, maki 9, "Shōgun kairiku yori semenoboru koto," p. 230.

[21] See Conlan, *State of War,* p. 9 for one example of how *Taiheiki* exaggerates numbers.

fact.[22] It describes actual encounters in far more limited, plausible fashion. For example, *Baishōron* mentions fifty troops dying in one encounter during the battle of Minatogawa, and it describes the destruction of the Kusunoki army as resulting in 700 deaths. Such numbers are consistent with the number of casualties in an overwhelming defeat.[23]

The narrative portrays individuals and shrines associated with Northern Kyushu vividly. These include warriors such as the Shōni and the Aeba, and also the important regional shrines of Kushida, Kashii, and Munakata. The Kyushu connection helps to determine who wrote the work.

The Question of Authorship

By analyzing the offices and ranks of figures mentioned in *Baishōron*, Koakimoto Dan has demonstrated that the work was completed, or at very least reached its current form, between the eighth and tenth months of 1351.[24] The timing is both significant and ironic, since this work devoted to glorifying the Ashikaga was written precisely at the moment when the two Ashikaga brothers, Takauji and Tadayoshi, had started fighting each other. The situation in Kyoto was chaotic, but in Kyushu only a handful of warriors still supported Takauji. The Shōni, one of whom might logically have been the author, sided with Tadayoshi. Nevertheless, Tadayoshi was killed, and his supporters later transferred their allegiance to the Southern Court. None of these could have retained favor with the Ashikaga beyond 1351.

---

[22] The *Kandabon Taiheiki* states that 300 Ashikaga warriors fought 30,000 Kikuchi enemies. See maki 15, "Tadarahama kassen [no] koto," p. 221. The *Seigen-in* version has the same numbers. See maki 15, "Tadarahama kassen [no] koto," p. 424.

[23] The battle in which Kitabatake Akiie died resulted in 700 dead. See NBIK vol. 1, docs. 1215-7, 1338 (Kenmu 5).urū 7.6 Isshiki Dōyū segyōjō, p. 367, and vol. 7, docs. 6995-8, 1338 (Kenmu 5).urū 7.6 Isshiki Dōyū segyōjō utsushi, pp. 15-16.

[24] Koakimoto Dan, Taiheiki Baishōron no kenkyū, Kyūko Shoin, 2005, pp. 352-61, 394-95. Koakimoto also showed that the work does not recognize Southern Court promotions and therefore betrays a Northern Court bias.

Thus the field of likely candidates for authorship narrows to an individual (or individuals) familiar with Kyushu, who witnessed the battles of Tadarahama and Minatogawa and steadily supported Ashikaga Takauji through the time when the work was written. The most plausible possibility is therefore a member of the Munakata family or someone closely affiliated with them.

Munakata Authorship

The Munakata, a family from Northern Kyushu, staffed the Munakata shrine. Some also served as Rokuhara administrators (*tandai*), Kamakura's judicial representatives in Kyoto.[25] For some reason, most such officials sympathized with the claims to legitimacy made by candidates of the Daikakuji lineage. Some, such as Iga Kanemitsu, actively supported the Daikakuji emperor Go-Daigo against Kamakura. The Munakata in Kyoto also came to support Go-Daigo.[26] This sympathy for Go-Daigo and the Daikakuji emperors pervades the early narrative, complete with indignation when Kamakura forced a Daikakuji emperor to abdicate in favor of his Jimyōin rival (Kōgon). Likewise, a lack of detail concerning important members of the noble Hino family suggests that the author was not in close contact with people affiliated with the Jimyōin emperors. However, these sympathies dissolved in 1336, once the unpopular Go-Daigo himself became a target of rebellion.

---

[25] Their ranks included Motouji, who served in 1315, and Nagauji, who served from 1313 through 1320, as well as a lay priest named Shinsei, who served in 1323-24 and 1327. See *Munakata shishi shiryōhen 1* (Munakata, 1995), doc. 261, Genkō 4.8.13 (1324) Rokuhara seisatsu, p. 610 for reference to the Munakata as serving as Rokuhara administrators (*bugyōnin*). See also Mori Yukio, *Rokuhara tandai no kenkyū* (Zoku Gunsho Ruijū Kanseikai, 2005), pp. 78-79. For a list of all known administrators, see pp. 140-54.

[26] See Mori, *Rokuhara tandai no kenkyū*, p. 77 for analysis of the *Rengeji kakochō* (KI, vol. 41, doc. 32137, pp. 252-58). This record of the Rokuhara dead reveals that only one administrator perished at Banba. The Munakata had abandoned Rokuhara by this time. Amino Yoshihiko discusses the duplicity of Iga Kanemitsu in his *Igyō no ōken* (Heibonsha, 1986), pp. 160-68. The *Baishōron* author mentions Iga Kanemitsu when describing Go-Daigo's new institutions of governance.

Minor but significant mistakes early in the narrative show that the author was not thoroughly familiar with the court. The claim that Emperor Go-Horikawa was the grandson of Go-Toba is incorrect.[27] The narrative also records imperial reigns as beginning not from the moment of an emperor's accession, but rather from the first full year of his reign.[28] These errors and inconsistencies contrast with the accuracy of the work's accounts of the battles of the 1330s.

The *Baishōron* author accepted the notion of inviolate imperial authority. Epitomizing these sentiments, the narrative portrays the eastern warriors as being unable to stand against the monarch, who in 1221 was felt to rule by moral suasion. They won the war nonetheless, simply because of Emperor Go-Toba's moral failings. These sentiments closely match those expressed in *Masukagami*, another fourteenth century narrative with a court perspective. *Baishōron* is unusual, however, in that a provincial warrior possesses attitudes resembling those prevalent at the court.

Because *Baishōron* has been seen as a counterpart to *Taiheiki*, both works' pro-Daikakuji bias has encouraged those who discuss the relationship between court and Kamakura through 1333 to ignore the rival perspective, that of the emperors and courtiers of the Jimyōin lineage. This silence particularly applies to claims that Go-Saga's testament required Daikakuji succession. Jimyōin documents suggest a different interpretation.[29] Until recently, the Jimyōin perspective and claim to legitimacy were little understood, although it was the Jimyōin emperors whom the Ashikaga supported and who are the forebears of the current imperial line.[30]

---

[27] Go-Horikawa was the grandson of Emperor Takakura, while Go-Toba was Takakura's son, hence Go-Horikawa's uncle.

[28] Perhaps the New Year *sechie* rites played a larger role in determining the start of an imperial reign than has been commonly assumed. *Baishōron* consistently dates an imperial reign to the year after the emperor succeeded to the throne. The one exception is that of Hanazono, who came to the throne on Enkyō 1.12.28 (1308). The fact that this happened so close to the New Year apparently led to this inconsistency, in that his reign should have been listed as starting from the following year.

[29] Murata Masashi, ed., *Fūjinroku* (*Murata Masashi chosakushū*, vol. 7 (Kyoto: Shibunkaku, 1986), pp. 13-14.

[30] For analysis of the Jimyōin perspective, see Conlan, *From Sovereign to Symbol*.

Although Munakata administrators linked to the capital may have had a hand in this work, not all of the Munakata immediately turned against Kamakura. Those in Northern Kyushu continued to support Kamakura officials through Genkō 3.4.2 (1333) before abandoning them, as did many others, in the fifth month of Genkō 3.[31] The Munakata with the strongest court ties later became the most influential at the shrine during 1333-36, but they quickly shifted allegiances from the Daikakuji emperor Go-Daigo to Ashikaga Takauji when Takauji rebelled in 1335. One Munakata collateral, Yakurō Ujiie, is described in his genealogy as following Lord Takauji and fighting on his behalf.[32]

Munakata Ujinori, the chief priest of the shrine, was ordered to quell "rebels" who, early in 1335, still supported the defeated and all but destroyed Kamakura bakufu.[33] He resigned his position on the fifteenth day of the third month, not long after the battle of Tadarahama, so as to fight for the Ashikaga. Ujinori and his son Ujitoshi traveled to Kyoto, where for nine years they fought in many battles.[34] Although Ujinori and Ujitoshi left few documents recounting their exploits, other relatives, who adopted the surname Asamachi, can be documented as shifting their allegiance to Takauji late in 1335.[35] Asamachi Mitsuyo fled with Takauji on Kenmu 3.2.18 (1336) to Onomichi, as the retreating forces made their way west, and then fought at Tadarahama on Kenmu 3.3.2 under the command of the

---

[31] For the head of Munakata shrine aiding Hidetoki, see *Hakata Nikki*, 1333.4.2, reproduced in *Munakata shishi shiryōhen* 1, p. 629. For the son of Munakata Ujikatsu taking part in the destruction of Hidetoki, see Genkō 3.6.2 (1333) Hizen Munakata Dotomaru chakutōjō, p. 632.

[32] See his genealogy, reproduced in *Munakata shishi shiryōhen* 1, p. 626 and 721.

[33] *Munakata shishi shiryōhen* 1, 1.21 Go-Daigo tennō rinji, p. 646.

[34] Teisei Munakata Daigūji keifu, in *Munakata shishi shiryōhen* 1, See p. 677 for the Munakataki tsuikō, which has Ujitoshi and others following Takauji to Kyoto in 1336 and remaining there for 9 years. For Ujinori's resignation, see doc. 315, Munakata mokuroku, p. 673. For another narrative of Ujinori and Ujitoshi, see pp. 704-5.

[35] *Munakata shishi shiryōhen* 1, doc. 309, Kenmu 2.12.20 (1335) Asamachi Zen'e mōshijō, p. 651. The *mokuroku* for the Munakata documents shows that on Kenmu 2.11.8 Ashikaga Takauji confirmed an Asamachi will, suggesting their early support, since this was just when his initial rebellion against Go-Daigo was becoming manifest.

Shōni.[36] Another Asamachi, Taneyasu, fought under the Shōni and the Aeba, and was a witness to the valor of others fighting in Kyoto in 1336.[37]

The Munakata can be verified as fighting in Kyushu and Kyoto in 1336, and as serving under commanders who occupy a prominent role in the narrative. On Kenmu 3.4.2, before the decisive battle of Minatogawa, they also received rewards for their services from Ashikaga Takauji.[38] Takauji rarely granted rewards before his authority stabilized. His bestowal of these lands on the Munakata, while still advancing on the capital, reveals the significance of the Munakata's valor at Tadarahama.

With close ties to the Ashikaga, the Munakata remained steadfast supporters of Takauji through the 1350s, even though Takauji's support all but collapsed in the west when he warred against his brother Tadayoshi. Ujiie, described in the Munakata genealogy as fighting bravely at Tadarahama, received an edict (*onkudashibumi*) from Takauji on Kannō 2.11.29 (1351) and a concurrent appointment to the *jitō* post of Miyanaga Katakuma, in the Kurate district of Chikuzen province.[39] This is around the time when *Baishōron* was written. In this case, one can therefore affirm that a veteran of Tadarahama remained in Takauji's good graces in 1351.[40] Ujiie ultimately lost his autonomy and transferred his records to the main

---

[36] *Munakata shishi shiryōhen* 1, Kenmu 3. 2.18 (1336) Asamachi Mitsuyo chakutōjō, pp. 652-53 and 1336.3.26 Ashikaga Takauji bugyōnin rensho hōsho, pp. 656-66. An unidentified Shōni wrote this document. Printed versions attribute it erroneously (as Seno Sei'ichirō has shown) to Shōni Fuyutsuke.

[37] For the genealogy of the Asamachi, see *Munakata shishi shiryōhen* 1, p. 617; for the military documents, see *ibid.*, doc. 324, Kenmu 3.25 9 (1336) Nagano Suketoyo gunchūjō utsushi, pp. 679-80. Taneyasu's name appears as Kyoku Yagorō. This document also mentions the Aeba, who figure in *Baishōron* as well.

[38] See *Munakata shishi shiryōhen* 1, Munakata mokuroku, doc. 317, p. 674.

[39] See his genealogy, reproduced in *Munakata shishi shiryōhen* 1, pp. 626 and 721. Yakurō Ujiie gave these lands to the head of the shrine in 1363. See the listing of Munakata documents on pp. 765-66.

[40] One can verify Ujiie's ownership of this Katakuma post, and the fact that he passed it to the Munakata main line in 1363. However, the edict from Takauji himself is missing. This is perhaps not surprising, since some of the most vivid military petitions were taken from the Munakata during the Tokugawa era.

Munakata line, and most were lost. Whether he or his brothers, nephews, and uncles were mostly responsible for the narrative is presently unknowable, but the probability of a Munakata connection remains high.[41]

Baishōron *as a Counterpart to the Oldest Versions of* Taiheiki

Baishōron seems to have been written in response to the earliest versions of *Taiheiki*, none of which now survives. Koakimoto Dan's research suggests that its narrative most closely matches the oldest *Taiheiki* variants.[42] Its author was aware of *Taiheiki* or had access to a shared narrative tradition that influenced both texts. For example, the parodic poem about watchfires at Amida-ga-mine appears in both works.[43] Likewise, *Baishōron* has Takauji rebel because he was forced to attack Kamakura while still in mourning for his father. However, his father died in 1331, not 1333. This same mistake, corrected in later versions of *Taiheiki*, appears also in the oldest extant version (the *Kandabon*) of this work.[44]

Baishōron also resembles *Taiheiki* in its coverage of the battle of Minatogawa and its focus on Kusunoki Masashige. *Jinnō shōtōki* by Kitabatake Chikafusa, one of the oldest accounts of the Southern Court, mentions Masashige as fighting at Chihaya in 1333 and briefly

---

[41] Other Munakata narratives, dating most likely from the late sixteenth century, resemble *Baishōron. Munakata shishi shiryōhen* 1, doc. 347, Munakata keifu, pp. 704-5. Some shrine histories emphasize the succession to office as well, a trait evident in the earlier passages of *Baishōron*. See *ibid.*, doc. 358, Munakata shamu shidai, pp. 706-710.

[42] For this fascinating analysis, see Koakimoto Dan, "'Baishōron' to 'Taiheiki'" in Taiheiki Baishōron *no kenkyū*, pp. 394-410. Koakimoto also suggests that the *Kandabon* version of *Taiheiki* is the oldest version of the work. Unfortunately, the *Kandabon* is incomplete, but the *Jingū chōkokanbon* represents a complete, albeit slightly later, copy based on it.

[43] Compare the *Kandabon Taiheiki,* maki 17, "Sanmon Nanto ni chō suru koto," p. 266 and Koakimoto, *Taiheiki, Baishōron no kenkyū*, p. 396.

[44] This error appears in the oldest *Kandabon* text of *Taiheiki*. See maki 9, "Ashikaga-dono jōraku no koto," pp. 85-87 and also the *Seigen-in* version, maki 9, "Ashikaga dono jōraku no koto," pp. 205-11. It was corrected in the later *Jingū chōkokanbon* version. See Hasegawa, *Taiheiki*, maki 9, "Ashikaga dono onjōraku no koto," pp. 215-16. For analysis, see Koakimoto , Taiheiki Baishōron *no kenkyū, pp.* 397-99.

acknowledges his role in establishing a Southern Court presence at Yoshino, but it omits the battle of Minatogawa and Masashige's death.[45] In contrast, both *Baishōron* and *Taiheiki* praise Masashige extravagantly. The former portrays him as a prudent and skilled warrior, while the latter has him so devoted to the imperial cause that he vows to be reborn fighting for Go-Daigo and ultimately becomes a vengeful spirit. This emphasis on Masashige stems from a perspective shared with *Taiheiki* or some other early source but foreign to Kitabatake Chikafusa.

Nevertheless, *Baishōron* shares some motifs with *Jinnō shōtōki*. Chikafusa argued that the Daikakuji line was Japan's legitimate lineage (*shōtō*). *Baishōron* exploits the same rhetoric, in early 1336, to argue that the Jimyōin emperors are legitimate. The ideas that pervade Kitabatake Chikafusa's work seem to have been widely discussed and disseminated, even though in this case they were applied to the Jimyōin rather than the Daikakuji lineage.

This Version of the Text

This translation is based on the seventeenth century *Rufubon* version of *Baishōron*, the best known, although not the oldest, complete text of the work.[46] The *Rufubon* was included in *Sankō Taiheiki* and *Dainihon shiryō*, and it was published separately, with scholarly analysis and annotation, in 1975.[47] Shuzo Uyenaka translated this text for his University of Toronto Department of East Asian Studies dissertation "A Study of *Baishōron*: A Source for the Ideology of Loyalism in Medieval Japan" (1978). The translation here is drawn, with his permission, from his thesis. Passages added to earlier *Baishōron* texts

---

[45] Kitabatake Chikafusa, *Jinnō shōtōki (Nihon koten bungaku taikei*, Iwanami Shoten, 1965), pp. 173, 189. See also Varley, *A Chronicle of Gods and Sovereigns* (Columbia University Press, 1980), pp. 245, 266.

[46] The *Kyōdaibon*, dating from 1470, is the oldest verifiable complete version of this text. A manuscript at Tenri may be older, but some questions remain concerning the colophon. It shares broad similarities with the *Kyōdaibon*.

[47] Yashiro Kazuo and Kami Hiroshi, ed., *Baishōron* (Gendai Shichōsha, 1975).

are printed in italics, so as to make visible some major ways in which later copyists stressed tropes of loyalty and praise of the Hosokawa.

A Note on the Translation of Honorary Titles

Because of promotion or reward for services rendered, a fourteenth-century warrior might hold an honorary court rank or office meaningful for him and for anyone reporting his deeds. For the intended reader of *Baishōron* and other such texts, this rank or office placed the warrior in a recognized hierarchy of prestige, if not of effective power. Its omission, too, can make a political statement. Nitta Yoshisada, who received titles from Go-Daigo between 1335 and 1338, is an example. *Baishōron* lists the latest promotion for each principal figure on the Ashikaga side, or mentions his title of governor (*kami*) or protector (*shugo*) of a province; but it gives Yoshisada only his older title of *Saemon no suke* (a junior officer post in the Left Gate Watch) thus suggesting that all later promotions, hence Go-Daigo's regime itself, were illegitimate. The text may also note a senior warrior's title of *nyūdō* ("novice" or "lay monk"), even though the man's elementary Buddhist vows have no effect whatever on his role in battle.

Offices and titles like these so resist economical, useful translation that the reader of another language is unlikely to grasp their significance. Moreover, attempts to translate them confuse the narrative and distract attention from the main thrust of events. Therefore such titles have generally been omitted from this translation. Specialists concerned with them will consult the original. The warriors mentioned are identified below by personal name and surname.[48]

---

[48] Over time *Baishōron* copyists, too, dropped some shifting titles. The oldest texts mention "Sanbōin *sōjō* Kenshun, known then as the Hino *risshi*," but the *Rufubon* calls him just "Sanbōin *sōjō* Kenshun." See Yashiro Kazuo and Kami Hiroshi, ed., *Baishōron* (Gendai Shichōsha, 1975, p. 286); and vol. 2 of the *Kyōdaibon Baishōron* (*Kokugo Kokubun* vol. 33 no. 9, p. 31); also Yashiro and Kami, *Baishōron*, note 73, p. 255.

BAISHŌRON
PART ONE

1. The Predecessor

It was in the spring some years ago. The 25th of the 2nd month being fixed as the final day of the Sacred Readings, a crowd of men and women, clergy and laymen, had gathered at the Bishamon-dō at Kitano. Some chanted darani or sutras, some sat deep in meditation, some recited poems. It was late at night. The wind rustled in the pines, and the fragrance of plum blossoms hung in the air. Everyone felt the holiness of the occasion. All hearts were at peace.

There was a short pause in the chanting. Someone said, "I hesitate to speak at such a time, but perhaps somebody can answer a question that I have wondered about for years. I would like to hear the full story of how the present Shogun came to overthrow his predecessor and, after establishing the basis of his good fortune, to surpass all others in glory. If anyone knows, please tell me."

There was a moment of silence. Then a certain old, ranking Buddhist priest, known for his wide knowledge and accomplishment in many arts, came forward. "Because of my great age," he said, "I have heard accounts of events that happened long ago. I will relate these events briefly. No doubt I have forgotten many things, but I ask those who remember them to assist me." The questioner and all others present listened joyfully, thinking him divinely inspired.

The priest spoke as follows.

The "predecessor" in question is Hōjō Takatoki, who was overthrown during the Genkō era [1331-33]. The line of warrior [Minamoto] Shoguns ended in Jōkyū 1 [1219]. Thereafter the nun Masako, the late Lord Yoritomo's widow, decided to have the shoguns appointed from among the court nobles. They ruled Japan from the

Kantō, appointing as adjutants (*shikken*) the descendants of Hōjō Tokimasa.

2. The Shoguns

In the reign of Emperor Keikō, the twelfth in the imperial line, the Eastern barbarians rebelled. The Emperor appointed Prince Yamato Takeru supreme Shogun and subdued the rebels.

Empress Jingū, the fifteenth of the line, was Shogun herself and, accompanied by the gods of Suwa and Sumiyoshi, subjugated the three kingdoms of Korea.

In the reign of the thirty-second Emperor, Yōmei, Prince Umayado, who was himself a general, put to death the minister Mononobe no Moriya.

The thirty-ninth Emperor, Tenchi, had Nakatomi no Kamatari put the minister Soga no Iruka to death.

The fortieth Emperor, Tenmu, who was commander-in-chief (*taishō*), put Prince Ōtomo to death. Emperor Tenmu is also known as the Kiyomigahara Emperor.

The forty-fifth Emperor, Shōmu, appointed Ōno no Azumahito general and killed Fujiwara no Hirotsugu, the Dazaifu deputy. It is Hirotsugu who became a deity of the Matsura Shrine.[49]

The forty-eighth in the line, Empress Shōtoku, appointed as commander-in-chief Sakanoue no Karitamaro, a middle counselor and the shogun of the Mutsu Headquarters, and she sent him on a punitive expedition against the deposed Emperor on Awaji[50] and his supporter Fujiwara no Nakamaro. Nakamaro is also known as Emi no Oshikatsu.

The fiftieth Emperor, Kanmu, sent Sakanoue no Tamuramaro, a middle counselor and the Shogun of the Mutsu Headquarters, to subdue the barbarian Akakashira and other villains in the far northeastern provinces.

---

[49] The Matsura Shrine (Kagami no Miya, the "Mirror Shrine") in northwestern Kyushu is much older than Hirotsugu, but his spirit was believed to have been incorporated into the divine presence there.

[50] Junnin, who was inserted into the list of recognized emperors and given this name only in the early Meiji period. These events took place in 764-765.

The fifty-second Emperor, Saga, had Sakanoue no Watamaro, the Shogun of the Government Headquarters in Mutsu, put Fujiwara no Nakanari to death.

The sixty-first Emperor, Suzaku, had Shoguns Taira no Sadamori and Fujiwara no Hidesato put Taira no Masakado to death.

In the Eishō era [1046-52] the seventieth Emperor, Go-Reizei, had Minamoto no Yoriyoshi, the governor of Mutsu, subdue Abe no Sadatō and others.[51]

In the Eihō era [1081-83] the seventy-second Emperor, Shirakawa, had Minamoto no Yoshiie, the governor of Mutsu and the Shogun of the Government Headquarters in Mutsu, execute Kiyohara no Takehira and his nephew Iehira.[52]

In the Kōwa era [1099-1103], the seventy-third Emperor, Horikawa, had Taira no Masamori defeat Minamoto no Yoshichika.

At the beginning of his reign, in Hōgen 1 [1156], the seventy-seventh Emperor, Go-Shirakawa, quarreled with his elder brother, Retired Emperor Sutoku. The Emperor had Minamoto no Yoshitomo, the governor of Shimotsuke, and Taira no Kiyomori, the governor of Aki, put to death Minamoto no Tameyoshi, Taira no Tadamasa, and others.

In the reign of the seventy-eighth emperor, Nijō, in Heiji 1 [1159], Taira no Kiyomori alone promptly subdued Fujiwara no Nobuyori, Minamoto no Yoshitomo, and others who had barricaded themselves in the palace, thus bringing peace to Japan.

Proud of his achievement, Kiyomori administered state affairs arbitrarily, defying imperial authority and acting atrociously. Therefore Cloistered Emperor Go-Shirakawa secretly issued a decree to Minamoto no Yoritomo, who sent his army and went on a punitive expedition against the Heike family and its supporters. The Emperor so strongly approved of this that Yoritomo was appointed to the offices of Shogun and protector of all Japan. He was also promoted to the rank of Major Counselor and Major Captain of the Right Inner Palace Guards. After his appointed, however, he resigned both offices. Such was his career after Jishō 4 [1180]. On Shōji 1.1.11 [1199] Yoritomo

---

[51] The Earlier Nine Years War.
[52] The Later Three Years War.

renounced the world because of illness. He died on the 13th of that month, in his fifty-third year.

Until then Japan had been ruled well, and there was no distress among the people. However, despite the fact that Yoritomo's son, Yoriie, succeeded him and was Shogun in the Kantō until Kennin 2 [1202], he performed many evil deeds. He was therefore killed at Shūzenji, in Izu, by order of his maternal grandfather, Tokimasa. He was in his twenty-third year.

The next Shogun was Lord Sanetomo, Yoriie's younger brother. He held the office for seventeen years, from Kennin 3 [1203] to Kenpō 7 [1219] (during which year the era changed to Jōkyū). He gradually rose in court rank until he held the office of Minister of the Right together with that of Commander of the Right Palace Guards. At the hour of the dog on Kenpō 7.1.27, Sanetomo went to worship at the Tsurugaoka Hachiman Shrine and was assassinated there, on the stone steps, by Yoriie's son Kugyō, a shrine official. He was then in his twenty-eighth year.

A force sent straightaway against Kugyō put him to death. No words can describe the widespread grief over the extinction of the shogunal line, which had continued for three generations. It moved over a hundred people to renounce the world.

However, the office of Shogun in the Kantō had to be filled. Lady Masako arranged for Court Regent Michiie's third son Yoritsune, whose mother was a daughter of Prime Minister Kintsune, to leave the capital for the Kantō, in his second year, on Jōkyū 2.2.29 [1220].

On Karoku 2.12.29 [1225], in his eighth year, Yoritsune had his coming-of-age ceremony. Hōjō Yasutoki, the Governor of Musashi, gave him his adult head-dress.

3. The Jōkyū War

Meanwhile Yasutoki and his deputy, Tokifusa, conducted affairs of state. In the summer of Jōkyū 3 [1221], Retired Emperor Go-Toba decided to destroy the Kantō Bakufu. First, he had Miura Heikurō Taneyoshi, and Sasaki Yatarō Takashige and his son Tsunetaka, and others,[53] executed by Iga Tarō Mitsusue and others. On the 19th of the 5th month, Kamakura learned that an imperial army was to set out immediately for the Kantō.

Accordingly the nun Lady Masako summoned her younger brother and the shogun's retainers. Weeping, she said, "I would be very sorry to live to see the graves of the three Shoguns trampled by the horses of western warriors. There is no reason for me to go on living. Kill me first, then go to join the Emperor."[54]

The retainers replied: "We are all deeply indebted to the Shoguns. Must we not treasure their remains? We will die in the west."

On the 21st of the same month—even though the day was so unlucky that the odds against survival were ten to one—Yasutoki and Tokifusa therefore left Kamakura at the head of an army.[55]

However, before his departure, Yasutoki told his father Yoshitoki: "The whole country has always been the imperial domain. Therefore, both in ancient times and in our own day, in this land and in China, no one who defied an imperial command has ever escaped retribution. For example, the former prime minister and lay priest Taira no Kiyomori harassed Retired Emperor Go-Shirakawa. As a result, the late Shogun Yoritomo secretly received an imperial order, initiated a punitive expedition against the Heike, and was fully rewarded for his service with offices and lands. And of course there is our house, beginning with my grandfather Tokimasa, whose rewards were greatest of all. This is why it would be all the more regrettable if I were subjected now to imperial censure. However, it is impossible to

---

[53] Neither Takashige nor Tsunetaka appears in the *Jōkyūki* account of Mitsusue's death. Takashige figures only in a list of warriors summoned to the trap prepared for Mitsusue at the palace. *Jōkyūki* does not mention Tsunetaka.

[54] The opposite of Masako's defiant and much longer speech in *Jōkyūki*. This change probably reflects a growing tendency during the fourteenth century to glorify imperial power.

[55] According to the almanac, an extremely unlucky day to start a military campaign. *Jōkyūki*, to the contrary, has Yasutoki exclaim, "Gentlemen, set out with all speed along the Tōkaidō behind your commander, Tokifusa, as soon as I have selected an auspicious day. Yes, the 21st of the 5th month is a day to begin a great undertaking. Go then, go!"

escape Heaven's decree, and we should therefore give up the idea of fighting and surrender."

After a short while, Yoshitoki replied to Yasutoki's earnest appeal. "You have spoken admirably," he said. "However, your words apply only when the ruler's government is righteous. When I look at what has been done in the country in recent years, I see that imperial governance has lost its substance and is no longer what it was in ancient times. For example, an imperial ordinance will be issued in the morning and repealed in the evening, and there is unrest everywhere because the imperial government appoints more than one governor to a province. The places that are still free from misfortune may owe their condition to being under Bakufu administration. Order and disorder are as incompatible as fire and water. Because things have come to such a pass, and because, after all, we would be acting to restore peace in the land, we should fight and put our trust in Heaven. If we eastern warriors gain victory, the rebellious subjects who influenced the Retired Emperor will be in our hands, and we should punish them severely. As for the throne, one of the Retired Emperor's descendants should be appointed Emperor. If he himself resists, then doff your helmet, unstring your bow, bow your head, and surrender. This point of view also has something to be said for it."

At his words the eastern warriors, led by Yasutoki, whipped their horses and advanced on Kyoto along three different roads. The commanders of the army were, on the Tōkaidō, Yasutoki, the governor of Musashi, and Tokifusa, the Governor of Sagami; on the Tōsandō, Takeda Gorō and Ogasawara Jirō; and, on the Hokurikudō, Nagoe Tomotoki, the Secretary of Ceremonial. The army, 190,000 mounted warriors strong, left Kamakura and stormed into the capital from three directions at once. The gates of the city were immediately broken down and the insurgents were all killed or captured. Consequently, Retired Emperor Go-Toba was exiled to the province of Oki, and in Jōō 1[1222] his grandson, Go-Horikawa, was appointed Emperor.[56] Go-Horikawa reigned for eleven years, from Jōō 1 to Jōei 1

---

[56] An erroneous claim of direct lineal descent from Go-Toba. In fact, Go-Horikawa's grandfather was Emperor Takakura. His father was Prince Morisada, who received the title of honorary emperor (*daijō tennō*) after Go-Horikawa ascended the throne.

[1232]. [57]

Emperor Shijō reigned for ten years, from Tenpuku 1 [1233] to Ninji 3 [1242].

Emperor Go-Saga reigned from Kangen 1 [1243] to Kangen 4 [1246]. [58]

Emperor Go-Fukakusa reigned for thirteen years, from Hōji 1 [1247] to Shōgen 1 [1259].

Emperor Kameyama reigned for fifteen years, from Bun'ō 1 [1260] to Bun'ei 11 [1274].

Emperor Go-Uda reigned for thirteen years, from Kenji 1 [1275] to Kōan 10 [1287].

Emperor Fushimi reigned for eleven years, from Shōō 1 [1288] to Einin 6 [1298].

Jimyōin [Go-Fushimi] reigned from Shōan 1 [1299] to Shōan 3 [1301].

Emperor Go-Nijō reigned for six years, from Kengen 1 [1302] to Tokuji 2 [1307].

Emperor Hanazono reigned for eleven years, from Engyō 1 [1308] to Bunpō 2 [1318].

Emperor Go-Daigo reigned for thirteen years, from Gen'ō 1 [1319] to Genkō 1 [1331].

The last two emperors have been Kōgon and Kōmyō.

Altogether there have been more than ninety emperors, from Jinmu, the first of the imperial line, to Go-Saga.

4. The Shoguns and the Adjutants

Next, in the period of 154 years from Jishō 4 [1180] to Genkō 3 [1333], the Shoguns and Adjutants in the Kantō were as follows.

There were nine Shoguns.

These three were from the warrior [Minamoto] house:

Yoritomo

Yoriie

---

[57] These reign years are not conventional, in that they refer to the first full year of an emperor's enthronement, rather than the year of his accession. The one exception is that of Hanazono, who acceded to the throne in 1308.12.28 (Engyō 1).

[58] Go-Horikawa's son, Shijō, died childless and was followed by Go-Toba's grandson through Tsuchimikado. The chronicler's knowledge of the imperial line was imperfect.

Sanetomo
These two were from the regental house:
Yoritsune
Yoritsugu
These four were imperial princes:
Munetaka
Koreyasu
Hisaaki
Munekuni
There were nine Adjutants:
Tokimasa, governor of Tōtōmi
Yoshitoki
Yasutoki
Tokiuji
Tsunetoki
Tokiyori
Tokimune
Sadatoki
Takatoki

These governed in support of the Shogun and maintained peace in the realm, meanwhile holding the office of governor of Musashi or Sagami. The Adjutants worked with talented men from their house and issued edicts (*kudashibumi*) and orders (*gechi*) in accordance with the Shogun's instructions. They treated as equals the retainers in charge of such matters as the banquet on the first day of the year, the first archery practice, the preparation of the outdoor seating, the receiving of the tribute horses, and the Shogun's bodyguards. When an Adjutant rose to become head of his house, he assumed the name Tokusō. He never held a court rank above the Lower Junior Fourth. He lived modestly, devoted himself to government affairs, revered buddhas and gods, and ruled the people with compassion. Therefore, the people obeyed the government as grass and trees bend before the wind, so that the realm enjoyed peace and ease generation after generation.

Takatoki was Adjutant for ten years, from Shōwa 5 [1316] to Shōchū 2 [1325]. In the summer of Shōchū 2 he renounced the world because of illness, and in Kareki 1 [1326] he appointed Moritoki and Koresada as his deputies. Thereafter the Kantō government became increasingly notorious for its injustices. Heavenly punishment was inevitable, especially because of its intervention in the matter of the imperial succession. Since ancient times the succession to the throne had been hereditary. The reigning Emperor appointed his designated his Heir Apparent, and no disorder surrounded the imperial throne.

5. The Imperial Succession

This is roughly what I have heard concerning the past.

Emperor Tenchi offered the throne to his brother Prince Tenmu, disregarding his own son, Prince Ōtomo. Tenmu retired to Mount Yoshino, to show that he did not wish to accede to the throne. Then Ōtomo attacked Tenmu. Tenmu went to the provinces of Iga and Ise, where he worshiped at the shrine of the Sun Goddess and raised an imperial army. He won the battle at the border between the provinces of Mino and Ōmi, and after finally suppressing Ōtomo's rebellion[59] he acceded to the throne. He was the Kiyomigahara Emperor.

When Emperor Kōnin succeeded to the throne, he saw reason first to put to death the consultant Fujiwara no Momokawa.

During Emperor Saga's reign, his mistress of staff (*naishi no kami*) incited the former Emperor, Heizei, to rebellious violence. By Emperor Kanmu's will, however, the Emperor retained the throne.[60]

Emperor Montoku's sons, Koretaka and Korehito, both showed equal promise, especially with respect to succession to the throne. They therefore held a wrestling match and a horse race, and the winner assumed the throne as Emperor Seiwa.

When Cloistered Emperor Toba died in the Hōgen era [1156-58], a struggle for the throne arose within ten days between Retired Emperor Sutoku and his brother [Go-Shirakawa]. By imperial order the army took up position in the capital and joined battle; but such was Heaven's dispensation that in the end the Emperor retained the

---

[59] The Jinshin War of 672.

[60] Fujiwara no Kusuko, mother of one of Heizei's concubines and rumored also to have been one of Heizei's mistresses. This incident, in which Heizei attempted to regain the throne, is known as the Kusuko Incident (810).

throne. Retired Emperor Sutoku was banished to the province of Sanuki, and those Minamoto and Taira warriors who had followed his orders were put to death.

Emperor Takakura was a wise ruler. The realm was at peace during his reign, and it appeared that imperial rule would long endure. Then Emperor Antoku ascended the throne in his third year, thanks to the machinations of his maternal grandfather, Taira no Kiyomori. Moreover, Kiyomori then governed exactly as he pleased, flouting the will of Heaven.

Next, in the Jōkyū era [1219-21], Retired Emperor Go-Toba threw the world into disorder and was therefore banished to the island of Oki. The Kantō [Bakufu] enthroned his grandson as Emperor Go-Horikawa.

Each of these successions for a time encountered difficulties, but in the end everything returned to normal.

When Emperor Go-Saga died in the Kangen era [1243-47], he left a posthumous decree to the effect that his first son, Go-Fukakusa, should accede to the throne; that when Go-Fukakusa abdicated he should have, as his own, 180 parcels of land that belonged to the Chōkōdō; that his descendants were to renounce any further ambition to reign; that Go-Saga's second son, Kameyama, was then to accede to the throne; that Kameyama's descendants were to reign thereafter in unbroken succession; and that he had good reason for issuing these instructions. Accordingly, Emperor Go-Fukakusa reigned from Hōji 1 [1248] to Shōgen 1 [1259].[61]

Emperor Go-Uda, Emperor Kameyama's son, reigned from Kenji 1 [1275] to Kōan 10 [1287].

Thus the three emperors who followed Go-Saga complied with his instructions, and their reigns were free of conflict. However Fushimi,

---

[61] This narrative shows that the author's sympathies were with Kameyama's line, since Go-Fukakusa never agreed that his descendants should renounce any ambition to reign. On the contrary, he argued that his succession to the Chōkōdō lands and the major chronicles of Go-Saga suggested that his descendants would rule. In the end, Go-Fukakusa successfully argued that Go-Saga had wished Kamakura to determine the succession. See Murata Masashi, ed., *Fūjinroku* (*Murata Masashi chosakushū,* vol. 7 (Kyoto: Shibunkaku, 1986), pp. 13-14.

Emperor Go-Fukakusa's son, ascended the throne despite his descent from Go-Saga's first son and reigned from Shōō 1 [1288] to Einin 6 [1298].

Jimyōin [Go-Fushimi], the son of Emperor Fushimi, reigned from Shōan 1 [1299] to Shōan 3 [1301]. These two successions were brought about on wrongful instructions from the Bakufu.

The descendants of Emperor Kameyama, Emperor Go-Saga's second son, were resentful with good reason. Therefore Emperor Go-Nijō, a son of Emperor Go-Uda, reigned from Kengen 1 [1302] to Tokuji 2 [1307]. However, this Emperor was not righteous, and the succession therefore reverted to the other line. Hagiwara [Emperor Hanazono], Emperor Go-Fushimi's younger brother, reigned from Enkyō 1 [1308] to Bunpō 2 [1318]. The succession then returned to the legitimate line. Emperor Go-Daigo, Emperor Go-Uda's second son, reigned from Gen'ō 1 [1319] to Genkō 1 [1331]. Such alternations in the succession, which violated Emperor Go-Saga's instructions, represented arbitrary Bakufu decisions. Thoughtful people everywhere were shocked, thinking that this must counter the will of Heaven.

Earlier, when Emperor Fushimi, the son of Emperor Go-Saga's first son, was on the throne, he secretly told the Bakufu repeatedly that if Emperor Kameyama's descendants were to reign in succession they would acquire real power, so that if the provincial warriors were to support the Emperor, they would eventually endanger the Bakufu. After Retired Emperor Go-Toba was banished to the island of Oki, in the Jōkyū era, the court conceived deep resentment, and never gave up the idea of destroying the Bakufu and subduing the realm; and the danger still existed, since they had not yet had a chance to do so. But of course, he said, the descendants of Emperor Go-Fukakusa, Emperor Go-Saga's first son, hoped for the sake of the realm that the Bakufu would remain secure.

As a result, the Bakufu came to suspect the throne and arranged to have the scions of the two lines, the senior line of Emperor Go-Fukakusa and the junior line of Emperor Kameyama, reign alternately for periods of ten years.

In Go-Daigo's time, the reigning Emperor's[62] emissary to the Bakufu was Grand Counselor Yoshida Sadafusa, and Jimyōin's [Go-Fushimi] emissary was the second son of the Hino Counselor.[63] These two traveled back and forth many times between Kyoto and Kamakura, and they often argued about the succession before the Bakufu.

However, Sadafusa declared, "In accordance with Emperor Go-Saga's instructions, the descendants of his first son, Go-Fukakusa, are still in possession of the Chōkōdō estate. The descendants of his second son, Kameyama, should therefore reign in unbroken succession. However, the Bakufu has repeatedly intervened to order changes, to the constant detriment of Kameyama's descendants, whose right to the throne is beyond question." As a result of these repeated protests, Emperor Go-Daigo, a descendant of Kameyama, gained the throne and reigned from Bunpō 1 [1317][64] to Genkō 1 [1331], in accordance with Go-Saga's instructions. In Gentoku 2 [1330], however, a Jimyōin son[65] became Heir Apparent.

Go-Daigo objected to Kamakura that this was an outrage and that never in the history of our land since the reign of Emperor Jinmu had a subject decided the succession. "Besides," he demanded to know, "how can Heaven approve an act clearly contrary to Emperor Go-Saga's instructions? Is it that easy for you to rule that the two lines are to reign alternately for periods of ten years? While a Jimyōin emperor reigns, his line might well be satisfied to have both the throne and the Chōkōdō estate. But when a descendant of Kameyama is not on the throne, what estates does his line have? Since a Jimyōin son is already Heir Apparent, the Chōkōdō estate should be ceded to the descendants of Emperor Kameyama during his ten years on the throne."

---

[62] Go-Nijō (r. 1301-1308), an elder brother of Go-Daigo and his predecessor as emperor. Both were sons of Go-Uda.

[63] Both Hino Toshimitsu and his son Sukena (the father of *Takemuki-ga-ki* author Hino Nako) traveled repeatedly to Kamakura, where Toshimitsu died in 1326. Sukena remained a staunch Jimyōin supporter. Another son, Kenshun, also remained prominent and would be instrumental in restoring the fortunes of the Jimyōin court.

[64] Go-Daigo's reign actually began in Bunpō 2 (1318).

[65] Kazuhito, a son of Go-Fushimi and the future Emperor Kōgon of the Northern Court.

Sadafusa presented these reasonable arguments repeatedly, but the Bakufu insisted on the Jimyōin prince's appointment. Emperor Go-Daigo was so angry that in the autumn of Genkō 1 [1331], on the 24th of the 8th month, he secretly left the palace and went to Mount Kasagi in the province of Yamashiro. Courtiers of all ranks accompanied him. He summoned Kinai warriors. The result was indescribable turmoil.

6. The Exile of the Former Emperor

The Bakufu's Rokuhara representative (*tandai*) raced down to Kamakura in three days. The Bakufu dispatched tens of thousands of mounted men to Yamashiro. Go-Daigo's force being small, he was captured and returned to the capital. He was confined there in the southern compound at Rokuhara.

That same year, two Bakufu emissaries went to the capital, investigated the crimes of the courtiers and others who had supported the emperor, and laid charges against them according to the gravity of their crimes. The next year, Genkō 2 [1332], they made Go-Daigo a "Former Emperor" (*sentei*) and decided to exile him to the province of Oki, following the precedent of Emperor Go-Toba's exile in Jōkyū. Sasaki Kiyotaka, the governor and protector (*shugo*) of Oki, accordingly crossed to Oki in advance to prepare the imperial residence.

Go-Daigo left the capital at midday on Genkō 2.3.7. From Rokuhara the procession moved west, away from the Rokujō riverbank, then south down Ōmiya, preceded by the square palanquin (*shihōgoshi*) that he was to board once outside the capital. Within the city he rode in a carriage with its curtains down, guarded front and rear by warriors under Bakufu orders. His consort (*jungō*), the Lady of the Third Rank,[66] followed. Then came two or three mounted gentlewomen in hunting costume. Of the courtiers, however, only the Rokujō Lieutenant (*shōshō*)

---

[66] Fujiwara no Renshi. Although not the formal empress, as quasi-empress she bore several important princes, including Tsuneyoshi, who became Go-Daigo's heir apparent in 1334, and, according to some accounts, briefly his successor. An imperial edict (*rinji*) preserved in the Yūki documents and dated Engen 1.11.12 (1336) may be from him. He was captured after the fall of Kanegasaki. Another son, Noriyoshi, succeeded Go-Daigo as Emperor Go-Murakami of the Southern Court.

Tadaaki (later known as Chigusa-dono) followed the Emperor along a side road. The Emperor's carriage stopped for a time before the south gate of Tōji, facing the Golden Hall. Every onlooker, high or low, gathered that he was praying and, moved to tears by his feelings, forgot to leave. No one in the whole land is not the Emperor's subject, but none attempted to save him by taking his place. Mist covered the blue sky and the moon hid; the Emperor's crimson brocade robe lost its color. Blossoms do not speak, but their sorrow was plain. The pathetic character of the scene was beyond words.

It had been decided to exile the eldest prince[67] to the province of Sanuki and the Myōhōin prince[68] to Tosa. The next day, the 8th of the month, the protectors of those provinces therefore took them from the capital. The sun and the moon might as well have fallen from the heavens. That was more than twenty years ago, but when I recall all that I saw then, it seems to me that not a thousand tears nor any flood of words, however skillful, could convey the sorrow of that time. There have always been instances of superiors meting out justice to inferiors, but never of an Emperor having to leave alone to go so far. People called it frightening.

In the Hōgen era Retired Emperor Sutoku was exiled to Sanuki, but his case cannot be compared with the present one because he had been in conflict with his younger brother, Emperor Go-Shirakawa, and because he was exiled on the latter's authority. In Jōkyū, Retired Emperor Go-Toba was banished to Oki, but again his case was different, since he had attacked his subjects with the intention of destroying the last of the three Kantō shoguns, blameless though they were. His actions were not in accordance with Heaven's laws, and he was therefore banished to Oki. In fear of Heaven's judgment, however, the [Minamoto] warrior house placed Emperor Go-Horikawa, one of Go-Toba's grandsons, on the throne. All acknowledged that this was a fine gesture. This time, violation of Go-Saga's instructions brought things to this pass. Heaven's judgment remained unfathomable, and one wondered what consequences might ensue. Blameless though he was, the Emperor was exiled to a distant island. The warriors in his escort

---

[67] Prince Takayoshi, Go-Daigo's eldest son since the death of Moriyoshi.
[68] Sonchō, Godaigo's fifth son, a priest at Myōhōin.

appreciated the depth of his feelings, and none among them failed to shed tears.

7. Go-Daigo Reaches Oki

After a journey of more than ten days, the party reached the harbor of Mio in the province of Izumo, where a ship was waiting. An old temple there served as the imperial residence that night. While still at Rokuhara the Emperor heard the autumn rain pattering on the board roof and composed a poem.

suminarenu	On an autumn morning,
itaya no noki no	I listen to the rain
murashigure	Falling on this strange board roof
kiku ni tsukete mo	And find my sleeves wet with tears.
nururu sode kana	

That residence had been bad enough, but this one was far worse, and all felt acute sympathy for him. Naturally enough, in these rustic wilds he could not even understand what people were saying. Life was so crude that he thought continually of the capital. Unable to sleep, he lay with his head lifted from the pillow, listening to waves crashing on the beach, and hearing men and horses hurrying to and fro. He was reminded of Genji's sleepless nights at Suma long ago, and of Ōshōkun's sorrow as she rode to the land of the Huns. Such thoughts ran through his head all night long. Sleepless as he was, he could not even dream of being back in the capital.

At daybreak he asked an attendant how far it was to the Izumo Shrine. The attendant said it was a long way. He turned to the warriors and said, "Do you know that the divinity of the shrine is Susano-o-no-mikoto, who long ago loved Inada-hime? He risked his life to kill a huge serpent at the headwaters of the River Hi, obtained a sword, married Inada-hime, and built a palace. He composed the *Yakumo tatsu* poem, which is still remembered. The first of the three imperial regalia is the sacred sword, said to be the one obtained by Susano-o." The emperor could not hold back his tears, and his face was full of sorrow.

The next day, the sea was calm and he boarded the ship. The men who had escorted him had been relieved of their duties and stayed behind at Mio. The two Bakufu emissaries who had come to the capital the previous winter also returned to the Kantō. Peace was over.

8. Go-Daigo Escapes to Mount Funanoe

Meanwhile Go-Daigo's son Ōtō-no-Miya, formerly Abbot (*zasu*) of Hieizan, had returned to lay life as Moriyoshi, the Minister of War (*hyōbukyō*). The year before, when Go-Daigo went to Kasagi, he had been rumored to be at Hase, in Yamato, but his exact location remained unknown. Now he was said to be in touch with the warrior monks of Tōnomine and Yoshino, with a view to wiping away the dishonor visited upon the throne, and so on. The Kinai was in turmoil.

In the winter of that year, Genkō 2 [1332], at Go-Daigo's command a great warrior named Kusunoki Masashige fortified Chihaya, a superb natural stronghold on Mount Kongō in Kawachi, and raised the imperial banner there.[69] The eastern warriors who had gone to Mount Kasagi the previous year therefore returned to the capital. The following spring [1333] their great army set out directly for Yoshino, via Nara, and defeated Ōtō-no-Miya. They killed Murakami Hikoshirō Yoshiteru,[70] then proceeded immediately to Mount Kongō, where they surrounded the fort. The Bakufu army, numbering in the tens of thousands, tried every possible strategy, but many picked men with strong bows defended that excellent stronghold, and untold thousands or tens of thousands of the attackers were wounded or killed.

A strange thing happened while the eastern warriors were dissipating their earlier gains. On Oki, Sasaki Kiyotaka's family had been taking turns since the previous spring guarding Go-Daigo's

---

[69] *Nishiki no mihata,* a long, narrow brocade banner embroidered in gold with a sun disk and bearing the names of the Sun Goddess (Tenshō Kōtaijin) and Hachiman (Hachiman Daibosatsu).

[70] According to *Taiheiki,* the Bakufu army was deceived when Murakami claimed to be the prince. Only when his head was examined later in Kyoto did the mistake become clear.

residence. One of Kiyotaka's warriors, Saburō, had long been close to Go-Daigo and heeded him. Now, perhaps inspired by Heaven, he secretly released him.

Go-Daigo boarded a boat and left that dreary island, accompanied by Chigusa Tadaaki.[71] However, no one knew which course to follow, and the boat drifted on the waves. Words cannot express the anguish in Go-Daigo's heart. He surely remembered now that although the sea can bear a ship, it can also capsize it.[72] And just as he was reflecting that an enemy attack now would put his very life in danger, Kiyotaka caught up from behind him with over a thousand ships.[73] All aboard paled.

Go-Daigo said to the steersman, "Have no fear. Quickly, steer towards them and drop a fishing line. When Tai Gongwang of China was fishing on the bank of the Wei River, Wen Wang took him home on his cart.[74] Do not be afraid." The man thought that this was the end, but he put aside concern for himself, obeyed the imperial command, and dropped a line.

The enemy approached and asked him whether he had seen a suspicious-looking boat. "Yes," he answered, "a boat like that sailed this morning towards Izumo, and with this fair wind it must have completed the crossing." The enemy looked the boat over, but fortunately the Jade Body lay hidden under a heap of cuttlefish, and they never even thought of looking there. Their suspicions allayed, they happily rowed away. Go-Daigo crossed just as he had hoped to do, because for some time past he had been offering many prayers to the Gods and Buddhas, and particularly to the divinities of the Twenty-Two Shrines—Ise, Iwashimizu, Kamo, Hirano, Kasuga, and so on.

Upon reaching the harbor of Mio in Izumo, Kiyotaka sent a message to his kinsman, Sasaki Magoshirō Takahisa, the protector of the province, to raise a force from the province and assist him. Takahisa

---

71 Tadaaki was Go-Daigo's chamberlain and wrote his edicts. When away directing an army, Go-Daigo wrote in his own hand but forged Tadaaki's signature.

72 *Xun Zi:* "The ruler is a ship and the people are the water. The water bears the ship but can also capsize it."

73 The Tenri and Kyōdai texts read, more plausibly, "over ten ships."

74 From the *Shiji.*

did not even reply, however, since Go-Daigo had already sent him a command to support him.

Meanwhile, Go-Daigo's boat had reached Notsu village on the Nawa estate in the province of Hōki. The steersman said, "There is here a wealthy man named Nawa Matatarō. He must have one or two hundred relatives who would fight to the last man. His Majesty might request his aid." He therefore received a command to show Chigusa Tadaaki the way, so that Tadaaki might appeal to Nawa for support. This Nawa Matatarō later became Nagatoshi, the governor of Hōki.

Tadaaki delivered his message at the gate of Nagatoshi's residence. Nagatoshi showed him in and asked where Go-Daigo was. Upon learning that Go-Daigo was still in the boat, he asked Tadaaki to wait a moment and went inside. He saddled a horse, led it out, and gave it to Tadaaki to ride, while he himself donned his armor and walked with over fifty men, including his brothers and sons, to meet Go-Daigo. Nagatoshi felt that, while Go-Daigo should properly lodge in his house, the site made the house hard to defend. He therefore burned it down and escorted Go-Daigo to Funanoe, a steep mountain in that province. There his men laid brushwood on the ground and served Go-Daigo a meal of parched rice. They then fashioned a palanquin in which to carry him, made of rope from their torn-up their clothes, and at the summit built him a temporary residence. At dawn they raised the imperial banner. The local people and provincial warriors hurried to join the imperial force.

The next day Sasaki Kiyotaka advanced to the foot of the mountain with over three hundred mounted warriors. Nagatoshi and his relatives fought all day, careless of their lives, and killed or wounded so many attackers that at last these withdrew. Meanwhile, every warrior in the provinces of Izumo and Hōki joined Go-Daigo's side. The exhausted Kiyotaka therefore returned to Izumo, boarded a ship, and set out for Wakasa and Echizen. The news spread, and the forces of the sixteen provinces of the San'yōdō and the San'indō all joined Go-Daigo. Such, it seemed, was Heaven's wish.

One hears that Gou Jian, the king of Yue, was defeated in battle and captured by the king of Wu. However, thanks to a plan devised by his wise retainer Fan Li, he escaped from prison and defeated Wu in a battle at Mount Huiqi. This victory was due entirely to Fan Li's forethought. The expression "washing away the shame of Huiqi" derives from this incident. Fu Chai, the king of Wu, was vanquished because he rejected a plan devised by Wu Zixu, a wise and loyal retainer accomplished in matters both literary and military. However, Emperor Go-Daigo's escape from Oki was not the result of a plan devised by a wise retainer. It was due solely to the will of Heaven.

9. Takauji Raises an Army

When Go-Daigo set off in the spring of the previous year, even those deeply indebted to the Bakufu grieved to see him leave on his long journey, and the most uncouth among peasant men and women joined those of more cultivated understanding in moistening the sleeves of their hempen garments with tears of sorrow. People everywhere prayed for the safety of the throne. It was therefore no mere coincidence that Akamatsu Nyūdō Enshin [Norimura][75] of Harima, and all the other forces in the Kinai and neighboring province had rallied to his support.

They awaited Go-Daigo's return, then on Genkō 3.3.12 [1333] made a two-pronged attack on the capital from Toba and Takeda. Rokuhara forces quickly rode to meet them, fought them, and drove them back. A messenger rode from the capital to the Kantō with news of this attack. Ashikaga Takauji, now the Shogun, therefore came up to the capital for the second time as one of the commanders of a punitive force. He entered the city late in the 4th month of the same year.

Back in Genkō 1 [1331], too, he had been a commander of the force that attacked the stronghold on Mount Kasagi. This time, however, he received the order to go within a few days of his father's death.[76] He

---

[75] The Akamatsu turned against Kamakura quite early in the conflict of 1331 and throughout the fourteenth century were staunch Ashikaga supporters.

[76] According to *Sonpi bunmyaku*, Takauji's father Sadauji (referred to in the original as Jōmyōji, his posthumous Buddhist name) died on Genkō 1.9.5 [1331]. This error appears also in the oldest (*Kandabon*) text of *Taiheiki* (Book 9, "Ashikaga dono jōraku no koto") but was corrected in the later *Jingū Chōkokanbon*. See Hasegawa, *Taiheiki*, maki 9, "Ashikaga dono onjōraku no koto," pp. 215-16. For analysis, see Koakimoto, Taiheiki Baishōron *no kenkyū*, pp. 397-99.

had not yet held the memorial service and was still overwhelmed with grief, but the lay priest (*zenmon*) Takatoki[77] nonetheless ordered him to start for the capital. He could only obey. No doubt his quality as a commander made him the Bakufu's best choice, but the order on this occasion was unreasonable, and Takauji apparently conceived a deep grudge. The other commander was Nagoe Takaie, the governor of Owari and a descendant of Tomotoki, of the Ministry of Ceremonial, who commanded the Hokurikudō force in the Jōkyū conflict. Both commanders reached the capital at the same time and also left at the same time, on the 27th of the 4th month. Takauji was to proceed to Hōki via the San'indō provinces of Tanba and Tango. Takaie moved to Hōki via the San'yōdō Harima and Bizen. Their goal was to attack Mount Funanoe, but in their first skirmish on the way there, at Koga Nawate,[78] Nagoe Takaie was killed. His men returned to the capital without fighting.

Takauji camped that same day at Shinomura, a holding of his in Tanba.[79]

His family had actually been harboring for generations the idea of destroying the Bakufu. Moreover, when he was at the Kagami post station in Ōmi, on his way to the capital, Hosokawa Kazuuji (Awa-no-kami) and Uesugi Shigeyoshi (Izu-no-kami) had conveyed to him the secret command that Go-Daigo had given them earlier. They had urged him repeatedly to take a stand for Go-Daigo, arguing that their receiving this command meant that the time had come to act.

Before the Hachiman Shrine in Shinomura, Takauji therefore flew his banner from the top of a huge willow. The spring sun rises in the

---

[77] Hōjō Takatoki (1303-1333), the fourteenth Kamakura Bakufu adjutant.
[78] In present Fushimi-ku, Kyoto.
[79] Takauji's mother, Uesugi Kiyoko, was born in the nearby Uesugi region and apparently gave birth to Takauji there as well, since much lore concerning Takauji's birth, as well as his grave and that of his wife and mother, can be found in nearby Ankokuji. In moments of crisis Takauji returned to Shinomura, and he made the shrine there an essential cultic site for the Ashikaga regime. Takauji's earliest documents confirm that his rebellion dates from the 27th of the 4th month, showing that the *Baishōron* narrative is correct. *Taiheiki* and other texts date his rebellion to approximately a week later. See *Kamakura ibun*, vol. 41, for Takauji's documents of Genkō 3.4.27 (1333).

east, and the willow is the tree of the east. By ruling the east the sun becomes the master of the realm. It is also said that a great commander comes from the east, and that when spring turns to summer he will move west and destroy the enemies of the court. Accordingly, a great many of the troops that had crowded into the capital hastened to rally to Go-Daigo.

Takauji then moved his camp from Shinomura to Saga, and it was rumored that he would attack the capital in a few days. In the capital, the Bakufu forces, which had lost more than ten battles since the 12th of the 3rd month, fortified Rokuhara and established an imperial dwelling there.[80] Tens of thousands of men entrenched themselves inside.

Meanwhile the large Bakufu army that had surrounded Kusunoki Masashige's stronghold on Mount Kongō since the previous spring had not won a single encounter and had been losing ground. They were very frightened when they heard that Takauji, acting on Go-Daigo's orders, would soon invade the capital. Nonetheless, many residents of the city, as well as Shikoku and Kyushu warriors, continued to give the Bakufu impressive service.[81]

10. Takauji Attacks Rokuhara

On the 7th of the 5th month, at the hour of the hare [6 a.m.], Takauji's forces proceeded from Saga and occupied Uchino. The front ranks took up position in front of the Office of Shrines (Jingikan), facing east. The Rokuhara forces went up through Shirakawa and positioned themselves beyond the Nijō-Ōmiya crossing, facing west.

At the hour of the dragon [8 a.m.] the two sides advanced. The din of humming arrows resounded, war cries went up, and a battle to the death began. The thunder of hooves and the whistling of arrows filled the sky and shook the earth. The two sides charged again and again. The dead and wounded were beyond counting. Among them, on

---

[80] See *Takemuki-ga-ki* 30. Kōgon, Go-Fushimi, and Hanazono moved to Rokuhara on Genkō 3.3.12 (*Takemuki* has 3.3.16).

[81] For example, the army of Aso Harutoki, who besieged Kusunoki Masashige in 1333. It survived long after other Kamakura institutions had been destroyed.

Takauji's side, was Shidara Gorō (Saemon-no-jō), whose loyal death in the vanguard of Takauji's forces was especially moving.

At the hour of the sheep [10 a.m.] the Rokuhara forces were defeated at Ōmiya and retreated. A loyalist force attacking from the south entered the capital via the Toba Road and Takeda, and occupied positions in several places around Kujō, while other forces attacking from various directions broke into the capital. The Rokuhara men therefore retreated into their fortress. Some braves among them, keen to win honor for their family and themselves, attempted sorties, and the battle continued for seven days.

Meanwhile, many on Go-Daigo's side favored using their great strength to surround the fortress immediately and kill all of the enemy. However, Hosokawa Kazuuji (Awa-no-kami) said, "The enemy will fight desperately If we do that, and our casualties will be high. If instead we open one side of our siege and allow them to flee, they will be in retreat, and we will wipe them out easily." This suggestion was carried out.

Many in the fortress changed their minds and came over to Takauji. The two Rokuhara administrators—Hōjō Nakatoki (Echigo-no-kami) of the north Rokuhara compound and Hōjō Tokimasu of the south— discussed the situation and concluded: "If we are to die, we would prefer to fall in battle here in the capital, but this would give us only personal fulfillment. We have His Majesty with us, and it would not help him or the Retired Emperors[82] for us to die fighting or to kill ourselves. We must first escort them out of the capital and await reinforcements from the Kantō, or send word to the forces besieging Mount Kongō, and only then join battle. Then we can quickly re-enter the capital."

They reported their position to the Emperor, who replied that the warriors should do as they saw fit. Accordingly, they left Rokuhara at midnight on the 7th day, proceeded east along the Kuzume road, crossed the Seta bridge, and came to a path across a field. It was now light. As the attending courtiers made their way through the thick, dew-laden summer grass that lined this unfamiliar mountain path,

---

82 Go-Fushimi and Hanazono.

their tears seemed to vie with the dew, for their sleeves were still wetter than the grass.

From roughly Moruyama on, skirmishers (*nobushi*) raced over hill and dale to attack the retreating force, of whom it is impossible to say how many were killed or wounded. That night the Emperor lodged at Kannonji in Ōmi.

The next day, the 9th of the 5th month [of Genkō 3, 1333], they were fleeing eastward when, at Banba in Ōmi, they were attacked by bandits (*akutō*) from Ōmi, Mino, Iga, and Ise. Claiming to be Go-Daigo partisans, the attackers raised their banner and blocked the road with their shields.[83]

Having fought in Kyoto on the 7th and survived the attacks of the skirmishers on the 8th, the previous day, the Rokuhara men and horses were too exhausted to go on. Nonetheless, some who valued their reputations fought all that day. However, there was no way out. The men agreed that they must perform the terrible act of killing the Retired Emperors, then all die in battle or by their own hand.

The commander, Nakatoki, said, "It would be disgraceful to survive and let His Majesty be captured, but if we die first, what happens afterwards will not matter." At the hour of the bird [6 p.m.] he therefore killed himself, followed by several hundred fellow warriors. Tokimasu had been struck by a stray arrow on the night of the 7th at Shinomiya-gawara. After his death, one of his retainers took his head and brought it to Banba, where Nakatoki viewed it before he committed suicide. The names of those who slit their bellies on this occasion were recorded then in the temple at Banba and therefore are still known.[84]

---

[83] According to *Masukagami*, the fifth son of Emperor Kameyama, the Itsutsuji Prince Moriyoshi, led a "waiting imperial force." Documents issued by him, describing the destruction of Rokuhara, appear in *Kamakura ibun*, vol. 41, doc. 32160, Itsutsuji Miya ryōji. This Moriyoshi is not to be confused with another, the more famous son of Go-Daigo.

[84] This document, the *Ōmi Banba no shuku Rengeji kakochō*, survives (*Kamakura ibun* no. 32137) and shows that 430 perished. The days correspond to those in the narrative. Of this list, 189 have their names recorded. Almost all were close Kamakura confederates. Only one was an administrator (*bugyōnin*) of Rokuhara; another was a member of the council. The rest, whose sympathies lay with the court, abandoned Kamakura with alacrity.

After this battle was lost, Emperor Kōgon and the Retired Emperors learned that Former Emperor Go-Daigo had entered the capital. When the same news reached Mount Kongō, the great force attacking Masashige's fortress lifted their siege and withdrew to Nara. They did not know what to do next. However, once Takauji had destroyed Rokuhara and become Shogun in the capital, on Go-Daigo's instructions he issued an order to all the warriors in the land to destroy the Bakufu, and the troops in Nara hastened to join him. Thereupon the commanders of the force attacking Masashige—Aso Tokiharu, Osaragi Takanao, and Nagasaki Shirōzaemon—surrendered in Nara and took holy orders there. They were imprisoned nonetheless.[85]

11. *Nitta Yoshisada Raises an Army*

Every man of the Bakufu paled when the news reached the Kantō that Takauji had accepted Go-Daigo's commission. In the middle of the 5th month, Nitta Yoshisada advanced under Go-Daigo's banner from Kōzuke to Serata, in the same province, and took up position there. He, too, was of the line of Yoshiyasu[86] and Yoshishige,[87] the sons of Yoshikuni, who himself was the third son of [Hachimantarō] Yoshiie, a descendant of Emperor Seiwa. Having received Go-Daigo's order in secret, Yoshisada and the families of his branch all rose up: the Yamana, Satomi, Horikuchi, Ōdate, Iwamatsu, and Momonoi, every one of them a superb warrior. Nagasaki Magoshirō, the protector of the province, hastened to engage Yoshisada's forces, but every warrior in Kōzuke had already joined Yoshisada. Overwhelmed, he withdrew. When Yoshisada led his great army to invade Musashi, all the warriors of that province joined him as well.

On the 14th of the 5th month Takatoki's younger brother, the novice Esei,[88] led a force toward Musashi. On the same day they camped on

---

[85] The Migita collection contains a document of praise written by Aso Harutoki. These men were killed by Go-Daigo in 1335, when Kamakura partisans launched a rebellion.
[86] The Ashikaga founder.
[87] The Nitta founder.
[88] Hōjō Shirō Yasuie.

the Yamaguchi estate.[89] The next day, the 15th, they fought all day at Bunbai and Sekito-gawara, and there is no telling how many thousands or tens of thousands were killed or wounded. Among them were Esei's most trusted retainers, Abu Saemon Nyūdō Dōtan, Awata, and Yokomizo Hachirō, all of whom died in the first encounter. The Kamakura forces therefore withdrew, and Yoshisada's army advanced on Kamakura. One would have thought from the turmoil in the city that the enemy had already invaded.

Accordingly, the Bakufu sent its forces out along three roads. The commander on the Lower Road was Kanazawa Sadamasa. Near Tsurumi, in Musashi, he encountered Chiba Sadatane, who had advanced from that province in alliance with Yoshisada. He was defeated and withdrew.

The commander on the Musashi Road was Hōjō Moritoki (Sagami-no-kami). He joined battle at Chiyozuka in Suzaki, but he, too, was defeated and killed himself rather than retreat a single step. Nanjō and Akui died there as well.

Osaragi Sadamichi (Mutsu-no-kami), the commander on the Middle Road, joined battle at Kuzuhara. The invading force fought so hard that Sadamichi, too, was defeated, and he withdrew after Honma Yamashirozaemon and many others were killed.

On the 18th of the 5th month, at about the hour of the sheep [2 p.m.], Yoshisada's force passed Cape Inamura and set fire to the houses on the beach.[90] The people in Kamakura rushed about in confusion when they saw the smoke. The scene was beyond words. Suwa, Nagasaki, and others of Takatoki's retainers defended the city without regard for their lives. Ōdate Muneuji, the commander of the force that attacked that day on the beach, was killed at Inase River. Yoshisada's force withdrew and pitched camp on Ryōzen.[91]

---

[89] A estate (*shōen*) overlapping present-day Sayama in Saitama-ken and Murayama in Tokyo. The Tenri and Kyōdai texts both give the place as Oyamada, an estate in present-day Machida, in Tokyo. Since Bunbai and Sekito-gawara, where the forces engaged the following day, are near Machida, scholars regard Oyamada as more likely.
[90] Yuigahama, the beach at Kamakura.
[91] A hill located to the northeast of Inamura, and just to the west of the Gokurakuji road into Kamakura.

From the 18th to 22nd of that month, there was not a moment when battle cries, the whistling of arrows, and the tramping of men and horses could not be heard at every approach to the city, including Kobukurozaka, Yamanouchi, and the road carved from the cliffs at Gokurakuji. Men had looked up to the Hōjō because such glory and prosperity as theirs had rarely been seen even in ancient times, but they could not avert the inevitable turning of joy into sorrow. Tragically, Takatoki committed suicide at Kasaigayatsu on Genkō 3.5.22 [1333], and several hundred of his relatives did the same.

A military force cannot move easily along the shore at Cape Inamura, because the cliff there is high and the path narrow. However, a strange thing happened: the tide suddenly went out, and the beach remained dry during the ensuing battle. People called this an act of divine protection. The city of Kamakura faces the sea on the south and is surrounded on the other three sides by mountains. The invading forces took up position on the peaks and descended the mountains, setting fire to houses here and there. Wind blew into the city from every direction, so that the whole city burned down. Kamakura had clearly opposed Heaven's will.

Yoritomo founded the Bakufu during Jishō. Thereafter the Bakufu acted humbly, revered the throne, treated the people with benevolence, and ruled the land. It established laws for the conduct of government and regulations to control the military. As a result, no signal fires were ever lit, people ceased to lock their doors, and for many years the country had been happy and prosperous. Now the Bakufu's time must have come, for in the summer of Genkō 3 over 700 of Tokimasa's descendants were destroyed at the same time. However, all the Bakufu's provisions remain in force. They constitute the body of law for ruling the country and regulating the way of bow and arrow.

Although the destruction of the Bakufu was Yoshisada's achievement, for some reason Yoshiakira,[92] then in his fourth year, accompanied him in a palanquin as [nominal] commander. After the destruction of the Bakufu he lived in the abbot's quarters (*bettō bō*) in the two-

---

[92] Takauji's eldest son. He became the second Ashikaga shogun.

story central hall (*nikaidō*) of Eifukuji.[93] Happily, all the warriors placed themselves under this young lord, whose face, people said, showed the fortunate signs of an everlasting shogunal reign.

Hosokawa Kazuuji, as well as his younger brothers Yoriharu and Morouji, had been sent down from the capital to crush the Bakufu. On the way they heard that the Bakufu had already been destroyed, but they continued on to Kamakura nonetheless and there assisted their young lord.

There was much excited talk throughout Kamakura, day after day, and the city was restless.[94] Wishing to settle the matter, the three brothers, Kazuuji, Yoriharu, and Morouji, went to Yoshisada to ask him to clarify the situation. Things settled down once Yoshisada had stated in writing that he had no ambitions. Thereafter he and his relatives went up to the capital.

12. The Unification of Japan

Meanwhile Go-Daigo had returned to the capital from Hōki. The courtiers of all ranks who came out to meet him were so beautifully dressed as to seem flowers in bloom. He was accompanied by Masashige and Nagatoshi, who had loyally given him distinguished service, and by a great number of other warriors. He chose to reside in the Nijō palace. Ever since Hōgen, Heiji, and Jishō, military houses had controlled the country and ruled it as they pleased; but now, for a change, in Genkō 3 [1333], Japan was unified under the throne.

The Emperor decided to return to the government of the Engi and Tenryaku eras [901-923 and 947-951].[95] His truly good and happy reign brought peace to the warriors and glory to the people. Governors and protectors were promptly appointed to every province, and courtiers to appropriate ranks. Warriors like Kusunoki, Nawa, and Akamatsu,

---

93 In Kamakura. Eifukuji had a two-story central hall (*nikaidō*) so remarkable that the Nikaidō, who patronized it, made the word their surname.
94 The people of Kamakura suspected rivalry between Yoshisada and Yoshiakira (the Ashikaga) and feared a power struggle between the two.
95 Agreed golden ages of imperial government.

from both the San'yōdō and the San'indō, displayed overweening pride in the favor that the Emperor had shown them.

The Emperor decided in his wisdom to establish a new office known as the Court of Settlements[96] (*Zasso Ketsudansho*) with eight bureaus, each headed by a high-ranking courtier, for the Kinai and the seven circuits. This court had the same function as the old Adjudicators (*Hikitsukeshū*).[97] Important matters were decided at the Record Office (*Kirokusho*); others matters were dealt with by a body known as the Kubodokoro, consisting of Iga Kanemitsu, Ōta Chikamitsu, Tomibe Nobutsura, and Kō no Moronao.[98] An Office of the Imperial Guard [Mushadokoro] was established as before, headed by members of the Nitta family and members of other families assigned to it in turn. The Emperor said, "These present-day arrangements are new, modified versions of old ones that had survived or been dropped. My declarations will stand as precedents for the future." There were constant reports of new imperial decisions.

The Shogun, who enjoyed the Emperor's supreme regard, was of course promoted and, in addition, named governor of Musashi, Sagami, and other several other provinces, in accordance with the precedent set in the case of Yoritomo. In the winter of that year, Prince Nariyoshi went down to the Kantō as Seii Shogun.[99] Ashikaga Tadayoshi accompanied him, escorted by most of the warriors from the eight provinces of the East. Kamakura had been devastated in the fighting of the previous summer but Tadayoshi's presence gave the people of the city some relief.

---

[96] This court dealt with minor claims, particularly concerning lands.

[97] This office was established in 1249 to promote the investigation of suits and appeals brought before the Council of State (Hyōjōshū) for judgment. It had two branches, one at Rokuhara and one in Kyushu.

[98] The *Baishōron* author misread the characters for the Kirokusho, an office established by Emperor Go-Sanjō in 1069. Go-Daigo reinstated it in 1334.

[99] Go-Daigo appointed Nariyoshi, his seventh son, Seii Shogun and sent him to Kamakura, where Nariyoshi nominally ruled, together with Takauji's younger brother Tadayoshi, from early in 1334 to the 8th month of 1335. The Nakasendai rebellion then forced him to flee.

13. Warriors and Courtiers: Fire and Water

Meanwhile, in the capital, where the Record Office and the Court of Settlements had been established, courtiers close to the Emperor nonetheless, in extraordinary cases, appealed to him directly about injustices. His orders were issued in the morning and revised in the evening, so that people's fortunes rose and fell as swiftly as a hand turns.

The Emperor generously remitted the capital sentences of those who had surrendered when the Bakufu fell, except for the direct retainers of Takatoki's family. He also issued orders confirming titles to estates under the standardized laws. However, this measure deprived some of their estates, and these people consequently bore a grudge. At the same time, a joke circulated at court: "Takauji does not exist."[100]

By destroying the Bakufu Go-Daigo had satisfied the wish of generations of Emperors to curtail warrior power. In Kamakura, however, the supreme authority was Tadayoshi, and the warriors of the eastern provinces submitted to him rather than to Kyoto. Go-Daigo feared that his hope of unifying the realm would come to naught. Meanwhile, those warriors who resented the court aspired only to seize the realm as Yoritomo had done. So it was that Genkō 3 [1333] ended with warriors and courtiers ranged against each other like fire and water.

The next year the era name was changed to Kenmu 1. The courtiers dressed up for the New Year's banquet (*gansan sechie*) and other court ceremonies, and the old days seemed to have returned. Outside, however, feelings were running high, and everything appeared to be in turmoil. People therefore feared that the good days could not last. Meanwhile, Prince Moriyoshi, Nitta Yoshisada, Kusunoki Masashige, and Nawa Nagatoshi received the Emperor's orders in secret and several times were on the point of setting out. Since it was difficult to

---

[100] Although Go-Daigo had favored Takauji and given him a high court rank at the beginning of the new regime, Takauji's name did not appear on the list of officers of important government organs. The emperor and his supporters seem to have quickly recognized him as a dangerous rival.

gauge how many men Takauji had at his disposal, however, any conflict might not go well. Under these circumstances the Emperor made several sudden, apparently casual visits to Kitayama on days when fighting threatened to break out, in order to keep those who mattered there informed.[101]

With the capital threatened by war, the Honma and Shibuya families,[102] supporters of the former Bakufu, rose in revolt in the Kantō early in the 3rd month and advanced on Kamakura from Sagami. The Kamakura force, commanded by Shibukawa Yoshisue, charged out and joined battle in front of Gokurakuji, where they defeated the rebels after a few engagements. When news of this incident reached Kyoto, Aso Tokiharu, Osaragi Takanao, and Nagasaki Shirōzaemon—the commanders of the forces attacking Mount Kongō, captured the previous year—were executed on the outskirts of the capital, in retaliation for the Honma and Shibuya uprising. Thereafter, disorder in the capital worsened and continued without letup.

It was then reported that a force commanded by Prince Moriyoshi would attack Takauji's residence on Kenmu 1.6.7 [1334]. Takauji's men surrounded his residence, while his reserve force filled Nijō. Things looked serious. Nothing happened that day, but Takauji expressed his indignation. The Emperor replied that this had not been his idea, but instead Prince Moriyoshi's.

Consequently, on the night of the 22nd of the 10th month, the Emperor arrested Moriyoshi when he visited the palace and confined him in the Guards Office (*Mushadokoro*). The following morning Moriyoshi was transferred to Tokiwai House[103] and kept there under the watchful eye of Takauji's men. The previous day, imperial guards (*banshū*), acting on the Emperor's orders, arrested scores of Moriyoshi's

---

[101] Different manuscripts given different versions of this sentence, which may be corrupt. Go-Daigo's empress was a Saionji and lived on the Saionji family's Kitayama estate. Kinmune, then the Saionji head, was so bitterly opposed to Go-Daigo that, according *Taiheiki*, he plotted to assassinate him. The relevant *Taiheiki* chapter is included in *Fourteenth-Century Voices I*.

[102] Kamakura housemen from Sagami.

[103] Tokiwai-dono, the residence of retired emperors since Kameyama, located north of Ōinomikado and east of Kyōgoku. Go-Fushimi and Hanazono occupied it at the time. It figures repeatedly in *Takemuki-ga-ki*.

retainers, including Nanbu and Kudō. In the 11th month Hosokawa Akiuji received custody of Moriyoshi and took him to the Kantō. No words could describe Moriyoshi's feelings on this unexpected journey. Apparently he was taken to Kamakura because the Emperor blamed him for the plot, although in fact the plot had been the Emperor's own. Moriyoshi was kept in Yakushidō-no-tani in Nikaidō. He is said to have remarked that he felt more bitterly toward the Emperor than toward Takauji.

14. The Battle of the Kantō

So Kenmu 1 [1334] ended. The disorder in the land only mounted in Kenmu 2 [1335]. Early in the 7th month, the family of Mikawa Shōun,[104] a priest at the Upper Suwa Shrine in Shinano and the father of Suwa Tokitsugu, together with the Shigeno, subjugated the entire province under the command of Takatoki's second son Shōjumaru, who called himself Sagami Jirō.

Ogasawara Sadamune, the governor and protector of Shinano reported this urgently to the capital. The court council reasoned that the rebels might move into Owari at Kuroda, along the Kiso Road, and decided first to dispatch the imperial army to Owari. However, the rebels had already subjugated one province and were advancing to attack Kamakura. Shibukawa Yoshisue and Iwamatsu Tsuneie resisted them all day at Onakage-ga-hara in Musashi, but the rebels fought so furiously that both men killed themselves. Oyama Hidetomo was sent, but the fighting became so difficult that he, his family, and several hundred of their retainers killed themselves at Fuchū in the same province.

Accordingly, Tadayoshi left Kamakura on the 22nd of the 7th month. On the same day he killed Prince Moriyoshi at his residence in Yakushidō-no-tani—an unspeakably awful thing to do. Tadayoshi fought all day at Idenozawa in Musashi, but he lost many men and abruptly withdrew along the Tōkaidō. Prince Nariyoshi and Ashikaga Yoshiakira, then in his sixth year, accompanied him. When they

---

[104] Mikawa Yorishige.

reached the Tagoshi post station,[105] they were attacked by old Bakufu supporters from Izu and Suruga. Although fewer in number, Tadayoshi's men defended their position very cleverly, so that when Kudō Iriezaemon, of Suruga, rushed to their aid with over one hundred mounted warriors, he and his men fought well and scattered the enemy. Tadayoshi then crossed Utsunotani Pass and hurried on to Mikawa, where he rested his men and horses.

Hosokawa Shirō Yorisada, known as Gia, was at Mount Kawamura in Sagami for a hot spring treatment. His son, Hosokawa Akiuji, sent him a message reminding him that he had so far done nothing for the imperial cause and advising him to return to the capital. Gia replied, "I regret not yet having performed a single act of service, even though I have been in enemy territory. Everyone would doubt me, if I were to live on. Therefore I will sacrifice my life now, so that my descendants should be free of worry and dedicate themselves to the struggle." He committed suicide in front of the messenger. Takauji heard of this and grieved deeply. It was in truth a brave deed, and one in full accordance with the way of a loyal retainer; yet it was also sad.

Perhaps because of this deed his descendants fought so loyally in every encounter, and such men as Hosokawa Tadatoshi and Hosokawa Masauji[106] died in battle. After peace was restored in Japan, Gia's sons built in his memory the Ankokuji temples in the capital and in Mutsu,[107] and Chōkōji in Sanuki. It was a wonderful thing, people said, that Gia had regarded his life as less important than a speck of dust. His death brought him great honor.[108]

---

[105] In Suruga.

[106] Tadatoshi was Akiuji's younger brother. Masauji was Akiuji's son.

[107] At Ashikaga Tadayoshi's urging in 1337, a temple named Ankokuji was built in each province (or, in some provinces, an existing temple was renamed Ankokuji) for the repose of the souls of those who had died in the war.

[108] This section seems implausible. These two paragraphs about Hosokawa Gia, which do not appear in the oldest version of the text, represent a later addition by the Hosokawa to glorify their ancestors. The focus on the way of the loyal retainer likewise represents an ideal that postdates the fourteenth century.

15. The Kamakura Loyalist Rebellion, or the Twenty-Day Bakufu

Takauji said to the Emperor, when the news about the fighting in the Kantō reached the capital, "I hear that rebels in the Kantō have risen up and attacked Kamakura, and that Tadayoshi, being short of men and lacking the skill to defend the city, has withdrawn along the Tōkaidō. I request leave to assist him." Takauji said this many times, but the Emperor withheld his permission.

Takauji therefore left the capital on the 2nd of the 8th month. He said, "This is not a personal matter, after all. It is for the sake of the realm." Many warriors then had turned against the court and gladly followed him. He reached Yahagi in Mikawa. The two commanders from Kyoto and Kamakura met him there. When they left Yahagi for the Kantō, their way was blocked by a force of supporters of the old Bakufu, who had fortified the village of Hashimoto in Tōtōmi. A certain Abu Tango-no-kami, a warrior in the vanguard, crossed the inlet, engaged the enemy, and scattered them, but he himself was wounded. Takauji was so impressed that he had Abu succeed to the estate of the late novice Abu Dōtan.

Other warriors began to follow Abu's example, fighting bravely without regard for their lives. This was the first of seven battles that they won, the others being at Sayo-no-Nakayama in that province; at Takahashi-nawate in Suruga; at Mount Hakone, on the Sagami River; on the Katase River; and at Kamakura itself. The enemy could not check their advance. Thus, when they stormed into Kamakura on the 19th of the 8th month, the Suwa Shrine priest, his father, and a son of lay priest Abu Dōtan committed suicide. Those who survived the attack either surrendered or were killed.

Sagami Jirō had returned to the city of his forefathers to rule for just over twenty days, from the end of the 7th month to the 19th day of the 8th. It is sad that he came to grief so soon. Among those who entered Kamakura with him, not one was an elder capable of assisting him. He had been very young.

Members of the Osaragi, Gokurakuji, and Nagoe families, who had just managed to save themselves by becoming acolytes at temples here and there,[109] had quickly returned to lay life; but none had recognized leadership qualities, and they therefore amounted only to a traitorous rabble. It was thought that they had failed because they had in truth acted against Heaven's will. This is known as the Kamakura Loyalist Rebellion (*nakasendai*) or the Twenty-Day Bakufu.

The Shogun and his brother entered Kamakura and moved into the abbot's Nikaidō residence. Those who had accompanied Takauji from the capital were pleased with the rewards that they received for their distinguished service. Since those who had fought for the old Bakufu were not executed or exiled, each was willing to confess his former misdeeds and become truly loyal to Takauji. People in the capital sent their relatives to congratulate Takauji for subduing the eastern barbarians.

The imperial envoy Nakanoin Tomomitsu brought the Kantō the message that the Emperor highly approved of Takauji's quick suppression of the rebellion in the eastern provinces, but that since the rewards to the warriors were to be made by the Emperor in the capital, Takauji should return there immediately. Takauji replied that he would hasten to comply. Tadayoshi then strongly urged him not to: "It was your military exploits that destroyed Takatoki and unified the realm," he said. "However, during your years in the capital, the courtiers and Yoshisada plotted repeatedly against you, and it is only by good luck that you are safe. You should not return, now that you are far from those rivals." Takauji therefore gave up the idea of returning to the capital. He built his residence on Wakamiya-kōji, on the site where generations of Shoguns had lived, and those of Kō no Moronao and other daimyo[110] stood side by side, giving Kamakura a very prosperous air.

Takauji granted confiscated lands in Shinano and Hitachi to the warriors who had accompanied him, as well as to Tadayoshi, as rewards for their distinguished service. And when Takauji heard that Yoshisada was on his way to the Kantō as the commander of a

---

[109] After the Kamakura Bakufu fell in 1333.

[110] This early use of the term daimyo probably means literally, in this context, "big names" rather than incipient magnates. Ultimately, however, it would become a favored term to describe warriors with considerable powers in the province.

punitive force, he immediately appointed Uesugi Norifusa protector of Kōzuke, Yoshisada's own domain.[111] Norifusa then went to Kōzuke to make his preparations. Things had come to such a pass that relatives and deputies of those who served the court hurried to the capital, while those whose loyalties were to the Kantō fled the capital. The streams of travelers going up and down the Tōkaidō had suddenly become as numerous as the threads in cloth. After the fall and winter of Kenmu 2 [1335], the realm knew no peace.

16. The Battle Between Yoshisada and Takauji

Meanwhile, news came that an imperial army numbering in the tens of thousands was on its way to the Kantō. Takauji therefore sent a large force under Kō no Moroyasu[112] along the Tōkaidō. He told Moroyasu to proceed to Mikawa and take up a position beside the Yahagi River and then recruit an army from the province, since it was Takauji's own; but that he was on no account to cross to the west side of the river. Having received Takauji's orders, Moroyasu took up position on the east bank of the Yahagi, while Yoshisada with his great force did the same on the west bank.

For two or three days they held each other, and there was no decisive battle. Then Moroyasu divided his eastern force into three sections. The left and right wings crossed the river and fought furiously on the west bank, but the centers of the two armies did not advance. Next, a warrior by the name of Horiguchi Sadamitsu charged out from Yoshisada's center and laid about him, fighting with consummate skill. The army on the west bank crossed the river and the fighting became so difficult that Moroyasu withdrew. He tried to hold the enemy at Sagizaka in Tōtōmi and then at Imami village in Suruga, but he could not do so.

Accordingly, on Kenmu 2.12.2 [1335], Tadayoshi set out at the head of an army numbering in the tens of thousands, and on the 5th he quickly rode to Tagoshi-gawara. He fought a confused battle all that

---

[111] Norifusa perished on Kenmu 3.1.27 (1336), as Takauji fled the capital. He was Takauji's uncle.

[112] The older brother of Kō no Moronao, often remembered wrongly as the younger.

day. The sound of the feet of men and horses was like thunder, and the sparks from the clashing weapons were like lightning. Words cannot describe how terrible it was. The fighting went on like this, and how many were killed or wounded there is no knowing. The odds being against Tadayoshi, many warriors from his side surrendered and joined Yoshisada. I shall not reveal their names, so as not to disgrace them. Meanwhile, Tadayoshi dug in at Mount Hakone. He cut a trench across the road at Mizunomi,[113] which he made his stronghold, and his remaining mighty warriors, including Nikki, Hosokawa, Kō no Moronao and Kō no Moroyasu, pitched camp there.

When Tomomitsu, the imperial envoy, reached Kamakura, Takauji undertook to return to the capital. However, he had not done so, and he felt very bad about that, since he had not wanted things to turn out this way. He said, "The Emperor granted me an audience and gave me his orders in person. Such were his gracious words and good wishes that, whatever may happen, I shall never forget his kindness. The present events are not at all what I had hoped." Accordingly, Takauji entrusted the conduct of political affairs to Tadayoshi and retired in secret to Jōkōmyōji,[114] accompanied only by Hosokawa Yoriharu and three trusted followers.[115] However, when he heard that his army was having a hard time fighting along the Tōkaidō, he said, "Life will have no meaning for me if Tadayoshi dies. Heaven well knows that I have no intention of disobeying an imperial order. Hachiman Daibosatsu will protect me."

When Takauji had sent out his forces in the past he may have anticipated such a development, since he had kept the Oyama, Yūki, and Naganuma families with him. These descended from three brothers,[116] the sons of lay priest Fujiwara (later Oyama) Masamitsu. These three had hastened to join Yoritomo when he first raised his army, and they served him faithfully during Jishō [1177-81]. They

---

[113] Mizunomi was a barrier (*sekisho*) in the mountains on the Tōkaidō, not far southwest of Ashinoko. It appears also in the passage translated from *Gen'ishū*.

[114] A Kamakura temple built by Hōjō Nagatoki in 1251.

[115] Later, he would personally write the prayer that appears as an epigraph to this volume.

[116] Oyama Tomomasa, Naganuma Munemasa, and Yūki Tomomitsu (*Sonpi bunmyaku*).

themselves descended from Fujiwara Hidesato, governor of Musashi and Shogun of the Government Headquarters in Mutsu, who in Shōhei [931-937] killed the rebel Taira Masakado, and whose descendants held the office of Shogun of the Government Headquarters in Mutsu for five generations. They were all accomplished in the arts of bow and horse, and their families had been famed for generations for their martial skills. Their force of over two thousand mounted warriors received Takauji's orders and left Kamakura as his vanguard on Kenmu 2.12.8 [1335]. Everyone thought that they were going to reinforce the army at Hakone, but Takauji had a different strategy. "If we go to Mizunomi," he said, we will only hold off the enemy there and gain no other advantage. However, if we advance with this fresh force beyond Hakone and then join battle, the enemy will be surprised and confused, and they will be easily destroyed."

On the night of the 10th of the same month, under cover of darkness, they therefore waited at the Takenoshita Road for dawn to break. Early in the hour of the dragon [8 a.m.] the enemy, under Prince Takayoshi[117] and Nitta Wakiya Yoshisuke[118] took up position in a field south of the shrine of the Ashigara deity—the deity who composed the poem, "If you loved me, you would have wasted away..."[119] Takauji's vanguard descended the mountain, sweeping over hills and fields, and joined battle at the foot of a small hill. The enemy could not hold their ground and retreated. Takauji's force followed up their victory by pursuing them for over ten miles. At Aizawabara there was a desperate battle. Takauji's force killed several hundred of the enemy. He was so impressed that he awarded the Ōta estate in Musashi to Oyama Tsuneinumaru[120]. It was a place to which the Oyama family had a good title. He also awarded the district of Seki in Hitachi to Yūki.[121]

---

[117] A son of Go-Daigo raised by Yoshida Sadafusa and groomed for the throne. When Go-Daigo initially fled the capital, Takayoshi fled with Nitta Yoshisada to Kanegasaki. He was killed in 1337 when this fortress fell.

[118] Yoshisada's younger brother.

[119] A poem from book 10 of the Kakuichi *Heike monogatari*. According to legend, the deity was away from home for three years and noted on his returned that his wife was still plump. He accused her of not loving him and divorced her.

[120] Assumed to be Oyama Tomouji, son of Suetomo.

[121] According to *Yūki-ke no ki*, Yūki Tomosuke.

These were the first of Takauji's awards in this war. Every man who knew about them became willing to fight fiercely without regard for his life. People thought this a good illustration of the saying, "Where there is tasty bait, there will be fish; where there are rich rewards, there will be heroes."

17. The Defeat of Yoshisada

On the following day, the 12th, the army from the capital retreated to Suruga and took up position at Mount Sano. Ōtomo Sadanori came from the capital at the head of an imperial force of over three hundred mounted warriors, but he told Takauji that he would come over to his side, and Takauji replied that he had no objection. When the exchange of arrows began, Ōtomo's force therefore joined Takauji's side and fought loyally for him. The enemy's position was soon broken, and many from the capital, including Nijō Tamefuyu, were killed. Tamefuyu had been a friend of Takauji, and Takauji had his head brought to him. The sight of it filled him with sorrow.

It rained that night, and Takauji camped in a mountain field overlooking the Izu provincial capital. His army, which had won the battles of that day and the day before, covered the ground like clouds. The rain continued through the night, but on the morning of the 13th Takauji attacked the provincial capital without waiting for a break in the weather. Meanwhile, Yoshisada lifted his siege of Mizunomi, and his force withdrew during the night. Takauji's army caught up with them when they passed the shrine of the Mishima deity and came to the Tōkaidō, and the battle continued for two hours, from the hour of dragon to that of the serpent [10 a.m.]. The shouts, the battle cries, and the whistling of arrows sounded like the six earth-quakes.[122]

The Awa Novice[123] was killed here. It was reported that Yoshisada had barely managed to cross the Fuji River with his surviving troops.

---

[122] There are three different accounts of the six earthquakes. The one most commonly accepted has them occur at the Buddha's conception; birth; enlightenment; first preaching; the moment when Mara urged him to live; and nirvana.

[123] Ogawa Makoto suggests (*Ashikaga ichimon shugo hattenshi no kenkyū*, p. 641-43) that he was Hatakeyama Iekuni.

Takauji's force, on the other hand, had won battles for three days (at Takenoshita, Mount Sano, and the Izu provincial capital) and had destroyed a great number of the enemy. On this day, the 13th, the two commanders, Takauji and Tadayoshi, joined forces and pitched camp, occupying all the territory from Fuchū to Kurumagaeshi and Ukishima-ga-hara. The colored hangings and crested banners of the various families fluttered in the wind, and it is impossible to say how many thousands or tens of thousands there were.

On the following day, the 14th, they met where Takauji was staying. One opinion held that the two commanders should return to Kamakura and rule the Kantō. The other held that, even if they controlled all of the Kantō, it was essential to win on the Tōkaidō and in the capital, and that they should therefore join forces and advance. Consequently they set out along the Tōkaidō on the 15th. When they reached Ukishima-ga-hara it was the middle of the 12th month, and deep snow covered Mount Fuji down to the surrounding plains. It was impossible to tell where the mountain ended and the sky began. The snow seemed too deep to be only this year's accumulation. The warriors who had gone over to the army from the capital at the time of the battle of Tagoshi-gawara, on the 5th, surrendered to Takauji at the Fuji River.

18. The Tenryū River

Eastern warriors had advanced to the west three times in Japan: Noriyori and Yoshitsune in Juei 3 [1184], Yasutoki and Tokifusa in Jōkyū, and Takauji and Tadayoshi that year, Kenmu 2 [1335]. The warriors were in high spirits, never doubting that Takauji would conquer the capital. However, they were sure that there would be battles at places along the Tōkaidō where mountains and rivers impede progress. When they came to the Tenryū River, however, they found that a strong bridge, guarded by the ferrymen, had been built across it.[124]

The river was deep and the current swift, and the work must have been extremely difficult. Takauji asked, "Who had you build this

---

124 This river was normally crossed by means of small ferryboats.

bridge?" The ferrymen replied: "We were hiding in the mountains and forests, and had hidden our boats here and there because of the recent disorders. Then Lord Nitta arrived and said, 'Although retreating, we are still a large force. We cannot cross on horseback because there is no ford. Crossing in boats would be slow and it would be a shame to lose a single one of our men. Hurry, build a floating bridge. Give us trouble, and you will be killed.' So we built the bridge in two or three days. It took five days and nights for Lord Nitta to send his force across, and when he saw that no one was left, he started across the bridge himself. Some men of his then ordered us to destroy the bridge as soon as he had crossed. Lord Nitta became very angry. He turned back from the middle of the bridge, to call to us and said, 'Even we, in defeat, managed to build this bridge. If we were to destroy it, the victorious eastern warriors could rebuild it in no time. As a rule, when a small force with its back to a river fights a superior enemy, one of the tactics is to burn the boats and destroy the bridges so as to make retreat impossible. It would mean eternal shame for me if it were said that I panicked at the prospect of an immediate attack and destroyed a bridge that the enemy would be sure to rebuild. Guard the bridge well.' Then he calmly crossed the bridge. This is why we have been waiting for you and guarding the bridge." All who heard this were moved to tears, feeling that Yoshisada was without a doubt a great commander and a model for every man born into a warrior family.[125] The warriors of the eight provinces of the Kantō, as well as of the provinces along the Tōkaidō, all joined Takauji. His army so filled the fields and villages when his army it reached Mino and Ōmi that there was hardly any room for men or horses to move.

Meanwhile, Adept *(ajari)* Yūkaku, at Enryakuji on Mount Hiei, recruited over a thousand monks to guide the warriors of the province. They quickly fortified the Ikishiro Shrine in Ōmi and took up position there. His plan was to hold Takauji's army in the province and wait for the imperial force from Mutsu, which would attack Takauji from the rear. Thereupon Takauji put Kō no Moronao in command of a large force, which, on the last day of the 12th month of

---

[125] *Gen'ishū*, too, tells this story.

Kenmu 2 [1335], attacked the shrine and took it during the night. The shrine stood on the shore of Lake Biwa, west of the Noji post station, and the survivors are said to have fled in boats.

Meanwhile, Takauji divided his army. He gave Tadayoshi command of the force attacking Seta and made Kō no Moroyasu his deputy. Hatakeyama Takakuni was given command of the force attacking Yodo, and Yoshimi Yoritaka that of the one attacking Imoarai. Takauji himself took charge of the force attacking Uji. The commanders of the imperial force defending Seta were Chigusa Tadaaki, Yūki Chikamitsu, and Nawa Nagatoshi. The attack on Seta was expected to begin on the 3rd day of the 1st month. Takauji left for Uji along the Tawara Road.[126]

Since Emperor Go-Daigo's unification of the country in Genkō 3 [1333], Kitabatake Akiie had been serving as the governor of Dewa and Mutsu under the Third Prince,[127] whose mother was the quasi-empress (*jungō*).[128] He was reported to have passed the Fuwa Barrier with a force recruited from fifty-four districts and was coming to attack Takauji from the rear. Nitta Yoshisada, the commander of the imperial force at Uji, tore up twelve feet of planking and erected a tower (*yagura*) and a wall of shields in the middle of the bridge. In this way he checked Takauji's force. In the evening of the 8th day of that month, Nogi Yoichibei and Nakaguki, Yamakawa and Yūki retainers, fought below the tower on the bridge, displaying matchless skill. Takauji was so impressed that he personally gave each a sword. It was the greatest honor of their lives.

Meanwhile, the exchange of arrows across the river continued day and night. A large number of warriors from Shikoku and Chūgoku, including lay priest Akamatsu Enshin, and commanded by Hosokawa Jōzen, arrived at top speed in Settsu and Kawachi. They had previously received Takauji's call to arms. At the hour of the bird [6 p.m.] on the 9th day of the same month they informed Takauji at his camp that they would defeat Go-Daigo's imperial force at Yamazaki

---

[126] This represents a crucial stage in the attack on the capital, since the advancing Ashikaga army had to cross the Uji or Yodo rivers. Successful invaders divided their forces in this way.

[127] Prince Noriyoshi.

[128] Fujiwara no Renshi.

before noon the next day, the 10th, and would send up a smoke signal. It was agreed that Takauji would attack at the same time.

After waiting anxiously for daybreak, Jōzen, Enshin, and the provincial warriors (*kokujin*)129 advanced to the gates of the enemy fortress and attacked. As planned, they defeated the Yamazaki force before noon on the 10th, then stormed into Koga and Toba, setting fires. While the imperial troops there were fleeing into the city, during the night of the 10th the Emperor moved to Enryakuji. The imperial palace burned down.130 In recent years, since the Kan'in palace was destoyed,131 this had been the only one left standing. All were astonished and saddened by this dreadful act. Alas, the residen-ces of courtiers of all ranks, as well as those of Chikamitsu, Masashige, and Nagatoshi were reduced at once to ashes. One has heard how the Afang Palace and Xianyang132 burned when the Qin army was defeated, but one can only imagine that disaster, since it happened in China. This one recalled the flight of the Heike from Kyoto in Juei 3 [1184; actually, Juei 2, 1183].

---

129 In thirteenth-century texts such as *Heiji monogatari* this term (literally "people of the province") simply means a provincial resident. However, in the fourteenth century it came to refer to provincial warriors without administrative office or status (such as houseman) recognized by Kamakura. This text represents one of the oldest examples of this meaning.

130.The Tominokōji palace (east of Tominokōji at the level of Nijō), built in 1317.

131 A residential building used by some of the Fujiwara regents. Emperor Takakura began to use it as his own *sato-dairi* (temporary palace) in 1168. Thereafter, succes-sive emperors used it for the same purpose. It burned down in 1259.

132 The Qin capital, built by the emperor of Qin in 212 B.C.

BAISHŌRON

PART TWO

19. *Takauji's Entry into Kyoto and Yūki Chikamitsu's Worthy Service*

Takauji entered the capital at the hour of the horse [midday] on Kenmu 3.1.11 and stayed with Tōin Kinkata.[133] So many warriors came to surrender that his office could not record all their names.

Meanwhile, Yūki Chikamitsu's actions truly exemplify the conduct of a loyal subject.[134] He won universal praise, not only from those who saw him do it, but even from those who only heard of it.

On the night of the 10th, Go-Daigo was on his way to Enryakuji when Chikamitsu caught up with his party, dismounted, removed his helmet, knelt before the imperial palanquin, and said: "The imperial army should have won the battle near Kamakura and brought peace. Things turned out this way only because Ōtomo changed sides at Mount Sano. I have resolved to sacrifice my life for you, if you will grant me leave from my duties. I will pretend to surrender, then cross swords with Ōtomo. I will die loyal to Your Majesty."

So resolved, Chikamitsu returned from Shimogamo. He knew that he would never again be received by the Emperor, and he could not restrain the tears that wet his armor sleeves. Watching him recede into the distance, the Emperor felt a mixture of hope and pity, and he, too, wept.

Meanwhile, Ōtomo advanced with his more than two hundred mounted warriors to the south gate of Tōji. Leaving the rest of his force just north of Kujō, Chikamitsu took his kinsman Masudo Akisuke and one or two retainers, approached Ōtomo, and announced a

---

[133] A ranking Saionji courtier who served both the Northern and Southern courts. His diary, *Entairyaku*, is an important source of political information on the period.
[134] Older variants of the text lack this sentence. The Kyōdai and Kanshō texts state that he was brave and met a tragic end.

wished to surrender. Ōtomo replied that he had no objection. As they proceeded together along either side of the stream near the crossing of Higuchi-kōji and Higashi-no-Tōin, Ōtomo said, "We are approaching Takauji's residence. I will therefore take your sword, as custom requires."

Chikamitsu replied, "If I come into Takauji's presence I will soon be appointed a commander and render worthy service. In any case, it would be disgraceful to surrender my sword on the battlefield. I trust you, however. Do not shame me." He removed the sword at his waist, took it in his hand, and started across to the west bank of the stream.

Ōtomo suspected nothing. "I will return your sword after our audience with the Shogun," he said. He was about to take the sword when Chikamitsu urged his horse up beside Ōtomo's, and in one motion drew the sword and struck the man. Ōtomo gave him no chance to strike another blow. He gripped Chikamitsu with all his strength and killed him on the spot. Over ten of Chikamitsu's relatives, struggled, but they, too, were killed.

Ōtomo had received a horizontal slash above his eyes, a mortal wound. He cut a heroic figure indeed when, lying in a palanquin with a cloth tied around his head, he brought Chikamitsu's head to Takauji. We hear the stories of Fen Yusi and Yu Rang in China,[135] but they lived long ago. Chikamitsu's last act of service stands out in both past and present. All who wielded the bow and arrow praised him as a brave warrior, and remarked with tears in their eyes that everyone should be like him. Masudo Akisuke, too, was killed. Ōtomo died the next day. He was incomparable. When an enemy attacked, he immediately counterattacked and killed him, and he lost his own life for Takauji.

20. The Arrival of Mutsu Forces and the Battle at Miidera

Meanwhile for three days, starting on the 13th of the 1st month, Prince Noriyoshi,[136] Kitabatake Chikafusa,[137] and a great multitude of men

---

[135] Chinese warriors who sacrificed their lives out of loyalty. Their deeds are recorded in the *Shiji*.

[136] He would later become Emperor Go-Murakami, Go-Daigo's Southern Court successor.

from Dewa and Mutsu arrived in Higashi Sakamoto[138] on the Yamada and Yabase ferries. They soon lodged the Emperor in the Higanjo at the main Hie Shrine,[139] and the warrior monks of Enryakuji joined them.

Word went out that the imperial force would burn down Miidera, since the temple had sided with Takauji. Accordingly, a fresh force from Shikoku and Chūgoku, commanded by members of the Hosokawa family, set out to reinforce Miidera at daybreak on the 16th day of the 1st month. A force from Dewa and Mutsu, under the command of Yoshisada and Chikafusa's son Akiie, set out for Miidera at the same time. Akiie's army attacked the temple from the main road and from the shore, and after a few hours of fighting the position defended by the monks of Miidera was overrun. The temple was burnt down, and Takauji's forces returned to the capital.

21. The Ashikaga Force Defeats Nitta and Yūki

Takauji and Tadayoshi then took up position at the Nijō riverbank. Their army stretched from Tadasu Wood in the north to the Shichijō riverbank in the south. At about the hour of the horse the imperial army commanded by Yoshisada, whose own banner flew beside the imperial one, advanced from before Jūzenji at Awataguchi to the Sanjō riverbank and took up position on the east bank of the Kamo River, facing west. Takauji's army went into the enveloping "crane wings" formation. The thousands of mounted warriors, flying their banners in the sky, startled heaven and earth with their battle cries, and the arrows they exchanged fell like rain.

They had hardly drawn their weapons before the fighting began, and in the melee the bodies of men and horses piled up in mounds. Blood poured into the river. Surely, not even the battle in which

---

[137] 1293-1354, one of the great supporters of the Southern Court, a noted ideologue and military commander.

[138] On the western shore of Lake Biwa, below Mount Hiei.

[139] The Higanjo was a building in the shrine complex where a Buddhist service called Higan'e was held every spring and fall. Go-Daigo, who had escaped to Enryakuji, now moved here under the protection of Kitabatake Chikafusa.

shields floated in blood[140] could have been worse. Over a thousand imperial warriors were killed, including Chiba Takatane and Funada Yoshimasa, Yoshisada's best warriors, and Serata of the Left Gate Watch.[141] Many were killed or wounded on Takauji's side as well.

Towards evening, when the imperial army seemed to be losing, Takauji's forces pressed their advantage and launched an attack. However Yoshisada, who bore his banner himself,[142] and Chikamitsu's father, Yūki Munehiro of Shirakawa, kept fighting back with over a thousand mounted men. When the fighting moved on to the riverbank at Nakanomikado, in front of Shirakawa Jōjuin, it looked as though Takauji's forces might not be able to hold their ground. However, the combined family forces of Oyama and Yūki, numbering over two thousand mounted warriors, fought furiously and incessantly. The defeated enemy retreated to the Shishi-no-tani hills. There seemed to be only a few survivors. It was late in the hour of the bird [7 p.m.] on the 16th.

Yūki Munehiro on the enemy side, and Oyama and Yūki on Takauji's side, were of the same family. They announced their names to each other before engaging in battle. The dead on both sides numbered over one hundred. Those on the enemy side and those on Takauji's bore the same family crest and wore *hitatare* with the same striped pattern. The Oyama and Yūki forces on Takauji's side, sure that they would be fighting such men in the battles to follow, tore off their right sleeves and attached them to their helmets.[143]

On the 17th of the same month, the directors of the Board of Retainers (*Samuraidokoro*), Sasaki Nakachika and Miura Sadatsura, inspected the enemy heads at the Sanjō riverbank and reported that there were over a thousand.

---

[140] A battle scene in the *Shiji*.

[141] The Yura in the text is probably an error for Serata, a Nitta collateral name. The Kyōdai text describes this warrior as the best (*ichi no mono*) of Yoshisada's men.

[142] Apparently his bannerman had been killed.

[143] Members of the same family wore armor with similar crests. At times they attached emblems (*kasajirushi*) on helmet or armor sleeves for identification. Remarkably, in this case the Oyama and Yūki removed their right sleeve, which would have made them easily distinguishable from their relatives who fought for Go-Daigo.

22. The Ashikaga Defeat and Retreat to the West

Meanwhile, Go-Daigo's imperial army took up position from Hachibuse on Kirara-zaka, on Mount Hiei, to the Sekizan Shrine.[144] Takauji's army, with its vanguard at the Tadasu riverbank, filled the capital and Shirakawa.

On the 27th of the 1st month, at the hour of the dragon [8 a.m.] the enemy army, divided into two forces, came down via the riverbank and Kurama-guchi. Takauji's army, also divided into two forces, promptly advanced to meet them, but after a series of engagements Takauji's forces were defeated and retreated down along the river. The enemy pressed its advantage and attacked them unsparingly. Takauji and Tadayoshi turned their mounts towards the enemy, seemingly determined to die. Brave warriors rushed in front of them one after another, to protect them, and engaged the enemy. Uesugi Norifusa, Miura Sadatsura, Nikaidō Gyōzen from Shimōsa, and Soga Tarōzaemon died in rearguard actions in various places along the route. Meanwhile Takauji and his army proceeded south down the riverbank, west along Shichijō, crossed the Katsura River, and pitched camp. This was made possible by those who had served by sacrificing their lives.

23. The Hosokawas' Fierce Fight

Thereafter Takauji's army retreated south along Ōmiya as one force, then along the Toba Road to Yamazaki. Prior to this, in anticipation of an enemy advance south through Senbon-guchi, a force from Shikoku commanded by members of the Hosokawa family waited in reserve in the vicinity of the Uchino riding ground of the Right Palace Guards. The enemy did not come this way, but a great deal of smoke was observed rising from various places in the southern part of the city, and many war cries were heard there. The Hosokawa warriors therefore moved east along Nakanomikado. At the Kamo River they encountered a large force flying the imperial banner. They routed the

---

[144] Two paths up Mt. Hiei from the south and southwest. They met a third of the way up the mountain.

force, killed the bannerman and stole the banner. They then drove the enemy to Nishi Sakamoto and, with a shout of triumph, burned down the temporary imperial residence there. Next, they proceeded south along the riverbank and saw another large force, extending from the Nijō riverbank to Shijō, blocking their way. They checked to see whether the force belonged to Takauji's army: it turned out to be an enemy force under Yoshisada and his main followers, lying in wait for them. The Hosokawa brothers, Jōzen and Akiuji, therefore raised their battle cries and engaged the foe. Completely routed, their opponents fled by way of Awataguchi and the Kujūmetsu Road.[145]

Having routed all of the enemy forces that had filled the capital, the Hosokawa brothers assembled their forces at the Shichijō riverbank and went looking for Takauji. Local residents told them that his army, divided into two forces, had retreated toward the Toba Road; and that one force had then headed west along Shichijō, while the other headed south along Ōmiya. The Hosokawa brothers hastened to cross the Katsura River with their forces. At about the hour of the Boar [10 p.m.] they reached Takauji's camp and reported that they had routed the enemy forces in the capital. Takauji immediately set out and entered the capital, proceeding east along Shichijō. The dawn of the 28th day broke as they reached the Shichijō riverbank.

Takauji's forces had had to withdraw from the capital despite their great numbers. Takauji was therefore deeply impressed by the way the Hosokawa brothers had stayed and routed the enemy. He presented Hosokawa Akiuji with a brocade hitatare, *together with a letter of commendation graciously written in his own hand. No feat of arms could be called more glorious. It inspired others to even greater efforts to render service without regard for their lives.* At the time people spoke of Hosokawa Jōzen as though he were a demon.[146]

---

[145] This road leads just north of Amida-ga-mine (near Shishi-no-tani) and on to Uji and Yamashina.

[146] The above paragraph does not appear in the Kyōdai text, the 1466 Kanshō text, or any other. It represents another example of the Hosokawa embellishing their exploits. The older versions have only the final sentence.

24. The Head Mistaken for Yoshisada's

At about the hour of the monkey [4 p.m.] on the same day, the imperial force on Mount Hiei came down again by way of Kaguraoka.[147] Takauji's army therefore rushed there and engaged them. One Shirakawa Kojirō, from Echizen, killed an enemy warrior who declared himself to be Yoshisada, cut off his head, removed his red-braided armor, and took them to Takauji's camp. Everyone was overjoyed, but the head turned out not to be Yoshisada's. Instead it was that of Kasai Saburōzaemon. Kasai had closely resembled Yoshisada in looks and build, and his red-braided armor had been very like Yoshisada's famous heirloom armor of thin metal plates. No wonder, then, that Takauji's men had thought at first that the enemy commander had been killed.

25. Takauji Retreats to Shinomura

There was no battle on the following day, the 29th. A few of Takauji's troops who had withdrawn to Yamazaki two days earlier, returned to the capital. At about midnight on the last day of the 1st month the battle of Tadasu-gawara began, and both sides fought as if this day were their last. Takauji's force was defeated, and Nikaidō Yukichika was killed.

Takauji had left the capital to subdue the eastern barbarians[148] at the beginning of the 8th month of the previous year, and in the course of subjugating Sagami Jirō,[149] and the Suwa priests[150] and their followers, he had fought at various places along the Tōkaidō until he reached Kamakura. That winter, however, a misunderstanding that arose between the Emperor and Takauji resulted in the battle at the Yahagi River. Defeated, Takauji's eastern warriors entrenched themselves at Hakone. In the battle at Ashigara, however, Takauji prevailed. Without resting he pressed on and stormed into the capital.

---

[147] Yoshida-yama.
[148] Hōjō Tokiyuki and his supporters.
[149] Hōjō Tokiyuki.
[150] Suwa Tokitsugu and Suwa Yorishige.

However, the question of ultimate victory or defeat remained to be decided this year. For now, short of weapons, the horses tired and the men dispirited, Takauji's army was beaten. That evening it pitched camp at Shinomura in the province of Tanba.[151]

26. Takauji Takes up Position at Hyōgo

The next day, Kenmu 3.2.1 [1336], some still advocated storming the capital, but the Hosokawa favored withdrawing first, then striking a decisive blow. Accepting the advice of Akamatsu and other western warriors, they said: "First we move our camp to the port of Hyōgo in Settsu, confiscate the ships there in order to obtain provisions, and let the men and horses catch their breath. Then, we will invade the capital, acting in concert with the warriors who will join us from all the provinces."

Takauji's army therefore proceeded over Mount Mikusa to Inamino in Harima and reached Hyōgo on 3rd day of the 2nd month. There, Akamatsu Enshin went to Takauji and said, "This position is difficult to defend, and you would be ill-advised to stay here. Let me take you and your brother to my fortress at Maya, while your army camps here. It is three miles from here to Maya."

However, a certain brave warrior said to Takauji, "Enshin's opinion has merit, but it concerns only the security of your own residence. Since last year, the realm has been divided, and in many provinces the two sides face each other with the outcome yet undecided. If you and your brother spend even a night at the fortress and word of it spreads, our side will be demoralized, and the enemy will gain the advantage. What matters is ultimate victory. Therefore, it would not be wise for you to go to Maya."

Enshin rejoined, "I expressed my opinion only because this position is hard to defend. I never thought of the effect it might have in other provinces. Certainly, what matters most is what people else-where would say. Therefore, even if you were in the fortress already

---

[151] This is near where Takauji grew up and also where he first rebelled against Kamakura, nearly three years earlier.

you would do better to leave." Akamatsu Enshin agreed. It was therefore decided to pitch camp at Hyōgo.

27. The Battles at Nishinomiya and Segawa

Meanwhile, Ōuchi Nagahiro and Kotō Takezane,[152] who had recently
received Takauji's summons (*migyōsho*), joined him at Hyōgo with five
hundred warships.

Having decided to attack the capital with these fresh forces, Takauji
left Hyōgo with his army on the 10th of the 2nd month. However
Kusunoki Masashige, appointed protector of Izumi and Kawachi,
rushed to the beach at Nishinomiya in Settsu and forced him to retreat.
The two sides held each other for the rest of the day, but that night, for
no apparent reason, Masashige withdrew. The following day, the 11th,
the Suō and Nagato forces, under the command of members of the
Hosokawa family, set out for the capital. Yoshisada met them on the
riverbank at Segawa in Settsu and fought fiercely. Minamoto Yoriharu,
Hosokawa Kazuuji's younger brother, was severely wounded. Neither
side made any headway in the battle, and both withdrew to regroup
and let the men and horses catch their breath.

28. Akamatsu Advises Takauji to Withdraw to the Western Provinces and to Obtain a Decree from the Cloistered Emperor

Late that night, Akamatsu Enshin went in secret to see Takauji. He
said, "Even if we were to defeat the enemy and invade the capital, we
would be too tired to accomplish anything worthwhile. Would it not
be better to move your army to the western provinces for a while, let
the troops recover their morale, rest the horses, and ready the
weapons, and only then proceed to the capital?

"In any battle," he continued, "the banners are fundamental. The
Emperor's army follows the imperial banner. Our side has no compar-
able banner, and we therefore appear to be enemies of the throne. The
Jimyōin Cloistered Emperor [Go-Fushimi] is, after all, of a legitimate

---

152 The Ōuchi, administrators for Rokuhara, were prominent in Suō. The Kotō were
key figures from Nagato.

imperial line (*shōtō*), and I doubt very much that the destruction of Hōjō Takatoki pleased him.[153] We should quickly obtain a retired emperor's decree (*inzen*) from him and fly the imperial banner before us.

"Our side was worsted in every battle last year," he went on, "because when we set out from the Kantō you were in the west, and we were therefore at a disadvantage. Nonetheless, you were fortunate enough after all to enter the capital. This time, when you attack from the western provinces the enemy in the capital will have to face you, and you will accomplish your purpose.

"First, the Hosokawa should go to Shikoku. I myself will take control of Settsu and Harima. In Kyushu, the two sons of Myōe of Chikugo,[154] Saburō and Shōgen, will soon join you. Myōe recently received your summons, and they will certainly give you service.

"Ōtomo Sadanori was killed by Yūki Chikamitsu in Kyoto in the 1st month of this year, and his successor, Chiyomatsumaru, is still a child; but several hundred of the family's retainers are serving in your army. Can there be any doubt that you will return to the capital next month with forces from Chūgoku, Shikoku, and Kyushu? First, though, you should return to the foot of Mount Maya."

Akamatsu gave Takauji this advice repeatedly. Takauji therefore withdrew from his position at Segawa around midnight and entered Hyōgo on the 12th day at the hour of the hare [6 a.m.].

---

[153] Kōgon had retreated with most of the Hōjō-related officials associated with the Rokuhara, although not their lower ranking administrators. (See the earlier section, "Takauji Attacks Rokuhara.") In the end, over four hundred of these men were defeated and committed suicide. Although some courtiers were wounded, they did not die here like the Kamakura warriors. Some renounced the world, but Go-Daigo refused to recognize this. Kōgon was then treated by Go-Daigo as if he had never reigned. This emphasis on Jimyōin legitimacy contrasts with the earlier narrative. As for the *inzen*, Go-Fushimi, the senior member of the Jimyōin line, fell ill at this time, so that the edict was ultimately issued by Kōgon, then styled Shin'in (Junior Retired Emperor).
[154] Shōni Sadatsune, the deputy governor at Dazaifu in Kyushu.

29. Takauji's Army Moves from Hyōgo to Muro-no-tsu

When Tadayoshi returned to the foot of Mount Maya, he meant to go on to the capital without regard for his own life. Takauji therefore argued forcefully with him and persuaded him to return to Hyōgo. They boarded the ships at about the hour of the bird [6 p.m.] on the same day, without deciding who would board first, and the men's eagerness to do so showed how keen they were to get away.

Long ago, however, in Jishō [Jishō 4, 1180], when he first took up arms, Yoritomo was defeated in the battle of Ishibashi, and when he boarded a boat at Cape Manazuru there were only six men with him, including Doi Jirō Sanehira and Okazaki Shirō Yoshizane. Miura Kotarō Yoshimori joined him at sea, on the way to Awa or Kazusa. *Miura seemed truly loyal, and Yoritomo trusted him.*[155] The warriors of the eight eastern provinces joined him as soon as the boat reached Karishima, in Awa, and he accomplished his purpose. Also, when Yoriyoshi and Yoshiie went on a punitive expedition to the far north, their force was once reduced to only seven men. Therefore many said that with these initial reverses Takauji was following in his family's fine tradition.

Meanwhile, seven or eight[156] of those who had served Takauji with forces under their own command left for the capital. They were said to have surrendered. All had rendered Takauji distinguished service since the previous year, when they were fighting in the Kantō, but because of Takauji's defeats they quickly furled their banners, removed their helmets, and altered their crests.[157] It is sad to ponder their feelings. When those brave warriors who attached more importance to loyalty than to their own lives learned what they had

---

[155] The Kyōdai, Kanshō, and other early texts lack this sentence.
[156] The oldest texts say eight or nine.
[157] Warriors attached the family crest of the Ashikaga, printed on a piece of cloth, to their helmets or sleeves as an identifying badge (*kasajirushi*). Those who went over from Takauji to Yoshisada are said to have modified their Ashikaga crests to make them look like Nitta crests, since both families were of Minamoto descent and the crests were similar.

done, they expressed their determination to render Takauji every possible service.

Takauji's ship set sail at about the hour of the dog [8 p.m.]. Suddenly, a wind blew up from the east: a following wind known as "the dragon."[158] The ship therefore reached Muro-no-tsu at about the hour of the tiger [4 a.m.]. Many who had been too late to board the ships the previous evening rode to Muro-no-tsu by land. Their service was admirable. Over three hundred ships accompanied Takauji's. The sea in the area where they made their passage is called Harima-nada.[159] The passage is difficult and no one makes it without a favorable wind. Takauji's fortunes had depended on the wind. Tadayoshi attributed it entirely to divine protection. He dropped relics[160] and a sword into the sea during the passage as an offering to the Dragon God.

30. The Ashikaga Army Splits Up Among Several Provinces. It Receives the Cloistered Emperor's Decree

The army stayed at Muro-no-tsu for a day or two, and a council of war was held there. Various opinions were expressed. One man said, "The imperial army will undoubtedly pursue us. Should we not station a commander in each province in order to protect Takauji's rear, until he reaches Shikoku and Kyushu?"

Takauji agreed. He immediately assigned these nine commanders to Shikoku: the three brothers Hosokawa Kazuuji, Yoriharu, and Morouji; and their cousins, the six brothers Hosokawa Akiuji, Jōzen, Kōkai, Tadatoshi, Masauji, and Shigeuji. He put Kazuuji and Akiuji in charge of rewarding warriors in Shikoku according to their services.

Akamatsu was assigned to Harima. Ishibashi Kazuyoshi of Owari was assigned to Bizen and stationed in Mitsuishi Castle, together with the Matsuda family. The Imagawa brothers Saburō and Shirō were assigned to Bingo, and took up positions at the ports of Tomo and Onomichi. Nunokawa Shosaku, of the Momonoi, and the Kobayakawa family were assigned to the province of Aki. Ōshima Yoshimasa of the

---

[158] The dragon stands approximately southeast by east in the Chinese zodiac.

[159] A *nada* is an area of ocean with strong winds and high waves.

[160] *Shari*, the relics of a Buddha or saint.

Nitta was appointed commander and Ōuchi Nagahiro protector of Suō. Shiba Takatsune was appointed commander and Kotō Tarō Takezane protector of Nagato.

After making these assignments, Takauji proceeded to Tomo in Bingo, where Sanbōin Kenshun, the imperial messenger, presented him with Kōgon's decree.[161]

This was a cheering development. Takauji was no longer an enemy of the throne, and it was a joyful occasion when he sent instructions to his commanders in the provinces to raise the imperial banner.

31. The Ashikaga Army Sails the Inland Sea and Reaches Tsukushi

Making a long, unforeseen journey was bad enough, but the sea route was unfamiliar to Takauji and many of his warriors. Afloat on the sea at high tide, the ships, numbering in the hundreds, seemed to be rising to the clouds and hanging in midair. Uncertainty filled the men, far from home and unsure of their destination. The clouds closed behind them. The noise of the wind forever blowing through the pine trees on the shore interrupted their sleep. Unable even to doze off, they could not stop thinking about their native lands. Words cannot express how discouraged they were in their desperate situation. Wretched and forlorn, they did not know whether they would live to return. The weather was favorable, however, and Takauji's ship reached Akama-no-seki[162] in Nagato on Kenmu 3.2.20 [1336].

On the 25th of that month, Yorinao, the eldest son of Dazaifu Assistant (*Dazai no shōni*) Myōe, came to greet Takauji accompanied by over five hundred members of his family. He presented Takauji and Tadayoshi with brocade *hitatare*. The occasion seemed to foreshadow Takauji's future success.

On the 29th, Takauji and his army left Akama-no-seki by ship and after a day's journey on the Inland Sea reached the port of Ashiya in Chikuzen, in Kyushu.

---

161 Kenshun, an uncle of the *Takemuki-ga-ki* author, was a crucial Ashikaga and Jimyōin supporter. For more on him, see the Introduction to *Ojima no kuchizusami*.
162 The Shimonoseki strait that separates Honshu from Kyushu.

32. Myōe Dies by His Own Hand

Towards evening, word reached Takauji's camp that Myōe had killed himself at dawn that day, at Uchiyama. His reason for doing so was as follows. Kikuchi Taketoshi, a son of Kikuchi Jakua Taketoki, who was on the court side, had attacked Myōe from Higo. Myōe had fought back in Chikugo as hard as he could, both on the 28th day of the 2nd month, two days earlier, and on the 29th, but lost. While evacuating his residence at the Government Headquarters, he saw many of the horses and weapons that he had prepared for Takauji and his commanders being reduced to ashes. He said, "It is unheard-of that Takauji and Tadayoshi should come to this remote region. I recently received from the Kantō a letter from Takauji, written in his own hand, in which he said that he was counting on me, and I therefore did what I could. After sending Yorinao to meet Takauji, I was defeated in battle and dishonored. It would therefore be pointless to prolong my old age. I have no other purpose than to give my life to support the Shogun's campaign here. If I can accomplish the ultimate military service for him, my descendants will continue to serve undividedly him as well." Then he hurried to Uchiyama, a mountain temple nearby, and after fighting a little longer disemboweled himself.

It was a sad moment when Myōe called a priest and gave him this message for his son Yorinao: "I am about to die for Takauji. Hold no memorial service for me. I wish you and all my surviving family members and retainers to unite and do your utmost to assist Takauji to establish his rule.[163] Let that be my memorial service. Your doing so will brighten even the dark world to which I go. No sutras and darani are to be chanted for me.

He continued, "They say that when Yoritomo first raised his army, during Jishō, Miura Yoshiaki fought Hatakeyama Shigetada at Kinugawa Castle and at the last told his sons: 'As one of a family who have been Minamoto retainers for generations, it gives this old man great joy to sacrifice his life for Yoritomo and so to bring credit to you. You must not die here with me. I shall defend this fortress, but you

---

[163] The older texts have "perform battle service" instead of "unite."

must go to join Yoritomo and serve him. The realm will inevitably come under Minamoto rule.' Yoshiaki wept as he spoke. Wada Kotarō Yoshimori,[164] Miura Kojirō Yoshizumi,[165] and the others knew that this would be their final parting. All tried to look brave, but both those who were leaving and those who were staying had to restrain their tears as they left the room. Yoshiaki was later killed by Shigetada, and the Miura family is therefore still known for its great deeds. Likewise I am sacrificing my life for Takauji, and my deed should not count for less than Yoshiaki's. Yorinao and the rest of you, never forget this!"

Myōe and Yorinao's two younger brothers, the governors of Echigo and Owari,[166] and other family members and retainers numbering over five hundred, died there in battle or by their own hand on the 30th of the 2nd month. By so doing they immortalized the family name, and it was a joyous occasion when Myōe's descendants received Takauji's praise.

Later, when Takauji had established his rule over the realm, he rewarded Yorinao with several estates; and when Yorinao returned to Kyushu he was honored with a variety of parting gifts from Takauji and Tadayoshi. These included a brocade *hitatare* and a *sake* cup from Takauji, and, from Tadayoshi, the white horse with a black mane that he had always ridden in battle. People recalled the old days when Zhu Maichen returned to his homeland wearing brocade.[167]

Presently, news of Myōe's death reached Takauji's camp at Ashiya. However, Yorinao denied the report and withdrew when Takauji asked him about it, even though he knew it was true. He did not wish to discourage Takauji's side.

33. Takauji's Army Leaves for Munakata; Yorinao's Council of War

The following day, the 1st of the 3rd month, Yorinao was assigned to the advance guard. Takauji's army left the port of Ashiya and, at the

---

[164] Yoshiaki's grandson.

[165] Yoshiaki's son.

[166] These two remain unidentified.

[167] He was appointed Governor of Kuei-chi, his homeland, by Han Wu-ti, and returned there dressed in brocade, a symbol of honor and success

hour of the bird [6 p.m.], reached the residence of Munakata Ujinori, the chief priest of the Munakata Shrine.[168] Ujinori presented Takauji and Tadayoshi with suits of armor and horses. Takauji learned there that Myōe had indeed committed suicide. He seemed to mourn him deeply.

Meanwhile, news came that the enemy had already taken up position at Hakata. That night Yorinao therefore did the same at Minoo Beach, some three miles ahead of Takauji's camp. He alone was summoned to Takauji's camp at Munakata, where they discussed the coming battle. Yorinao said, "My father was defeated in the recent fight at the Dazaifu Headquarters because I had taken my men to meet you and he therefore he had too few. He knows that area well, however, and I am sure that he himself is safe. No doubt some of the local warriors will join you at tomorrow's battle. As for that Kikuchi Taketoshi, I will easily dispatch him with a single blow." He tossed off this speech casually, leaving the impression that one could fully rely on him.

One man said to Takauji: "The men who followed you from the Kantō are willing to die for you. However they are on foot, since they left their horses at Hyōgo, and it is uncertain whether they will arrive here tonight. I suggest that you stay here tomorrow, just one more day, and place them in the vanguard for the battle. It would be a pity to leave here without them."

There was no agreement, but about midnight there were reports from various quarters that Kikuchi had already left Dazaifu to attack Takauji. The question of the force left behind was therefore no longer relevant.

34. A Good Omen at the Kashii Shrine

At the hour of the dragon [8 a.m.] on Kenmu 3.3.2, Takauji and his army left the camp at Munakata to meet the enemy. After some fifteen miles they passed at about the hour of the sheep [2 p.m.] before the Kashii Shrine, where priests brought Takauji cedar branches and said, "The

---

[168] The Munakata, hereditary chief priests of the Munakata Shrine, were also administrators for Kamakura. Some lived in Kyoto, but many more fought for Takauji. They could well be the source of the *Baishōron* narrative.

enemy are all wearing as their emblem leaves of bamboo grass. Yours should be cedar. They attached cedar sprigs to the sleeves of Takauji, Tadayoshi, and the other warriors. This seemed truly auspicious. This shrine is named Kashii[169] because when Empress Jingū was here, at the time of her expedition against Silla, she touched a chestnut tree, and it gave off a sweet fragrance. The chestnut was therefore designated the shrine's sacred presence (*shintai*), while the cedar was made its particular treasure.

At any rate, an old man in white personally attached a cedar sprig to the sleeve of Takauji's armor. Takauji gave him a sword in a plain wooden scabbard. Later, when Takauji asked for the old man, the priests said that they had no idea who he was. Takauji took this as a sign of divine protection, the old man being a god in human form. He grew even more confident, and his army displayed heightened morale.

35. The Ashikaga Army Confronts the Kikuchi Army at Tadarahama

Takauji's army left Kashii and advanced to a place called Akasaka. Takauji sent out scouts. They discovered a dry beach known as Tadarahama, three and a half miles long and with a brook at its southern end. The Hakozaki Hachiman Shrine was there, surrounded by a hundred-acre pine wood. To the south was Hakata; there was a hill about a mile to the east; and to the west the sea stretched away to China. The place reminded one of the sad story of Lady Matsura, who pined away, waving her scarf.[170]

Between Akasaka, where Takauji took up position, and the pine wood, the sand sparkled like jewels. The enemy crossed the brook and drew up facing north, with the pine wood at their rear. They were reported to number over 60,000 mounted men.[171] In the vanguard of Takauji's army were Kō no Moroyasu, as well as those who had followed Takauji from the capital: Ōtomo, Shimazu, Chiba, Utsunomiya,

---

[169] Literally, "fragrant chestnut tree."

[170] According to a legend recorded in the *Man'yōshū,* the *Hizen Fudoki,* and elsewhere, she climbed the hill mentioned and in vain waved her scarf to call back her departing lover, Ōtomo Sadehiko, who had been sent to lead an expedition to Mimana.

[171] Needless to say, a gross exaggeration.

and over 300 mounted warriors. These drew up facing the main enemy force. Takauji's advance guard to the east was Shōni Yorinao and his force of over 500 mounted warriors; these dismounted and took up position. In all, Takauji's force numbered fewer than 1,000 men.

Yorinao wore a yellow-braided breast protector and arm guards bound at the edge with cord of the same color. This was the famous armor that his ancestor, Mutō Kojirō Sukeyori, had received from Yoritomo at the time of the Ōshū expedition in Bunji 5 [1186][172] and that had been in his family for generations. Wearing this armor and his helmet, a drawn short halberd in hand, and riding a piebald horse, Yorinao went by himself to see Takauji and Tadayoshi. He said: "The enemy are many, but they may come over to your side. Kikuchi's own force cannot number over 300. If I sacrifice my life fighting at the forefront of your army, the enemy will be like dust before the wind. I suggest that we should advance under our banner." He seemed fully reliable. Naturally, everyone present agreed that Takauji and Tadayoshi should advance.

36. Takauji's Appearance, and His Orders

Takauji wore that day the red brocade *hitatare* that Myōe had presented to him through Yorinao; a suit of armor braided with Chinese twill; and two swords, one named Crunchbone, [173] which had been in his family for generations. He carried a rattan-wrapped bow and *kabura* arrows. His horse, a dark grey, was one that the chief priest of the Munakata Shrine had presented to him the previous day.

On that day Takauji had Atsutadaigūji Takanori[174] of Noda wear the suit of armor Kosode ("Short Sleeves"), which had been in the

---

[172] Yoritomo's punitive expedition to Mutsu against the Fujiwara family in 1189.

[173] Ōbami, according to *Genpei Jōsuiki* 16 the sword with which Minamoto Yorimasa (1104-1180) killed the *nue* (a monstrous creature with the head of a monkey, the body of a tiger, and the tail of a serpent) at the imperial palace. *Heike monogatari* 4 only mentions Yorimasa receiving a sword named Lion King (Shishi-ō) as a reward for his deed.

[174] Originally Atsuta Daigūji ("chief priest of the Atsuta Shrine"). However, the title came to be used as the name of the Owari family, which held the office.

Ashikaga family for generations.[175] In general, that family has many secret traditions regarding battle dress. Long ago, when Minamoto Yoriyoshi went on his punitive expedition against Abe no Sadatō, he struggled hard for twelve years. Since they fought on dark nights and in the snow, it was feared that in a melee Yoriyoshi might be mistaken for an enemy. Kiyohara Takenori got the idea of having him wear seven emblems, the so-called Seven Signs, all of them being items of military equipment, that would not allow the enemy easily to pick him out. It is said that Takauji gave some thought to his dress on this day, in accordance with this example, although he did not go as far as seven emblems.

Takauji said: "I never meant to come so far from the capital, but war involves both advance and retreat. If we meet this renowned enemy and for lack of a strategy lose our last battle, will our family not also lose its long-standing reputation for military skill, and will we not leave a bad name behind us? I have an excellent plan. If Tadayoshi and I were to advance together and find the going hard, who would be left to accomplish our purpose? If I stay in the rear, however, even by myself, the forces in the front will fight with some confidence. Even if the odds are against us, I would be able to take over with my guardsmen and defeat the enemy. Therefore Tadayoshi should advance first." Everyone praised this idea, saying that no one else could have thought of it. They also said that Takauji's tactics had won the battle at Ashigara the year before, after leaving Hakone, and they advanced under his banner.

Tadayoshi wore the red brocade *hitatare* given him by Myōe and armor braided with purple leather. His sword fittings were decorated with a bamboo grass leaf pattern, and he carried and a bow and arrows. He rode a chestnut horse that had been given him the day before by the chief priest of the Munakata Shrine.

---

175 Perhaps Atsutadaigūji had been designated Takauji's double, a common practice.

37. The Battle Begins; Soga and Niki's Hard Fight

The warriors who had come with Takauji from the Kantō were on foot, but all vied as they advanced to be first. Among them was Soga Morosuke, wearing a red-braided suit of armor, cut off below its cross-patterned borders, over a padded garment of shot silk. He carried two swords over four feet long; a large, unlacquered bow; and, on his back, a quiver with twenty or thirty arrows. With his helmet on, he cut a strange figure as he stood before Tadayoshi's mount.

Under the banner stood Niki Yoshinaga in a yellow-braided suit of armor. Tadayoshi had received this armor from the chief priest of the Munakata Shrine and then presented it to Niki, thus greatly honoring him.

When Niki rode his chestnut horse to the front, what seemed at least twenty or thirty thousand of the enemy charged out from the east wing, which faced the Shōni force, brandishing their swords and shouting battle cries. They were so powerful that it seemed not even demons could resist them.

However, Tadayoshi's force remained calm. First the foot soldiers shot arrows, and when the enemy hesitated for a moment, the mounted warriors seized the opportunity and charged. Just then, a north wind blew up clouds of sand, making things difficult for the enemy and causing them to falter. At the sight, Tadayoshi's center, too, fought fiercely.

Meanwhile, Soga Morosuke killed an enemy officer and cut off his head, and soon came before Tadayoshi riding on the officer's large red-tinged grey horse. When he showed Tadayoshi his prize, Tadayoshi was highly pleased. "Morosuke," he said, "you have gotten yourself a good horse. Now you can take on a thousand or even ten thousand of the enemy." Morosuke charged the enemy again, every inch a matchless warrior.

Niki Yoshinaga charged the enemy and fought without regard for his life, killing many, and rejoined the ranks with blood on his horse and armor.

Taking advantage of victory, Tadayoshi's force pursued the enemy past the Hakozaki pine wood and all the way to the Hakata beach.

38. The Ashikaga Victory and Aeba's Feat of Arms

Meanwhile the local troops on the enemy side put up no resistance but fled and scattered as fast as they could. Kikuchi Taketoshi and his men alone turned back and fought as if it were their last day on earth. Tadayoshi's force seemed to be in trouble and withdrew, one part passing through the pine wood and the other along its eastern edge.

Unfazed, Tadayoshi ordered his bannerman to raise the banner high. He sent a messenger to Takauji, who had taken up position in the rear, saying, "I shall sacrifice my life holding my ground here. Meanwhile, you must cross over to Nagato or Suō so as to save your life and accomplish your purpose." He cut off the right sleeve of his *hitatare* and sent it with the message. Those who saw this wept. However, his brave warriors seemed to strengthen their resolve even more.

Meanwhile, an enemy force of about three hundred riders under a worn imperial banner emerged calmly from the northern edge of the pine wood and was about to cross the stream. The bannerman of Chiba Tanesada rode into the water by himself to keep them from crossing. At the sight, the enemy stopped and held their position.

Takauji then raised his banner and came up from the rear with the force that had withdrawn earlier from the front. With mighty war cries they charged the enemy. Tadayoshi drew his long sword when he heard them and urged his horse forward. Yoshinaga, Morosuke and his other men charged, each vying to be first.

The two armies spent some time facing each other across the stream. Then one of Shōni's retainers, a man by the name of Aeba, came to Shōni. He wore armor braided with red leather, with white braiding at the chest and shoulder, and rode a red-tinged grey. Aeba said, "This is the place for you to die. I will go first." He then crossed the stream. His son followed him across, wearing black-braided armor and riding a black horse. They charged into the enemy ranks and laid about them. Fearing that the two might be killed, a great many of Takauji's warriors followed them and joined the fighting. As a result, the Kikuchi force was defeated and fled.

Aeba and his son sustained several wounds, but these did not prove fatal. After Takauji had returned to the capital, Aeba had the honor of receiving a sword from Tadayoshi for his battle service in that decisive encounter.

39. Takauji's Offering at the Hakozaki Shrine

Tadayoshi quickly started with Yorinao in pursuit of the defeated enemy, even though it was the hour of the bird [6 p.m.]. They reached Dazaifu that night at about the hour of the boar [10 p.m.]. Tadayoshi first inspected the remains of Myōe's residence, which had been reduced to ashes, and he seemed deeply grieved. The troops, however, had more confidence in Takauji than ever, for they believed that that his strategy had won the day.

Takauji camped at the Hakozaki temple.[176] The shrine priests welcomed him. He refrained from making a formal offering because he had been defiled by battle, but he bathed and saluted the Hachiman Shrine[177] from before the gallery. He then donated to the shrine a sword in a plain wooden scabbard, with a cord tied in a latticework pattern, given him by Kira Mitsuyoshi. Wishing also to donate land to the shrine, he asked to see the shrine documents in order to obtain a model for his letter of endowment. Among these he found a letter of endowment written long before by Chinzei Hachirō Tametomo.[178] Feeling truly grateful to his family's tutelary deity, he turned toward the shrine's main hall and pressed his palms together in veneration. His reverence seemed profound.

40. Takauji and Tadayoshi Reunited

The next day, the 3rd of the 3rd month, Tadayoshi sent a messenger named Mutō Buzen Jirō, a Shōni kinsman, to Takauji to say, "Our victory in yesterday's battle was by no means due to our human

---

[176] Presumably the temple (*jingūji*) associated with the shrine.
[177] The Hakozaki Shrine proper.
[178] Minamoto Tameyoshi's eighth son, who subdued most of Kyushu in the late Heian Period. *Heiji monogatari* tells his story.

prowess. I believe that we owe it to divine protection. Our triumph was auspicious. When we climbed the mountain near Dazaifu yesterday, at about the hour of the bird, enemy warriors surrendered and joined us. Yorinao interceded with me on their behalf. We are expecting you here, but I am sending you this message in the meantime."

The distance from Hakozaki to Dazaifu is said to be about twelve miles. At the hour of the horse Takauji reached the monks' lodge on the mountain. While he and Tadayoshi met there, the warriors who had surrendered the previous day were assigned to guard the gate. This was a noble act indeed.

The victory had been due to Takauji's strategy, but it was said that the quick destruction of the enemy had been due to Shōni Yorinao's deeds.

41. Takauji's and Tadayoshi's Tribute to Myōe, and their Subjugation of Kyushu

While there, Takauji took the time to ask about Myōe's last deeds, and the circumstances of his death and those of his sons, kinsmen, and retainers. He grieved deeply, for which the souls of the departed must have been very grateful. Not only Myōe's relatives, but every warrior present was moved to tears and felt that to give up life for this leader mattered less than a drop of dew.

Tadayoshi suggested holding a memorial service during the mourning period for Myōe. He strictly forbade his men even to raise their voices, and his own feelings were revealed by a stream of tears. Yorinao went to see Takauji when he learned of this. He said, "I gather from stories of olden times that many have sacrificed their lives for their lords, including Miura Yoshiaki, Kanō Yoshimitsu, and Sanada Yoichi Yoshitada. My father is not the only one to have done so. Your sympathy for him honors me greatly, but we must set out to destroy Kikuchi Taketoshi without further delay." Having had a variety of dishes brought to Takauji's quarters, he personally served him fish and fowl as well as *sake*.[179]

Takauji did not disagree. There was a banquet that night, and after that he even held meetings with people. Then he appointed Isshiki Noriuji and Niki Yoshinaga to commanders a force that included Kyushu warriors and the Matsura league[180] in the vanguard, and he sent them to attack the Kikuchi base in Higo. The Kikuchi castle was captured within half a month, after fierce fighting around it. No rebels against Takauji remained in all of Kyushu.

42. The Ashikaga Army Leaves Tsukushi at Akamatsu's Request

Meanwhile, the warriors who had failed to embark with Takauji at Hyōgo had been arriving and reporting on events in the capital. Takauji said, "It must have been like this long ago when Minamoto no Yoshiie and Fujiwara no Hidehira organized couriers to bring them news from the capital."

There were two opinions on the question of returning to the capital. One was to return immediately, before Takauji's allies in various provinces lost heart, and the other was to wait until autumn to secure provisions. Undecided, Takauji stayed where he was from the 3rd of the 3rd month to the 3rd of the 4th month. Akamatsu Norisuke[181] then arrived in great haste from Harima. He said, "Nitta Kingo Yoshisada advanced on our fortress[182] at the head of a large force, and he has taken up position there. There are enough men in to defend it. Besides Enshin's family, we have troops who were on their way from the capital to Kyushu and hurried to join us. However, we have not stocked enough supplies. We will not be able to hold out if you delay your return to the capital. We trust that you will set out quickly."

The report from Ishibashi Kazuyoshi, the commander at Mitsuishi in Bizen, was similar to Akamatsu's: an enemy force commanded by

---

[179] Buddhist practice requires abstinence from meat during a period of mourning.
[180] A tightly-knit group of families from the Matsura area.
[181] The son of Norimura (Enshin).
[182] The Shirahata fortress in Harima, also referred to below as the Akamatsu fortress.

Nitta and Wakiya was advancing on his castle, which lacked sufficient supplies.

Accordingly, Takauji stationed Isshiki, Niki Yoshinaga, and the Matsura league, as well as other local warriors and other forces, in Kyushu, and set out from Dazaifu on Kenmu 3.4.3 [1336]. Ōtomo, Shōni, and other Kyushu warriors cast off and left the Hakata harbor. Takauji and Tadayoshi stayed at Fuchū in Nagato for a few days and then left by sea.

Takauji's ship belonged to a descendant of the boatman whose twelve ships at Kushizaki, in the same province, had been used by Minamoto Kurō Yoshitsune long ago in Genryaku, at the battle of Dan-no-ura. After destroying the Heike, Yoshitsune gave the boatman a letter, written in his own hand, exempting those ships from government service in any port or harbor in Japan, and his descendant still had this letter. That one of these ships was chosen for Takauji now perfectly followed that good example. Kotō, the protector of Nagato, had arranged this.

43. The Army is Divided into Land and Sea Forces at Shōni Yorinao's Urging

Takauji finally reached the port of Tomo, in Bingo, on the evening of the 5th of the 5th month. While he was there, his supporters in various provinces sent word urging him to hurry back to the capital.

Accordingly, a council of war was held, and various opinions were expressed. One was that Takauji and Tadayoshi should go by sea, and the commanders and warriors from Shikoku and Chūgoku by land. Another was that Takauji and Tadayoshi should go by land with the whole army. A third was that they should all go by sea. Each opinion was advocated so strongly that no decision had yet been reached, when Shōni Yorinao approached Takauji. "Far be it from me," he said, "to disagree that you and Tadayoshi should go by sea. However, whether or not you are to rule the realm will depend on how you now divide your army. We have had reports that the enemy has already surrounded our castles in Harima and Bizen. Peace can be established only once the enemy is destroyed. However, the rebels cannot be destroyed by a sea battle alone. Fortunately, both you and Tadayoshi are here. You should go by sea and Tadayoshi by land. I will be in the vanguard of the land forces, and, in accordance with my father Myōe's last request, I will fight in commemoration of the hundredth day after his death. This will be his memorial service. That is my only wish in all the world."

Shōni spoke so earnestly that Takauji gave his approval. It was decided that Takauji would go by sea and Tadayoshi by land. Accordingly, the army was divided into two.

The Ashikaga family chief of staff (*shitsuji*) Kō no Moronao, other senior warriors who had come with Takauji from the Kantō and the capital, and warriors from Shikoku and Kyushu were assigned to accompany Takauji by sea. As for Tadayoshi's forces, Kō no Moroyasu and other younger warriors who had accompanied Takauji from the Kantō and the capital, together with Shōni, Ōtomo, and other Ashikaga retainers from Nagato, Suō, Aki, Bizen, and Bitchū were assigned to go by land.

That spring, in the 2nd month, when Takauji had been on his way to Kyushu, he had instructed the protector of these provinces to prepare saddles, armor, bows and arrows, shields, and provisions, in proportion to the size of each province, and they had done so. Takauji's intention was to distribute these things among the warriors who came from the more remote areas to join him.

44. The Army Advances by Land and Sea, and the Arrival of Forces from Shikoku

On the 10th of the 5th month the sea and land forces left Tomo in Bingo. The ships were unmoored and the horses arranged in ranks. In the vanguard was Shōni Yorinao with, it was said, over 2,000 mounted warriors. For some time the land and sea forces could see each other, and it was observed that a rush hat was attached to the crosspiece of Shōni's banner. This was because of a long-standing belief in the Shōni family that the spirits of the family ancestors would appear and remain in the hole at the top of the post.

Takauji's ship had gone over three miles when a large number of ships became visible, rowing towards them. The lead ship trailed bunting bearing the Ashikaga crest. Someone said, "This might be a trick by Kusunoki, pretending to be on our side in order to approach us." The idea caused some anxiety, but it was not so. The ships bore members of the Hosokawa family, Toki Rokurō Yorikiyo, the Kōno family from Iyo, and other warriors, all from Shikoku. There were said to be over 500 ships, with over 5,000 mounted warriors.

45. Good Omens for the Ashikaga Army

Takauji reached Kojima in Bizen on the 15th of the 5th month. This area was held by the Sasaki family. Kaji Akinobu, therefore built him a temporary residence near the beach and prepared a bath and so on for him. Takauji rested there.

That night, two black lines of cloud were observed stretching for some time across the full moon. Takauji's troops joined their hands in worship. It was a very good omen.[183]

While Takauji was in Kyushu countless strange phenomena occurred at various shrines, and there were other good omens as well. A particularly auspicious one occurred while he was at Dazaifu in Kyushu. Speaking through a maidservant at the Sumiyoshi Shrine, the deity of the Kushida Shrine in Hakata said to Takauji, "I will keep watch over you and Tadayoshi all the way to the capital. You will arrive safely, but you will have to fight. Offer a white banner, a suit of armor, a sword, a bow some arrows, and some humming arrows (*kabura*)." This oracle was so miraculous that Takauji had these things prepared. The woman who had received the oracle strung the bow and fitted a humming arrow to it in the presence of Takauji's messenger. She said: "Many doubt me, but here is the proof. If Takauji is to establish his rule over the realm, not one of these arrows will miss its mark." She then shot three arrows at a slender bead tree branch and never missed. No woman of humble birth could have done this.

---

[183] The Ashikaga crest consisted of two dark horizontal bars in a circle.

Also, the spirit of Tenjin's messenger appeared, shining, in each battle, inspiring great confidence in Takauji's men.[184] Finally, Takauji had a sacred dream on his way down to Kyushu, as a result of which an old, pale grey horse was stationed to one side of his ship.[185]

46. A Letter from Tadayoshi Sets Out His Battle Plan

Every warrior in the Ashikaga army, from the top on down, sported on the front of his helmet the words, "All hail the Three Treasures and Kanzeon Bosatsu"; and on the 18th of each month Takauji had the *Kannon senbō* litany chanted for the dead. On his way down to Kyushu, he summoned all the priests from his more than 300 ships and found their number sufficient. It goes without saying that he continued this practice on his way back to the capital.

Seven miles separate Karube-gawara in Bitchū, where Tadayoshi camped on the 17th of the 5th month, and Takauji's location as Kojima in Bizen. On that day the following message arrived from Tadayoshi: "We now have commanders, protectors, and local warriors from Bitchū, Bingo, Aki, Suō, and Nagato in our force, and yesterday Miura Takatsugu hurried to join us from Mimasaka. Since the Shōni and Ōtomo forces are with us as well, it is impossible to say how many warriors we have. I hear that the Shikoku warriors have joined your naval force, and I congratulate you on this. However, we are still hearing that the Akamatsu fortress in Harima and the Mitsuishi fortress in Bizen are under attack, and that, finally, a force under Ōeda Ujitsune, of the Nitta family, rushed here a few days ago and entrenched itself in Fukuyama castle in Bitchū. Tonight I am therefore assigning my forces to their positions, and tomorrow at dawn I will attack the castle and set it on fire. I am hurrying this message off to you so as to put you on guard, since that castle is close to Kojima, where you are camped."

---

[184] "Tenjin" is probably Tenman Tenjin, the deified Sugawara no Michizane enshrined at Dazaifu. Uesugi Kiyoko mentioned a comparable divine manifestation in the passage quoted as an epigraph to this volume.
[185] The meaning of the original sentence is unclear.

47. The Nitta Forces Flee the San'yōdō

The next day, the 18th, the *senbō* service was held, and when it was over a servant who had gone up the mountain to pick some arbutus (*yamamomo*), then in season there, ran back down and reported, "Tadayoshi's great force has already taken Fukuyama Castle. They stormed in and set it on fire, and the enemy have fled." Since this had happened on the day of the *Kannon senbō* service, Takauji took it that Tadayoshi's victory had really been due to divine protection, and he felt confident.

The Ashikaga land force then invaded Bizen and drove off Wakiya Yoshiharu,[186] who had been attacking Mitsuishi castle. This news prompted Tadayoshi to send a courier bearing his congratulations.

Takauji soon set sail from Kojima. The land and sea forces lit signal fires day and night, as previously arranged, so that, even when separated by mountains, Takauji and Tadayoshi knew each other's position. Meanwhile, the force attacking Mitsuishi in Bizen withdrew to the capital. Nitta Yoshisada therefore lifted his siege of the Akamatsu fortress and withdrew as well.

48. Takauji Examines the Abandoned Enemy Banners

Meanwhile, the land force pitched camp at Kakogawa in Harima. The sea force reached the harbor of Muro in the same province. The next day, Akamatsu came to see Takauji at his ship and gave him a register of the warriors who had joined him in his castle, as well as over a hundred banners that the enemy had abandoned at their points of attack when they withdrew. Takauji examined each, and each family crest was identified. "Seeing these," he said, "I have nothing to say about those who were on the enemy side from the beginning. However, I also see here the banners of a few warriors who once rendered me distinguished service in war. It is sad to imagine the inmost thoughts of those who joined Yoshisada in order to avoid our

---

186 A younger brother of Nitta Yoshisada.

temporary hardships. They will eventually rejoin us." Takauji looked very pleased, and people appreciated the generosity of his feelings .

Takauji entrusted the banners to Akamatsu and told him to make a note of how many there were, saying that he would decide later what was to be done with them.

49. The Passage over Harima-nada on the Advice of the Boatman Magoshichi

Now, the sea between this place, Muro, and Hyōgo is called Harima-nada. The passage over it is so difficult that no one would ever venture to make it without a good following wind like the one that favored Takauji on his way down to Kyushu. Takauji therefore waited for favorable weather. The members of the sea force were impatient at the delay, since the land force was advancing, but at the hour of the dog [8 p.m.] on the 23rd of the 5th month, a light west wind carrying rain began to blow. Takauji rejoiced and said, "This wind must be a gift from Heaven. Quickly, unmoor the ships."

However, a man said, "We are unfamiliar with seafaring and are in no position to express an opinion. Takauji should summon the boatmen in the larger ships and ask what they think. Accordingly the boatman of Takauji's ship, from Kushizaki; the boatman of Chiba Tanesada's, from Okihashi; and over ten others from the Ōtomo and Shōni ships, and those from Nagato and Suō, assembled before Takauji. They all said, "The wind is favorable now, but it may turn against us when the tide rises as the moon comes up. If we set out now, we may encounter difficulties on the way."

One of the ships was that of Uesugi Shigeyoshi.[187] Its boatman, Magoshichi, was from Tsubaki-no-ura in Abu county in Nagato. He said respectfully to Takauji, "I think that you are very fortunate to have this following wind. The rain began when the wind started to blow, and it will stop when the moon comes up. It may become a little strong, but it will still be a following wind." He alone said what Takauji

---

[187] The adopted son of Norifusa.

himself had been thinking. Very pleased, Takauji graciously appointed him an officer of the Left Gate Watch.

Takauji said, "Long ago, in the Genryaku era, Minamoto no Yoshitsune crossed the sea from Watanabe despite a high wind, just because the wind was favorable." He sailed without even waiting for the rain to stop. Some wondered how he could have accepted one man's opinion when so many boatmen had warned him that the passage would he dangerous. However, there was no point in arguing, since he was already on his way. When he sailed the total number of ships in his fleet, large and small, reportedly exceeded 5,000; however, not more than 3,000 left that night.

50. The Ashikaga Land and Sea Forces Reach Harima

Takauji's ship anchored at Hisaku-no-ura, three miles east of Muro, to await the tide at the rising of the moon. The rain stopped, as expected, and his ship therefore set out at moonrise. The wind was indeed strong, but it was behind them. All the ships hoisted their sails and ran before it.

Towards daybreak they found themselves at sea amid towering waves and felt lost, seeing no mountains nearby. However, most of the ships, including Takauji's, anchored off Ōkuradani in Harima on the evening of the 24th day.

The ships from Shikoku had made up the core of the naval force, and they had preceded Takauji. These anchored in Awaji strait, off Suma and Akashi. At night, they lit watch fires fore and aft in every ship, and it really looked as though the waves were burning.

The land force positioned themselves facing Ichinotani, between Shioya, where Doi Jirō Sanehira had camped long ago,[188] to as far back as Ōkuradani and Inamino. They lit watchfires.

---

[188] In *Heike monogatari* 9.

51. The Ashikaga Army Is Divided
in Preparation for the Battle at Hyōgo

Since the land and sea forces could see each other, couriers went back and forth many times that night with messages about the battle to be fought at Hyōgo on the following day, the 25th of the 5th month. Takauji divided his army as follows. The center, under Tadayoshi and his deputies Kō no Moroyasu, Ōtomo, Miura, and Akamatsu, consisted of the forces from the three provinces of Harima, Mimasaka, and Bizen. The mountain wing, under Shiba Takatsune, consisted of Kotō, the protector of Nagato; the protector of Aki and Suō; and the forces from these three provinces. The beach wing, under Shōni Yorinao, was made up of the forces of his relatives with lands in Chikuzen, Buzen, and Hizen; the Yamaga and Aso forces; and the forces from Satsuma. All these were assigned to fight together in this wing.

It was the 5th month, and the nights were short. Nonetheless, everyone waited impatiently for dawn, each man telling himself that he would be the first into battle. Their feelings were admirable, yet also touching.

52. The Positioning of the Two Armies on Land and at Sea

At the hour of the hare [6 a.m.] on the 25th the Hosokawa commanders, whose more than 500 ships from Shikoku made up the main naval force, spread their sails as on the previous day, since the following wind was still blowing, and sped along within sight, to port, of the Minato River, where the enemy had taken up position, and Hyōgo Island.[189] Their purpose was to block the enemy's line of retreat.

The imperial banner on Takauji's ship bore a gold sun disk and the names of the Sun Goddess and Hachiman in gold characters. It glittered in the sun. The banner was unfurled and fluttered in the breeze, and they beat the drum, as was the custom when Takauji's ship set sail. The thousands of ships spread their sails at the same time, jostling one another so that even the three-mile-wide strait of

---

[189] Hyōgo-no-shima, a crucial port west of Sakai, destroyed at the time of the Ōnin war.

Awaji seemed to be too narrow. As they rowed along in formation, one could not see the water.

The land forces likewise began to move. They seemed to fly through Ichinotani. Late in the hour of the dragon [9 a.m.] they came within sight of the island at Hyōgo. The enemy had taken up position from the mountains behind the Minato River down to the village, with their banners flying and their shields in lined. This was Kusunoki Masashige's force.

Also, a large force[190] proceeded to the Suma junction on the Harima Road and took up position there. At the beach front, an enemy force apparently over 10,000 strong stood with its back to a young pine grove on Wada Point, flying *nakaguro* banners.[191] Actually, it was divided into three.[192] The vanguard appeared to be about 500 strong and the next force about 2,000. The third stood at the pine grove.

53. The Shōni Force Advances to the Van of the Ashikaga Army

Time passed. At the hour of the serpent [10 a.m.] Takauji's three forces— mountain, Suma junction, and beach—all began to advance at the same time. Perhaps because they were faster, Shōni's beach force of over 2,000 mounted warriors took the lead under his banner.

Over 500 of these warriors got some one hundred yards ahead of the rest, and over fifty of these were even further in front, when two of them raced about thirty yards ahead of all the others. One was rode a black horse and wore a pink *horo*.[193] The color of his armor braiding was not clearly visible. The other rode a tan horse with a black mane and tail ("buckskin") and wore yellow-braided armor. Both were relatives of Shōni Yorinao.[194]

---

190 Tadayoshi's.

191 The Nitta family crest.

192 According to *Taiheiki*, these three were commanded by Nitta Yoshisada, his younger brother Wakiya Yoshisuke, and Ōdate Ujiaki.

193 A sort of cape that protected against enemy arrows. A crimson-dyed *horo* was thought to reflect a warrior's resolve to fight to the death in battle. A *horo* could also serve as a fallen warrior's funeral shroud.

194 Unusually, this passage does not describe a warrior's armor fully, but instead limits its description to what the narrator presumably observed.

The one with the *horo* was Mutō Buzen Jirō, and the one with the yellow-braided armor was Muto Tsushima Kojirō. Both were very young. The ships were only about a hundred yards from the shore, and those aboard could watch as though watching a performance from stands.

54. Yoshisada's Defeat at the Battle of Hyōgo

When rapid drumbeats sounded from Takauji's ship, the men in the naval force raised their battle cry. The great land force responded three times, and the *kabura* arrows began to sound. The six earthquakes' roar could not have been louder.

Before this spectacle the enemy vanguard pulled back without shooting a single arrow. The two warriors in the lead changed direction and charged into the enemy's second rank.

Fearing that the two would be killed, the rest of the great force followed. As a result, the enemy was defeated. In this battle at Wada Point, while smoke rose from farmhouses at the edge of Hyōgo, the enemy force on the Harima road could not hold. The same was true for the mountain force.

Meanwhile, the Shikoku force was landing near at Ikuta Wood, to prevent the enemy at Hyōgo from retreating, when they encountered Yoshisada and some 3,000 warriors, who were withdrawing in defeat from the battle at Hyōgo. The men on the ships hesitated to land, since the enemy was on horseback. *However, the Hosokawa brothers and cousins advanced, each vying to be first.*[195] Among them were Jōzen, his younger brother Tatewaki Senjō, Furuyama Yūzō, Sugita, Usami, and Ōba. These disembarked their horses and mounted, and eight of them charged into the great force.

However, the enemy were too many. They were forced back into the water and returned to their ships. Then one Niinomi Kodayū, from Sanuki, declared that he would sacrifice his life for his commander. He dismounted and remained alone on the shore to fight. At the sight, Jōzen and fifteen other mounted warriors rushed ashore again and

---

[195] This sentence is missing from the Tenri text, one of the oldest variants.

fought. The rest of the force then disembarked and went up on the shore. As a result, Yoshisada was defeated and fled towards the capital.

55. Masashige's Death in the Battle at Minatogawa

Jōzen heard that Kusunoki Masashige was still at the Minato River and fighting fiercely against the center force. Ignoring Yoshisada, he rushed to join Tadayoshi in the fight. Late in the hour of the monkey [5 p.m.], Masashige, his younger brother Shichirō Masasue, and some fifty other warriors committed suicide together. Over 300 others had died in action. It was said that, altogether, over 700 had died on the beach, at Hyōgo, and at the Minato River. In such a battle, there were naturally many killed and wounded on Takauji's side as well.

56. Masashige, the Brave Warrior and Far-sighted Strategist

Once the enemy force at the Minato River was defeated, Takauji pitched his camp at Uo-no-midō,[196] where he had stayed on his way to the west. There, a Kō retainer,[197] who had beheaded Kusunoki, brought the head to Takauji. There could be no doubt, upon inspection, that it was Kusunoki's.

This was a sad story. That spring, when the capital learned that Takauji and Tadayoshi had left Hyōgo for Kyushu, the Emperor [Go-Daigo] had been pleased, and all the courtiers had rejoiced, thinking that there was now nothing to worry about. Masashige then advised the emperor to have Yoshisada executed, and to call Takauji back and effect a reconciliation with him; and he offered to serve as the imperial envoy.

The courtiers called this strange advice and ridiculed it in various ways. However, Masashige said again to the Emperor: "It was thanks only to Takauji's deeds that Your Majesty destroyed the former Bakufu. I admit that Yoshisada subjugated the Kantō, but still, it is to Takauji that all the warriors in the land have rallied. This is proven by the fact that even those warriors who used to live in the capital have

---

[196] Unidentified; possibly near the Sakase-gawa in Settsu.
[197] Possibly Moronari, a son of Moroyuki; or Morohide, a grandson of Moroyasu.

followed the 'defeated' Takauji to Kyushu and have deserted Your Majesty's 'victorious' army. This shows that Yoshisada cannot command respect. As far as I can see, Takauji and Tadayoshi will subdue the western provinces and return by the end of the 3rd month. When that happens, there will be absolutely no way to stop them. Your Majesty and your courtiers are very wise, but in the matter of military strategy my humble opinion is not wrong. I beg Your Majesty to reconsider the matter without delay." Masashige wept. People saw that he was truly a far-sighted warrior.

His advice was rejected, but Masashige nonetheless set out for Amagasaki to engage Takauji, and while there he sent the capital this message: "The imperial side will undoubtedly lose this battle. The human mind is not infallible, but these are my reasons for saying so. At the beginning of Genkō [1331-33], when I received the emperor's secret orders and promptly took up position in the fortress on Mount Kongō, I did what I had set out to do, with the help of warriors from Kawachi. I knew then that this was because everyone supported the Emperor.

This time, however, when I received an imperial order and assembled an army in my capacity as protector of Izumi and Kawachi, even my own relatives showed reluctance. You can imagine how the other warriors and residents of these provinces felt on the subject. This shows that the people have turned against the Emperor. Therefore my life no longer has any purpose. I shall be the first to die."

What happened then matched his prediction. No one on either on side, the enemy's or Takauji's, failed to lament his death. Such a man, they said, truly deserved to be called a brave warrior possessed of wisdom and strategic ability.

57. The Ashikaga Army Enters the Capital

The next day, the 26th of the 5th month, Takauji left Hyōgo and camped at Nishinomiya.

Upon learning that Takauji's great army had killed Masashige at the Minato River and was advancing on the capital, the Emperor again, as in the evening of the 27th of the 1st month, withdrew to Enryakuji.

The first into the capital were Niki Yoriaki and Imagawa Yorisada,[198] together with forces from Tango and Tajima. Altogether several thousand mounted warriors entered the capital from Tanba, under the imperial banner.

Takauji established his headquarters at the Hachiman Shrine on Otoko-yama. Tadayoshi entered the capital on the last day of the 5th month. Many of those who had abandoned Takauji that spring, when he left for Kyushu, surrendered. Those who had accompanied Takauji and rendered service were present. There was a marked difference between the happy faces of those who had served well and the gloomy faces of those who had not.

58. The Ashikaga Attack on Enryakuji

On the 5th of the 6th month the Hosakawa force led an attack on Enryakuji. They began fighting at Nishi-Sakamoto and advanced on foot to Kirarazaka. Chigusa Tadaaki was killed in this action.

The enemy then took up position on Ōgatake.[199] Takauji's forces advanced through the thick woods on the mountainside and took up position. Tadayoshi, the commander of the attacking army, pitched camp in front of the Sekizan Shrine.

They attacked the summit from three directions. The warrior monks of Miidera and the Chūgoku forces advanced along the Imamichi road. The main division, consisting of the Hosokawa forces and those from Shikoku, as well as the main Ashikaga army, advanced along Kirarazaka. Shōni Yorinao and the forces from Kyushu advanced along the mountain pass through Sasanomine and Yokawa.

There was daily fighting, and whenever Takauji's army seemed to be winning, the warrior monks of Miidera readied pine torches. Apparently they intended to set fire to Enryakuji. This was shameful.

---

[198] An older cousin of Imagawa Ryōshun (Sadayo).
[199] The main peak of Mt. Hiei.

59. The Ashikaga Army Withdraws in Defeat to the Capital

On the 20th of the 6th month, Takauji's side was defeated in a battle at the Imamichi road, and all three divisions were driven down to Nishi-Sakamoto. Kō no Morohisa and several tens of warriors were killed on the mountain in this action. Tadayoshi's camp at the Sekizan Shrine was now no longer of use, and the whole army withdrew into the capital.

Tadayoshi, the commander of the army, established his head-quarters on Sanjō-bōmon. Takauji fortified Tōji, lodged the Emperor [Kōgon] there, and had it guarded.

That spring, when Takauji and Tadayoshi took up position on the Kamo riverbank, they had been unable to coordinate the efforts of their forces because of their numerical inferiority. This time, Takauji therefore ordered that, even if the fighting did not go well, no one was to abandon Tōji. The forces filled the capital, and disorder was inevitable.

60. Yoshisada's Army Attacks the Ashikaga Forces in the Capital

Rumor had it that the forces on the mountain were going to attack the capital. Takauji therefore prepared by dividing his army. First, the Hosokawa forces and those from Shikoku took up position at Uchino. A large force commanded by Kō no Moronao stood ready at Hōjōji-gawara.

At dawn on the last day of the 6th month, a large army under the command of Yoshisada attacked the Hosokawa position at Uchino. The Hosokawa men fought without regard for their lives, but they were defeated and withdrew into the capital. The enemy army, divided into two forces, advanced south down Ōmiya and Inokuma, and set fires here and there. At the same time Moronao's force was fighting at Hōjōji-gawara. The Ashikaga won that battle.

61. The Battle for the Capital, and Nagatoshi's Death

Tadayoshi, the commander, had taken up position at the Sanjō riverbank and sent out scouts. The enemy had already penetrated down to Hachijō-bōmon, near Tōji, and he could see smoke. Many feared that Takauji's residence was in danger and urged Tadayoshi to go down there.

Shōni Yorinao had taken up position at the residence of Ōtsuki Tadatō, at the Aya-no-kōji and Ōmiya crossing. It had been previously arranged that Yorinao's force would assemble quickly at the Sanjō riverbank, then proceed in whatever direction Takauji ordered. Yorinao was therefore standing there with his force of 2,000 mounted men. He said to Tadayoshi, "There are many brave warriors at Tōji, which will be safe even if the enemy reaches its moat or its fence. If you go to reinforce Tōji, Moronao's northbound force will have a hard time at Hōjōji-gawara. You must under no circumstances move a step from here today. I will go straight to Tōji."

Yorinao proceeded west along Sanjō. The two enemy forces had advanced to Hachijō-bōmon, the one under Nitta Yoshisada moving along Ōmiya, and the other, under Nawa Nagatoshi, moving along Inokuma. However, Niki Yoriaki, Uesugi Shigeyoshi, and others opened the small gate of Tōji and burst out. They fought so hard that the enemy could not hold their ground, but instead withdrew in two corps along the roads by which they had come. However, they were then attacked by the Hosokawa and Shōni, who fought running battles with them all over the city. Nawa Nagatoshi was killed at the Sanjō-Inokuma crossing by Kusano Hidenaga, from Buzen.

62. The Ashikaga Force Defeats Nitta Yoshisada

Yoshisada wanted to fight Hosokawa Jōzen and got close to him several times, but whenever Yoshisada himself seemed to be in danger, his mighty warriors rushed to protect him and died to save his life.[200]

---

[200] The passage in italics, absent from the oldest versions of the text, represents another Hosokawa embellishment.

Report had it that his force was reduced to two or three hundred mounted warriors and that he retreated along the Nagasaka Road.

To the south, in the Kinai, the enemy attacked along the Toba Road, but Kō no Moronao promptly routed them. From Uji, the enemy penetrated as deep as the vicinity of Hōsshōji (a temple at Kujō-gawara). However Hosokawa Yoriharu, previously assigned to the force at Uchino but now been called upon to command a force himself, drove them back to near Sugatani and routed them. The enemy at Takeda were attacked and routed by the forces from Tango and Tajima under the command of Imagawa Yorisada.

On the 30th of the 6th month, Takauji's force fought several battles in different places and by the hour of the sheep [2 p.m.] had won them all. This was auspicious, being due, apparently being to divine protection.

63. The Inspection of the Heads
and Sannō Gongen's Dream Revelation

On the following day, the 1st of the 6th month, the enemy heads were inspected at the Sanjō riverbank. There were said to be over a thousand. Before that, a strange thing happened. Many people reported that Sannō Gongen[201] had appeared in their dreams, looking angry and saying, "If the battle is lost on the mountain, the Buddhism of my mountain will be destroyed. Therefore the site of the battle must be changed. Its outcome will be for Heaven to decide." Takauji's forces did indeed withdraw from the mountain, and their victories on the 30th of the 6th month were auspicious.

64. The Battle at Uji
and Kō no Shigemochi Composes a Poem

To the south, the enemy occupied Uji and the area around the Iwashimizu Hachiman Shrine, and in the capital there were daily rumors that they were going to attack. However, the 7th month passed

---

[201] The deity of the Hiyoshi (or Hie) Shrine, the guardian shrine of Mount Hiei.

without incident. On about the 20th of the 8th month it was decided to drive the enemy from Uji. Over 2,000 mounted warriors belonging to Kōno Tsushima Michiharu and his relatives set off under the command of the Hosokawas. They were defeated and turned back.

Advancing by way of Kohata and Inari-yama, the enemy took up position at Amida-ga-mine, overlooking the Imahie Shrine. There they lit watchfires. At the sight Kō no Shigemochi composed this poem:

> Although they appear numerous,
>
> there can not be more than forty-eight—
>
> the watchfires on Amida Peak.[202]

It was a good one.

66. The Battle at Kamo Tadasu-gawara

From daybreak on the 23rd of the 8th month there was continuous fighting all day at the Kamo riverside at Tadasu. The commander, Moronao, fought without regard for his life and received two wounds. His brave warriors fought on as if it were their last day on earth. Yoshisada was defeated and withdrew, but many on his side were killed.

67. Takeda is Captured on Hosokawa Tadatoshi's Recommendation

However, the enemy on Amida-ga-mine still held their position, On the night of the 24th of the month, a council of war was therefore held at Tōji. Various opinions were expressed.

One was that they should advance on foot, protecting themselves with shields, break through the moat and fence, and defeat the enemy. However, Hosokawa Tadatoshi said, "The enemy entrenched on Amida-ga-mine do not amount to much as warriors. They are mountain men from nearby provinces in the Kinai. They prefer to fight when entrenched in a fortress. My relatives and I will take the Shikoku force and first proceed to Yodo and Takeda. We will drive the enemy, who are good runners, to the river. Then we will charge up the Kohata

---

[202] A *kyōka* comic poem. The Buddha Amida had made forty-eight salvific vows. This same *kyōka* appears in *Taiheiki* 17 ("Sanmon no chō Nanto ni okuru koto").

heights and over Inari-yama, and attack them on horseback from the rear. We are certain to scatter them, since they have not fortified the rear of their position. However, the defeated troops will doubtless go north along Kujūmetsu Road and through Shirakawa, and head towards Awataguchi. Tadayoshi should therefore meet them in the vicinity of the Shichijō riverbank."

This opinion was adopted. Without even waiting for daybreak, the Hosokawas headed south along the riverbank, completely ignoring Amida-ga-mine. The enemy occupying Yodo and Takeda had prepared for an attack by cutting the footpaths between the rice fields at Takeda, where they were narrow, and by making fences, erecting a tower, and building a gate.

The large Hosokawa force began their attack, but three warriors charged about two hundred yards into the lead, each vying to be the first. When they approached the tower, one, on a black horse, first brought his mount to a sudden stop, placed his drawn sword back in its scabbard, spread his arms wide, and seized the latticework door of the gate under the tower, to prevent its being lowered. As he sat on his horse with his neck protector tilted to one side, an enemy warrior who was trying to lower the gate grabbed him. While they struggled, the other two warriors rushed up and charged past them, scattering the enemy men, so that all three got through the gate. The rest of the great force followed. They quickly destroyed the fort at Takeda and drove every last one of the enemy into the Yodo River. It had rained heavily from the evening of the 23rd to the 24th, the day before, and the river was in flood. None of those who fell into it survived.

The one who had been in the lead, on the black horse, was Hosokawa Tadatoshi. While holding the tower gate he had been wounded under his helmet, and his horse had also received several cuts. However, they managed to get back to Tōji.

One of the other two warriors was Furuyama Hyōzō, one of Hosokawa Tadatoshi's retainers. He had ridden flank to flank with the priest Ganken,[203] the enemy commander, who had returned to lay life. Both fell from their horses while they grappled, but Hyōzō took

---

[203] Otherwise unknown.

Ganken alive. The last warrior was Nagano Saburō, from the province of Ise. All three had fought without regard for the lives, and Takauji was extremely impressed.

68. The Hosokawa Force Destroys the Court Force at Amida-ga-mine

The Hosokawa force then climbed the Kohata heights and by way of Inari-yama approached the rear of the enemy position on Amida-ga-mine. Accordingly, the pursuing force at the Shichijō riverbank also closed in. In its vanguard was Shōni Yorinao.

Alarmed, the enemy in the fort raised a cry. The Ashikaga forces immediately rushed in from the mountainside. The enemy were defeated without putting up any resistance. Many of them were killed there, and the rest, reportedly very few, fled along Kujūmetsu Road and through Shirakawa.

69. Moronao and Others Repel a Court Force Attempting to Invade the Capital

On the 28th of the 8th month of the same year, the men on Mount Hiei decided to engage that day in one last battle. Go-Daigo bestowed his *hakama* on them. They tore it up and each attached a piece to his helmet as an emblem.

The enemy began their attack at night. The Ashikaga warriors were therefore assembled into one large force under Moronao, and they fought as though it were their last day on earth. They were in high spirits, having won the battles on the 23rd and 24th. The fighting in the capital ended on that day.

70. The Battle of Ōmi, and Go-Daigo's Return to the Capital

However the enemy on Mount Hiei had not yet been subdued. In the middle of the 9th month, Ogasawara Sadamune therefore set out at the head of a force of over 3,000 mounted warriors made up of members of his family and of units from the provinces of Kai and Shinano. They proceeded along the Tōsandō to Ōmi and approached Seta. There, the

113

warrior monks of Enryakuji had torn up the bridge. The Ogasawara force therefore pitched camp in the vicinity of Noji. Another, commanded by Wakiya Yoshisuke, crossed Lake Biwa and launched a fierce attack, but the Ogasawara men defeated them.

However the place was hard to defend. The Ogasawara men therefore withdrew for the time being. The enemy immediately attacked once more when they reached Kagami-yama. They fought back, routed the enemy, killing many, and rushed to Ibuki-yama, where they took up position.

Ogasawara reported the situation to the capital. It was obvious that the enemy at Higashi-Sakamoto, both the fighting monks and the warrior forces, had been able so far to hold their position essentially thanks to support from Ōmi. Takauji therefore decided that a force should be sent to conquer Ōmi and cut the supply lines to Higashi-Sakamoto. He ordered Sasaki Dōyo to help Ogasawara subjugate Ōmi. Sasaki left the capital at the end of the 9th month. His force reached Obama in Wakasa by way of the Tanba Road, and since Sasaki knew the area well his men stormed into the province of Ōmi from the north. United with the Ogasawara force they conquered the whole province, which disheartened the fighting monks and warrior forces on Go-Daigo's side. Accordingly, on the night of Kenmu 3.11.22 [1336], Go-Daigo called for peace and returned to the capital.[204] Takauji and his retainers went to the Kamo riverbank to meet him.

71. Yoshisada and Prince Tsuneyoshi Depart for Hokuriku

The night Yoshisada, who had received Go-Daigo's secret orders,[205] set out for the Kantō along the Hokurikudō with the Heir Apparent[206] and Go-Daigo's first son.[207] When he left, Yoshisada offered a red-braided

---

[204] Takauji had sent him an ultimatum to do so.

[205] Go-Daigo ordered Yoshisada to retreat to the north with the two princes and regroup, with a view to returning. He may have meant to pass the throne to one of them.

[206] Prince Tsuneyoshi, Go-Daigo's sixth son and heir apparent. His mother, Fujiwara no Renshi, was Go-Daigo's favorite consort.

[207] Prince Takayoshi, Go-Daigo's eldest son since the death of Moriyoshi, but, unlike Moriyoshi, one groomed to inherit the throne.

suit of armor called "Thin Gold," a family heirloom for generations, to the Sannō Shrine. It is said still to be there.

Many unfortunate things happened on the way. They were caught in a great snowfall on Mount Arachi, and many of the members of the force perished from the cold. However, Yoshisada reached Echizen safely and entrenched himself in the peerless fortress of Kanegasaki at the port of Tsuruga.

72. Go-Daigo's Escape from Kasan-no-in to Anō

Accordingly, Shiba Takatsune, the protector of that province; Kō no Moroyasu; Niki Yoriaki; and Hosokawa Yoriharu set out for Echizen.

Emperor Godaigo was residing at Kasan-no-in[208] with his quasi-empress[209] and two or three ladies-in-waiting. Takauji had his warriors mount guard all around the residence. People had called that unthinkable even when Go-Daigo had been brought from Mount Kasagi to Rokuhara in the fall of Genkō 1 [1331]. Now it saddened everyone that such a thing should have happened twice in one reign. The sun and the moon might as well have gone dark.

There was talk that Go-Daigo might be exiled again to the provinces. Meanwhile, he slipped out of Kasan-no-in. The uproar in the capital was indescribable. Tadayoshi, fearing that the enemy might rise up from within the capital immediately ordered his forces sent to guard Tōji. Everyone tightened his helmet cord and rushed to Takauji's residence.

Takauji showed no sign of dismay. He met with his chief advisors and said, "We could not relax the guard on Go-Daigo while he resided at Kasan-no-in, and this placed an intolerable burden on us; and it would have been a terrible thing to exile him to a distant province as the former Bakufu did. I had been wondering what to do. That Go-Daigo has now escaped is the most fortunate aspect of this whole, serious business. Presumably he is hiding somewhere in the home provinces. If he has settled down quietly, doing whatever he likes,

---

[208] The former residence of Sadayasu, one of Emperor Seiwa's sons. Go-Daigo was, in effect, under house arrest.

[209] Fujiwara no Renshi.

there is nothing wrong with that. How things will turn out is up to Heaven, not to the power of man's shallow intellect."

Those who heard him said to each other; "It has long been obvious that we are fortunate to have such a matchless Shogun as our commander, but even so, it is amazing that he was not troubled by the escape of Go-Daigo, a formidable enemy."

Meanwhile, it was reported that Go-Daigo had gone to place called Anō in the Yamato mountains. Everyone called it well named.[210]

73. The Fall of Kanegasaki and the Restoration of Peace

Kanegasaki in Echizen fell on the 6th of the 3rd month of the following year, Kenmu 4 [1337]. Yoshisada had left the fortress some time before.[211] His son Yoshiaki committed suicide, as did Prince Takayoshi. The Heir Apparent was captured by Ashikaga warriors and returned to the capital. Everyone, high or low, who witnessed this wept, thinking that such a thing had never happened before. It was said that, having run out of provisions, the troops in the fortress killed their horses to eat them, so that they were able to hold out about twenty days longer. It is sad to imagine their lives in the next world, since they had lowered themselves in this life to the level of hungry ghosts.

Thus throughout the country, wherever Takauji's banner went, the enemy forces were soon defeated, and as the days and months passed peace was restored.

74. The Most Reverend Musō's Praise of Takauji's Virtues

In the course of a sermon, the Most Reverend Musō[212] once praised Takauji's and Tadayoshi's virtues. Of Takauji he said, "A man born to become a king, a minister, or a leader of men is so destined by the power generated by his good deeds in previous lives; it is not a matter

---

[210] Although some manuscripts have "Anō," this one has simply *ana*, which can be understood to mean to mean "hole" or "trap."
[211] He had fled to the fortress of Somayama, about 25 miles north of Kanegasaki. He was killed a year later, in 1338, in the battle of Fujishima.
[212] Musō Soseki, 1276-1351.

merely of what he does in this life. The Shogun, especially, occupies a very important position, since it is his duty to assist the Emperor and suppress rebellion.

"I have heard only at second hand about affairs in China. In our own country, Sakanoue no Tamuramaro, Fujiwara no Toshihito, Minamoto no Yorimitsu, and Fujiwara no Yasumasa all suppressed rebels, but their authority did not extend over the whole country. From Jishō [1177-81] on, Yoritomo also held the office of Shogun and took affairs of state entirely into his own hands. He did not let his personal feelings affect his administration of justice, but the punishments he meted out were nonetheless too harsh, and he therefore appeared to lack humanity.

"Takauji, the present Shogun, possesses not only benevolence, but also still greater virtues. First, he is courageous. Often, in his battles, his life seemed in danger, but he kept smiling and his face betrayed no fear. Second, he was born with charity and hates no one. He has forgiven many sworn enemies, treating each as if he were his only son. Third, he is generous; there is nothing stingy about him. To him gold and silver are like earth and stones, and when he gives weapons, horses, and so on away, he does not match the gift to the man but distributes them at random. I have heard that he has received gifts beyond counting on occasions like the 1st day of the 8th month, but that he has given them all away, so that by evening no one could remember what they had been. Truly, a Shogun with these three virtues is rare in this latter age." Musō talked this way whenever he preached a sermon.

75. Takauji's and Tadayoshi's Deep Devotion to Buddhism

Prince Shōtoku built forty-nine temples and instructed the nation to observe the fast days. Emperor Shōmu built Tōdaiji and the Kokubunji, and Fujiwara no Fuhito built Kōfukuji. These things occurred in ancient times and were all a result of divine incarnation.

Likewise Takauji and Tadayoshi, in our own time, should not be regarded as ordinary men. They devote themselves to Buddhism above all, and they built Tenryūji, founded by Musō. Takauji offered a prayer in

*which he vowed to copy out the Tripitaka,[213] and he personally painted a
Buddhist image, wrote an inscription on it, and signed it. Even after a
heavy bout of drinking he always holds a meditation session with
everyone present.[214]*

76. Takauji's and Tadayoshi's Good Government,
and Their Respect for Musō

Tadayoshi built a temple named Ankokuji in each of the sixty-six
provinces, and he similarly erected a stupa in each province. In this
way he fulfilled his desire. His behavior shows him to be an upright,
sincere man untainted by dishonesty. For this reason Takauji
entrusted the government of the realm to him. Tadayoshi declined
resolutely more than once, but he finally agreed after Takauji begged
him to accept. Thereafter Takauji never interfered in government
affairs, even in the most trivial matter.

Once, when they were together, Takauji said to Tadayoshi, "Since
you rule the realm, please behave responsibly and never go sightseeing or waste your time. There is nothing wrong with viewing
cherry blossoms or autumn leaves, but sightseeing and so on should
be limited to special occasions. I ask you to be prudent because I think
that I myself will be mingling casually with retainers, eliciting their
support and guarding the imperial court." Tadayoshi appreciated this
advice, which, he thought, an ordinary man would never have given
him.

This is how Takauji and Tadayoshi came to accept Musō as their
master. Before Genkō, when Hosokawa Akiuji was on his way through
the northern provinces to Awa, to recruit troops for the imperial
cause, he had an audience with Musō at Erinji in Kai and received his
teaching. Later, Musō gave spiritual guidance to Takauji and
Tadayoshi. Thanks to the urging of the priest Musō and the layman

---

[213] The *Gen'ishū* account of the battle of Tōji (1355) describes Takauji's fulfillment of
this vow.

[214] The oldest Kyōdai text lacks these two paragraphs, although the 1466 (Kanshō 7)
copy of the latter half of *Baishōron* contains them.

Akiuji, Takauji and all those below achieved everlasting glory. This was wonderful and auspicious indeed.

77. Takauji's Magnanimous Rule and the People's Willing Submission

Takauji and Tadayoshi once came together, summoned Kō no Moronao and many members of the former Bakufu's Council of State, and enacted a number of government regulations. Takauji said, "According to what I have heard of ancient times, the Heike were wicked and tyrannical during the twenty years when Yoritomo suffered in exile in Izu and devised his farsighted plan of raising an army. In order to put an end to the inexpressible grief of the people, Yoritomo raised his army in Jishō 4 [1180] and suppressed the rebels in Genryaku 1 [1184]. The war lasted for five years.

"What I have heard about his rule suggests that rewards and punishments were made clear, which is something that the ancient sages did well. However, there were still many harsh punishments and this gave rise to suspicion within the Minamoto family, and between it and others. As a result, many were executed for no particular misdeed. This was most unfortunate.

"The intention of this government is to rule without causing suffering. We should therefore placate even those who were our sworn enemies, assure continued tenure of their ancestral estates, and bestow especially generous rewards on those who perform military deeds. I trust that everyone will assist the government with this aim in mind."

Tadayoshi was particularly pleased. Moronao and all the members of the old Council of State appreciated Takauji's generous feelings. None among them failed to wipe tears from his eyes.

There is no need here to discuss Yao and Shun, since they lived in China. Here in Japan, however, those who born under such a Shogun as Takauji, even in this Latter Age, have had the good fortune to enjoy prosperous and peaceful lives.

78. The Celebration of Ashikaga Rule
and the Origin of the Name of This Book

It was decided that the Heir Apparent, the son of Retired Emperor Kōgon, would ascend the throne.[215] The order was issued to hold the Daijōe, and on the day of the ceremony the courtiers adorned the capital like so many flowers.[216]

Now all the Shogun's sworn enemies in every province have either surrendered or been destroyed. His authority has pacified the entire land, and there is no more talk of war. And since Heaven protects the benevolent and wise, Takauji's and Tadayoshi's rule will last longer than the Zhou dynasty's 800 years, and even the sands of the stormy sea could never outnumber the years that Takauji's descendants will flourish.

Here the speaker concluded his story.

He who recorded it did so at the Kitano Shrine. He therefore wished that Takauji's glory might blossom like the plum trees and that his descendants might flourish for as long as the pines. He also bore in mind the saying, "When wind blows through the pines, plum blossoms send forth their fragrance." Therefore he called the book *Baishōron*, "Of Pine and Plum."

---

[215] Prince Okihito, Kōgon's eldest son, became heir apparent in 1338 and succeeded to the throne in 1349 as Emperor Sukō.

[216] *Entairyaku*, *Moromori ki* and other sources record planning for a Daijōe (Sukō's formal enthronement) that was never performed. The planning began in Kannō 1.4 [1350], the month when the *nengō* was changed from Jōwa to Kannō, but according to *Kō nendai ryakki* the event, scheduled to begin on 10.22, was canceled because of *tenka jōran* ("chaos in the realm"). This suggestion in *Baishōron* that the Daijōe took place after all is curious and could have some bearing on the date or process of the work's composition. However, its significance remains unclear.

THE NORTHERN EMPERORS' JOURNEY TO ANŌ, 1352

From *Taiheiki* 30
"Jimyōin-dono Yoshino e senkō no koto"

INTRODUCTION
The Kannō Anarchy

Both *Baishōron* and Hino Nako's second *Takemuki-ga-ki* entry cover Go-Daigo's flight from Kyoto in 1331. This event irreversibly confirmed the split between the Northern (Jimyōin) and Southern (Daikakuji) imperial lines. The main narrative in *Baishōron* starts then. It ends in 1336-1337 with Go-Daigo's escape to the remote village of Anō; the fall of Kanegasaki (the Southern Court's stronghold in the north) and, above all, the success achieved by Ashikaga Takauji his brother Tadayoshi, for whom, as late as 1350 or 1351, *Baishōron* foresees ten thousand years of glory.

That was not to be. Southern Court resistance continued.[217] The balance seemed to favor the North and the Ashikaga when, in Jōwa 4.1 (1348), Kō no Moronao, Takauji's chief lieutenant, drove the Southern emperor (by this time Go-Murakami, Go-Daigo's son) from Yoshino back to Anō. However, a succession feud then broke out between Takauji and Tadayoshi.[218] Chaos known as the Kannō Anarchy (*Kannō no jōran*) ensued in 1350-1352. In principle the chaos ended late in 1352 with the carefully contrived accession of the Northern emperor Go-Kōgon. However, more trouble lay ahead, starting with Go-Kōgon's flight to Mino in 1353 (*Ojima no kuchizusami*).

The Kannō Anarchy began when, in Kannō 1.8 (1350), Moronao marched on Kyoto, demanding a governing role for Takauji's son Yoshiakira. Tadayoshi responded by ordering Moronao and his son Moroyasu killed. Two months later (Kannō 1.10), however, Tadayoshi had to flee Kyoto, and Takauji obtained a Northern Court edict (*inzen*) commanding his destruction. The next month Tadayoshi surrendered

---

[217] The following summary of events is derived from Thomas D. Conlan, *From Sovereign to Symbol*, Oxford University Press, 2011, pp. 118-129.
[218] Tadayoshi wished his own newborn son to succeed Takauji, rather than Takauji's son Yoshiakira. The feud figures in Imagawa Ryōshun's *Nantaiheiki*.

to Go-Murakami, who ordered him to attack Takauji. In Kannō 2.2 (1351) Takauji surrendered to Go-Murakami and Kitabatake Chikafusa. He only barely managed to return to Kyoto. Meanwhile, on the very day when Tadayoshi's men killed Moronao and Moroyasu, Tadayoshi lost the little son whom he had hoped to see succeed Takauji.

After surrendering to the South, Takauji headed east to suppress Tadayoshi, while the Southern Court moved from Anō to Nara. During Kannō 2.12 Chikafusa was issuing orders in Kyoto, although the tides of wars then drew him elsewhere. In the east Takauji defeated Tadayoshi. Early in 1352, on the anniversary of the deaths of Moronao and Moroyasu, Tadayoshi was poisoned.

Twelve days after Tadayoshi's death, Chikafusa attacked Kyoto. Yoshiakira fled the city, leaving behind all three Northern emperors: the retired Kōgon (whom Hino Nako had known well) and Kōmyō, and the reigning Sukō. Kitabatake Chikafusa's son, Akiyoshi, took them and the heir apparent (Naohito, a son of Kōgon) prisoner. Go-Murakami and his officials escorted them to Iwashimizu Hachiman. However, Chikafusa failed to hold Iwashimizu. Early in Kannō 2.6 the Southern Court retreated and took the three Northern emperors to Anō. From Kannō 2.12 (1351) to Kan'ō 3.8 (1352, Go-Kōgon's accession [*senso*]) there was no emperor, reigning or retired, in Kyoto.

THE NORTHERN EMPERORS' JOURNEY TO ANŌ

The enemy [the North] then fled the capital, but the Yoshino Emperor [Go-Murakami] refrained from entering it. Only Kitabatake Chikafusa and Akiyoshi, father and son, did so and saw to various matters there. The senior nobles and privy gentlemen accompanied their sovereign to Iwashimizu Hachiman.

On the 23rd [Kannō 2.12.23, 1352] an imperial messenger, Nakanoin Captain Tomotada, brought the Yoshino Emperor the Three Regalia from the palace in Kyoto.[219] When the Previous Emperor [Go-Daigo] surrendered the Regalia to the Ashikaga, he substituted forgeries that he sent to Jimyōin House (*Jimyōin-dono*). To this end he sacrificed the Jewel's case and bestowed the Sword and Mirror on courtiers in his intimate service: the former as a ceremonial sword for the use of the Palace Guards and the latter as a dressing mirror. These were not the real Regalia, but they had already served in three enthronement rites (*daijōe*)[220] and for over twenty years had daily received the imperial salutation to Ise (*go-shinpai*), as well as kagura in the Seishodō.[221] For that reason the divine spirit undoubtedly inhered in them; hence protests that they were too awesomely sacred for such profane use.

On the 27th, Kitabatake Akiyoshi led over 500 mounted men to Jimyōin House, after first securing every nearby gate and crossroads.

---

[219] The issue of the regalia at this time is insoluble. According to *Taiheiki* 17 ("Genkō gubu no hitobito kinsatsu seraruru koto"), when Tadayoshi ordered Go-Daigo in Kenmu 3 (1336) to surrender the regalia to the reigning Jimyōin emperor Kōmyō, Go-Daigo entrusted to a woman official (*naishi*) counterfeit regalia that he had had prepared in advance. Conlan discussed the regalia in *From Emperor to Symbol*, pp. 59-63 and on p. 122 dismissed the *Taiheiki* account as "implausible and contradicted by Go-Daigo's behavior in 1333, when he used Izumo shrine objects as his regalia." On the same page Conlan noted, among other things, that even Tōin Kinkata, the author of *Entairyaku*, did not know whether or not the regalia were real.

[220] For Kōgon, Kōmyō, and Sukō. Actually, Sukō had no Daijōe. See the final note to *Baishōron*.

[221] Kagura was performed in the course of a Daijōe.

The three Empresses (*nyōin, kōgō*) collapsed in despair, crying, "Oh no, the warriors are going to kill the reigning and retired Emperors!" Meanwhile the women officials (*naishi*), senior pages (*ue warabe*) and senior gentlewomen (*jōrō nyōbō*) fled in terror and scurried aimlessly about.

Akiyoshi entered calmly through the small gate to the west and announced through Shijō Grand Counselor Takakage: "His Majesty commands the removal of the imperial seat (*kōkyo*) to the southern mountains until peace returns." The Emperors and the Heir Apparent, too aghast to speak, could only weep and wring the tears from their sleeves.

At last the Junior Retired Emperor [Kōmyō] said, "I assumed the imperial dignity only after the realm had lapsed into chaos, and, as far as I can see, what has happened is no fault of mine. Nothing in the world has gone as I would have wished. The Big Dipper (*hokushin*) no longer shines, and the capital is in darkness. I should much prefer to seek the shadows of retirement and follow in the footsteps of Kasan of old,[222] and I can only lament that even now that should be impossible. The imperial fortunes have shifted to the South, and your every hope is now met. If it pleases His Majesty [Go-Murakami] to allow me to do so, I shall retire into obscurity in some distant wilderness. You will convey my words to him."

Akiyoshi could not request an imperial reply. "His Majesty has spoken," he said, "and I cannot pursue the matter with him further." He had two carriages brought up and, remarking that time was passing, urged the imperial persons quickly to board them. The senior Retired Emperor [Kōgon], the Junior [Kōmyō], and the reigning Emperor [Sukō], did so together with the Heir Apparent and left through the south gate. Moonlight shone dimly enough as it was through the misty blossoms, and more dimly still through their tears of farewell. The Empresses lay prostrate within their blinds or behind standing curtains, and sobbing could be heard here and there from galleries or gentlewomen's rooms. Carriage wheels creaking, they descended Higashinotōin under the dawn moon, while first light revealed the boughs of their capital and

---

222 Emperor Kazan (r. 984-986) was deposed by Fujiwara no Kaneie, renounced the world, and devoted his life to religious practice and wandering.

bells sounded in the cloud-topped Eastern Hills. A throng of courtiers followed them as far as Tōji, but Akiyoshi forbade them to proceed further. Only the Sanjō Captain Sanetoshi[223] and Atsunao, the head of the Office of Physic (*Ten'yakuryō*) accompanied them to Toba, amid the unaccustomed presence of warriors. Meanwhile, night gave way to day. At Toba the carriages stopped, and the imperial persons were made to board instead shabby *ajiro* palanquins.[224]

They spent that day traveling to a place called Anō in the remote fastnesses of Yoshino. Even the imperial dwelling there, revered by the local people as the residence of their sovereign, was built of unbarked logs, had bamboo eaves, and was surrounded by a brushwood fence. To all appearances it was uninhabitable even briefly, and yet now, after their capture by the enemy, it had become, so to speak, their home in exile: a long-crumbling retreat roofed with ill-fitting cryptomeria boards through which, during the lonely nights, visiting showers of rain wet their sleeves. At dawn cold winds sighed through the forest, moonbeams gleamed on the tops of the surrounding pines, and at nightfall the cries of monkey bands set the clouds racing.[225] No distant account of the miseries of life in this mountain wilderness—so Their Majesties often assured one another, amid unceasing tears— could convey their reality.

---

223 An older brother of Ōgimachi Sanjō Hideko (1311-1353, Yōrokumon-in), Kōgon's empress (*kisaki*, elevated from the office of *naishi-no-suke* held years before by Hino Nako), and the mother of Sukō and Go-Kōgon.
224 Made of woven *hinoki* or bamboo strips.
225 This sentence draws on *Wakan rōeishū* 495, by Ōe no Mochitoki.

Casual Verses from Ojima:
OJIMA NO KUCHIZUSAMI

Nijō Yoshimoto

INTRODUCTION

Nijō Yoshimoto (1320-1388), a major literary figure, was also in his time head of the Fujiwara house and regent to the Northern Court emperors Kōmyō, Sukō, and Go-Kōgon. Remembered especially as an expert on waka and renga, he also wrote on such technical matters as the proper form for court ceremonies (*Omoi no mama no nikki*) and the art of falconry (*Sagano monogatari*). Such other works as *Sakakiba no nikki*, *Kumoi no minori*, or *Sakayuku hana* describe events at which he was present, sometimes in a central role.[226] He often adopted as narrator the persona of a gentlewoman, an old woman, a nun, or an old man, but in *Ojima no kuchizusami* he speaks as himself. The work concerns the Northern Court's flight to Mino in 1353.

In the summer of Bunna 2 (1353) a Southern Court army under Kusunoki Masanori (Masashige's third son) took Kyoto.[227] Go-Kōgon (r. 1352-1371) fled first to Mount Hiei (Bunna 2.6.6) and then, a week later, to Ojima, a locality in present Gifu-ken, west of the Ibi River. Yoshimoto accompanied him as far as Sakamoto, on the shore of Lake Biwa. On 6.17 the Southern Court regent (Nijō Moromoto) dismissed all officials associated with Go-Kōgon's accession the previous year. Yoshiakira, Ashikaga Takauji's son and successor, counterattacked and entered the capital on 7.26, but the threat posed by the Southern forces still barred the Northern Court's return.

---

[226] Matthew Stavros translated and studied *Sakayuku hana* ("Imperial Progress to the Muromachi Palace, 1381") in *Japan Review* 28, 2015; and Royall Tyler's *The Miracles of the Kasuga Deity* (Columbia University Press, 1990) includes a translation of *Sakakiba no nikki*. Yoshimoto was long credited with *Masukagami*, which he was believed to have written during Ōan (1368-1374). However, Ogawa Takeo ("*Masukagami* no sakusha: seiritsu nendai, sakuzō no saikentō," *Mita bungaku* 32, September 2000) has shown that *Masukagami* must date at the latest from the late 1340s, rendering Yoshimoto's authorship implausible.

[227] The following paragraphs rely on Itō Kei, *Shinhokuchō no hito to bungaku*, Miyai Shoten (Miyai sensho 6), 1979, pp. 192-193. Itō drew most of his information from *Entairyaku*.

Yoshimoto was probably suffering already from a malarial fever (*warawayami*) when Go-Kōgon started for Mino (Bunna 2.6.13). After turning back from Sakamoto he retired to what he called "a grass hut" at the foot of Ogura-yama, west of the city. However, on 6.27 he set out for Mino after all, presumably in response to a direct appeal from Go-Kōgon. *Kuchizusami* covers his journey there, his stay in those provincial wilds, Takauji's arrival, and Go-Kōgon's return to Kyoto, which he reached on Bunna 2.9.21.

On the way to Mino, Yoshimoto was often too ill to continue and had to break his journey wherever he happened to be. Nonetheless, he acknowledged in verse, as any other literary-minded medieval traveler would have done, the poetically famous places (*utamakura*) that he passed. Some of his poems convey an optimism about the imperial future not obviously warranted by the current situation but fitting for a man in his position. The living conditions at Ojima appalled him. His account of the return to capital has a more triumphal tone than the circumstances might seem to justify.

The introduction to the preceding translation from *Taiheiki* briefly reviews the events of the Kannō Anarchy (1350-52), during which three Northern Court emperors, reigning or retired, were captured by the South and taken to Anō in the Yoshino mountains. In principle, the anarchy ended with Go-Kōgon's accession on Kannō 3.8.17, amid "heavy rain and fierce winds."[228] Some historians therefore see his accession as initiating a "New Northern Court" (*shinhokuchō*). However, the three emperors were still at Anō, where Chikafusa died in Bunna 3.4 (1354). Only in the last days of that year did Southern Court forces return them to Kyoto, when they again occupied the city. Ashikaga Takauji and the Northern Court fled.

For two or three months thereafter the Northern Court moved from place to place. Once more there was no emperor in Kyoto. Relative stability returned only once the North had defeated the South decisively at Tōji on Bunna 5.3.13 (1355).

---

[228] Thomas D. Conlan, *From Sovereign to Symbol: An Age of Ritual Determinism in Fourteenth-Century Japan,* Oxford University Press, 2011, p. 136, citing *Entairyaku* for that date.

Yoshimoto and Go-Kōgon

Takauji was still in the east when in Bunna 2 (1353), between Go-Kōgon's accession and Chikafusa's death, the Northern Court was obliged to flee to Mino. For Yoshimoto the journey must have been a nuisance at best, and also a considerable disappointment.

Go-Kōgon was the second son of Kōgon, whom Hino Nako served during his accession in 1331. *Takemuki-ga-ki* mentions Kōgon's visits to Kitayama, the Saionji estate where Nako lived as Saionji Kinmune's widow and the mother of his son. It also tells how, early in Kenmu 5 (1338), Kōgon entrusted Prince Iyahito, the future Go-Kōgon, to the care of Nako's father, Hino Sukena, at the Hino family home.[229]

Yoshimoto, too, had a Saionji tie, since his wife was a second cousin of Kinmune.[230] He also knew several Hino, among them three of Nako's uncles (sons of Sukena): the chamberlain (*kurōdo*) and *densō* Sukeaki;[231] the Tendai abbot Kōei; and the Shingon prelate Kenshun.

Kenshun, abbot of Sanbōin (Daigoji) and Tōji, was a major Northern Court figure. Tōin Kinkata wrote in *Entairyaku* (Enbun 1.7.5, 1356), "Kenshun Sōjō controls the whole realm in the palm of his hand"; and, after Kenshun's death (Enbun 1.7.17), "His glory knows no bounds. No courtier or warrior had comparable power."[232] In *Kuchizusami* Yoshimoto mentions Kenshun three times. He crosses paths with Kenshun on his way to Mino; in Mino, Kenshun welcomes him on Go-Kōgon's behalf; and a storm obliges Kenshun to cede his temple residence to Go-Kōgon. Actually, Go-Kōgon owed his accession less than a year earlier to both men.

The accession ceremonies for Kōmyō (a son of Go-Fushimi) and Sukō (Kōgon's eldest son) had been held in the residence of Yoshimoto, who had also had sponsored Prince Iyahito's coming-of-age.[233] The Kannō Anarchy then confronted him with an unprecedented challenge.

---

[229] *Takemuki-ga-ki*, no. 37. Sukena died later that year.

[230] Itō, *Shinhokuchō no hito to bungaku*, p. 46.

[231] The *densō* transmitted imperial documents, set the agenda for council meetings, recorded minutes, and so on. As Conlan observed (*From Sovereign to Symbol*, p. 131), during the Kannō Anarchy Sukeaki served a court that did not properly exist.

[232] Conlan, *From Sovereign to Symbol*, p. 146.

[233] Itō, *Shinhokuchō no hito to bungaku*, p. 46.

With the three emperors, the South had also taken the imperial regalia. The North urgently required a new emperor but had no retiring emperor to whom a new one might succeed. It also had no regalia for the new emperor to receive.

Yoshimoto and Kenshun therefore devised a solution that granted Go-Fushimi's empress, Kōgimon-in, retired emperor (*daijō tennō*) rank so that she could play the retiring emperor's part in legitimating the succession. It also circumvented the absence of the regalia (the sword, jewel, and mirror).[234]

When Hino Nako handled the sword and jewel in 1331, in preparation for Kōgon's accession, she knew that the "real" sword had been lost at Dan-no-ura.[235] Unlike the *Taiheiki* author, she also knew that Go-Daigo had not taken the mirror. This much already suggests confusion in her time about the genuineness and even the location of the regalia. Kitabatake Chikafusa asserted in *Jinnō shōtōki* (ca. 1340) that the "real" sword and mirror were substitutes made in the [mythical] reign of Emperor Sujin, the original sword being kept at Atsuta and the original mirror at Ise. For Chikafusa, the only original among the current regalia was the jewel, "the protective talisman that sovereigns have kept safely in their personal possession reign after reign from the age of the gods."[236] It is therefore unclear how authentic the available regalia were in 1352, when the Southern Court made off with them. However, they were at least physical objects imbued, if necessary by expedient means, with ritual authority.

Yoshimoto and Kenshun bypassed the need for their presence. Their reasoning relied on Kenshun's mastery of Shingon ritual and on

---

[234] Conlan, *From Sovereign to Symbol*, p. 138, citing *Entairyaku* for Kannō 3.8.17 (1352) Bunna 1.12.6 (1352); and quoting Tōin Kinkata's expression of "fear and indignation" over the procedure adopted (*Entairyaku*, Kannō 3.9.26).

[235] See *Takemuki-ga-ki* 3.

[236] H. Paul Varley, tr., *A Chronicle of Gods and Sovereigns: Jinnō Shōtōki of Kitabatake Chikafusa*, Columbia University Press, 1980, pp. 217-218. This is how Nako herself thought of the jewel. No record seems to identify what it was. Even the learned and inquisitive Emperor Hanazono claimed not to know what was in the case that he sketched and that Nako eventually rewrapped. (*Hanazono-in shinki* for Gen'ō 2.1.21 [1320], cited by Conlan, *From Sovereign to Symbol*, p. 62.) On pp. 122-123, Conlan cited further evidence of controversy on the subject.

a principle defined by Yoshimoto as *nyozai no rei*: ritual performed *as though* the missing objects were present. Rightly conceived and performed ritual would authenticate the succession and render physical objects superfluous.[237]

This solution made possible both Go-Kōgon's accession and a reaffirmation of Takauji's authority.[238] Yoshimoto may have favored it all the more because, just as the Northern imperial house had lost the regalia, his own had lost its records of procedure, ritual, and precedent. In 1252 the chronicles of the regental line had passed to the Kujō and Ichijō when Yoshizane (1216-1270), Yoshimoto's grandfather and the Nijō founder, was disinherited.[239] Yoshimoto, too, had little choice but to start fresh. In fact, when the South took Kyoto in mid-1353 and annulled all appointments associated with Go-Kōgon's accession, it also confiscated what house documents he had left.[240]

Yoshimoto mentioned writing *Kuchizusami* in order to record a "rare event" and so "while away the time on the journey's sleepless nights." Perhaps he really did hope after this picturesque reverse that a more promising future lay ahead.

---

[237] Conlan, *From Sovereign to Symbol*, pp. 137-138, referring for *nyozai no rei* to *Entairyaku*, Bunna 1.12.31 (1352).

[238] Nonetheless, Kenshun did what he could to supply a material support for the accession rite. A week or so after the Southern Court fled Iwashimizu in the 5th month of Kannō 3 (1352), he found or claimed to have found there, abandoned, the case that had held the mirror. This empty case seems to have figured in the rite. (Conlan, *From Sovereign to Symbol*, p. 136, citing *Entairyaku* for Kannō 3.5.19 and 7.1, and *Tadatōki* [Kotsuki Tadatō] for Kannō 3.8.3.)

[239] Conlan, *From Sovereign to Symbol*, p. 137, citing Itō, *Shinhokuchō no hito to bungaku*, pp. 67-70.

[240] Itō, *Shinhokuchō no hito to bungaku*, pp. 192-193.

135

OJIMA NO KUCHIZUSAMI

I had retired to a grass hut at Nakanoin, below Ogura-yama, suffering from a malarial fever and feeling more acutely than ever that I might soon draw my last breath. The thought so disturbed me that I tried every spell, went to the oldest, holiest monks for suitable, protective talismans, and ordered prayers. However, none of this brought any relief. It only made things worse. I was at my wits' end.

Then the breeze from east of the barrier[241] repeatedly brought me this message: "What encourages you to linger a moment longer in so cruel a world?" Indeed, I had no reason to believe myself safe even in hiding among the rocks,[242] and the sound of the wind blowing through the pines reached me too often and too loudly: no, I could trust no mountain trail to offer me passage unseen.[243] After the 20th of the 7th month I therefore left my grass hut late in the night, with the dawn moon in the sky, and set out on the road to the east. I felt miserable. It was unprecedented for someone like me to pass beyond the barrier, but I still derived consolation from the thought that there was no reason the Gods and Buddhas should not keep me from harm.

That night I reached Sakamoto. The monks of the Mountain gave me a gratifying welcome. They swept the dew from straw matting and very kindly invited me for the night into a nearby lodge. I therefore passed the night there.

The expected fever arose the next day, which I spent in idle melancholy. The next morning I crossed the lake by boat. The crossing did not take long, but the boat tossed about so much that the experience was very unpleasant.

---

[241] The Ōsaka barrier. Go-Kōgon is already at Ojima.

[242] From *Kokinshū* 952.

[243] From *Kokinshū* 955.

Today I managed to reach Moruyama. The name is impressive enough[244] but the place offers nothing much to see. No doubt this is where the great Tsurayuki spoke of "heavy winter rain,"[245] and that moment from the past came straight to mind:

> *moruyama no shitaba wa imada irozukade*
> *uki ni shigururu sode zo tsuyukeki*
>
> At Moruyama, the lower leaves have not colored yet,
> and cold, dreary showers wet my sleeves with dew.

I felt too unwell to write more. In this way I continued on to a place called Noji-no-shinohara. I knew it well by name as an *utamakura*, but this was the first time I had actually been there.

> *tsuyukesa o omoiokuran hito mo gana*
> *noji no shinohara shinobu miyako ni*
>
> How I long for someone to note my dewy tears,
> where at Noji-no-shinohara I so miss the capital!

Then I passed the hill named Kagami-yama. I wanted to go and have a look at it, but I had a long journey ahead and was in too great a hurry, so I merely passed on by.

> *harubaru to yukusue tooku kagamiyama*
> *kakete kumoranu miyo zo shiraruru*
>
> Far along my way, I see Kagami-yama
> promise a future of unclouded reigns.

I must have been feeling perfectly miserable, because I found myself praying silently for better times ahead.

Oiso Forest consisted exclusively of *sugi* trees; there was no other kind. The view across the foothills offered a great deal to please the eye. I had come a long way, and the sun was low. They put my palanquin down, and I called out a villager, to ask where I might be able to spend the night. An old nun came forth, presumably the best educated person there. "This forest is very beautiful," I said. "What is it called?"

---

[244] Moruyama (now read Moriyama) is an *utamakura*.

[245] *Kokinshū* 260: *shiratsuyu mo/ shigure mo itaku/ moruyama wa/ shitaba nokorazu/ irozukinikeri* ("Bright dew and cold showers fall abundantly at Moruyama, where color has touched every lower leaf").

"This forest has long been famous," she answered. "Its name describes my years."[246] So witty a reply in such a place showed her to be no rustic, and I was deeply touched.

> *ima wa mi no oiso no mori zo yosonaranu*
> *misoji amari mo sugi no shitakage*
> Aging as I am, Oiso Forest is no stranger to me,
> for beneath these sugi trees my thirtieth year has passed.

My illness still troubled me, and I spent the night there. The next day I had a reprieve. The journey was not going smoothly, and the count of days kept mounting.

Crossing a river named, I believe, the Yasu-gawa:[247]

> *itsumade to sode uchinurashi yasugawa no*
> *yasuge naki yo o watarikanuran*
> How long, O Yasu-gawa, must I wet my sleeves
> in this life, always so perilous to cross?

Toko-no-yama in Inukami, the Isaya-gawa, and other such spots offered so few distinguishing features that I hardly knew which was which, but I was still curious to visit anywhere with a name in poetry. However, on such a journey it would have been tasteless of me to seem to affect literary refinement, so I passed them by. I felt like imploring the denizens of these wilds never to breathe a word of the sadly reduced figure that I cut among them.

Ibuki-yama soared far off, beyond the clouds, yet loomed very near when I crossed its lower slopes. Somewhere named Ono I encountered the Sanbōin prelate Kenshun, a son of the Hino grand counselor Toshimitsu. I explained that I was on an urgent journey in the direction of Ōmi. The bearers put down my palanquin next to a chapel sheltered by a grove of trees, and he and I talked. He seemed astonished to find me so greatly reduced by illness on this long trip through the hinterland. Then he continued straight on toward the capital. The name of this place, too, appears often in old poems, but

---

246 The *oi* of Oiso means "old age."

247 This river flows from Suzuka-yama into Lake Biwa. Yoshimoto's poem contrasts the sound *yasu* ("easy," "pleasant") with the experience of life.

this is not where Prince Koretaka lived, and the association struck me as untenable.[248]

Further on, I came to where the purest water flowed from under a rock surmounted by tall pines. The place seemed hardly to belong to this world. It must have been Samegai.[249] Nearby was a simple bridge and a small, pretty chapel. Here, too, the water issuing from the rock was incomparably pure. I called for a gourd dipper and washed my hands before continuing on. The water was extremely auspicious.

> *ima yori ya ukarishi yume mo samegai no*
> *mizu no nagarete sue mo tanoman*
> From this day onward shall the Samegai waters
> dispel that painful dream and promise a bright future.

The Fuwa barrier hut was a ruin already long ago, and there remained of it only a length of board eaves and a woven bamboo fence that, indeed, could not possibly keep out the autumn wind.

> *mukashi dani arenishi fuwa no seki nareba*
> *ima wa sanagara na nomi narikeri*
> The Fuwa barrier, a ruin long ago,
> by now survives only as a name.[250]

The evocative name "Fuji-gawa" is associated with the barrier, and I made a point of asking about it. It sounds substantial enough, but actually the stream looked too small to last ten thousand ages. Still, there it was, flowing on reassuringly as before.

> *sate mo nao shizumanu na o ya todomemashi*
> *kakaru fuchise no seki no fujigawa*
> Even so, I hope to leave an undying name,
> as long as the current of the Fuji-gawa runs.

---

[248] Koretaka (b. 844), a son of Emperor Montoku, figures prominently in *Ise monogatari*, especially nos. 82 and 83. *Heike monogatari* 8 tells how he lost out to his brother and rival, Korehito. The Ono where he took refuge was in the hills north of Kyoto.

[249] A spring famous in poetry.

[250] The Fuwa barrier is particularly famous in poetry as a relic of a distant past.

I gathered that Oyama in Mino[251] is fairly near Ojima. My destination was therefore no great distance away. That day at last I felt a little better. According to a local peasant, the celebrated Hitotsumatsu ["single pine"] is still there, as it was long ago, but to my lasting regret I made no great effort to locate and visit it.[252]

> *ukarikeru mino no oyama no matsu goto mo*
> *ge ni tagui naki yo no tameshi kana*
> Despite my misfortune, the Oyama pine in Mino
> yet promises an incomparable reign.

So it was that, after a two or three day journey made in five or six, I reached Ojima at last. I had never seen anything like it. To right and left rose mountains heaped with unbroken cloud. For utter gloom, "such a place" surpassed all others.[253] It was autumn, and the prospect of the mountains filled my heart with dejection beyond words. Here, stags' calls and insect voices stirred me far more than had the same seasonal sounds under those pines.[254] This was not Obasute-yama, no, but my travel here had still left me unconsoled.[255] It had been so upsetting in every way that I went straight to where the Nijō counselor[256] was lodged and installed myself there.

This lodging[257] had eaves of *kaya* rushes and a woven bamboo door. The wind blew in freely through the widely spaced veranda boards.

---

251 A sacred hill and the site of a major shrine (Nangū Taisha) in Tarui-chō, Fuwa-gun, Gifu-ken. It, too, is an *utamakura*. Tarui is where, below, Takauji and Go-Kōgon meet.
252 *Shinkokinshū* 1407, by Ise, mentions the Hitotsumatsu at ""Mino no Oyama."
253 *Kakaru tokoro*, an expression from the "Suma" chapter of *Genji monogatari* (Tyler, *Genji*, p. 244) and a recognized renga *yoriai* (allusion) identified with the chapter.
254 Presumably ones he had just left, below Ogura-yama.
255 A celebrated *utamakura* and the setting of the Noh play *Obasute*. *Kokinshū* 878: *waga kokoro/ nagusame-kanetsu/ sarashina ya/ obasuteyama ni/ teru tsuki o mite* ("My heart remains unconsoled—ah, Sarashina!—when I see the moon shine down on Obasute-yama"). The place name is taken to mean "mountain of the abandoned crone."
256 Fujiwara no Yoshifuyu, Yoshimoto's uncle, then in his thirty-fifth year.
257 As distinguished from Genji's in "Suma." In connection with Go-Toba's exile to Oki, *Masukagami*, too, alludes to Genji's house at Suma (Perkins, *Clear Mirror*, p. 55; Tyler, *Genji*, p. 239), while it evokes Go-Daigo on Oki rather as "Suma" evokes Genji, gazing soulfully and elegantly seaward from his dwelling (Perkins, *Clear Mirror*, p. 211; Tyler, *Genji*, pp. 244-245).

The place was intolerable for a single night. Eager to get away soon as possible, I moved that very day to the provisional Ojima palace (*tonkyū*). It was dark, it was raining, and my *nōshi* got all wet. The locals seemed to find a gentleman in formal headdress (*kanmuri*) a wonder to behold, because a crowd of them stared at me. As for the palace, it sported a board roof, rare in these parts, which merely continued the slope of the hillside. There was no break in the cloud and fog. Summoned immediately into the presence, I reported to His Majesty on developments in the world. He gave me a moving account of, among other things, his forced journey here from the Mountain.

For that night I went to Zuiganji. The temple offers much worth seeing. It is built up against a mountain, and what with the rocks and trees, and the flow of the stream, its setting would be a delight even in the capital. I was ill all the next day, and I spent a trying night. There was nothing I could do to dispel the misery of these nights away from home.

> *itodo mata uki ni uki sou tabine kana*
> *ukaregokochi no yume no magire ni*
> How nights far from home heap misery on misery,
> when one restlessly seeks relief in dreams!

His Majesty made Lord Tokimitsu's[258] office available to me, and in two or three days I felt settled in the palace. Through Kenshun I reported to him on events in the world and on my own condition.

"Your coming all this way shows that the old covenant of union (*yuka o narabeshi chigiri*) remains unchanged," Kenshun remarked.[259] I replied,

---

[258] Hino Sukena's third son after Fusamitsu and Ujimitsu, hence Nako's brother.

[259] This remark refers to the *Nihon shoki* passage in which Amaterasu gives Ama-no-Oshihomimi the treasure-mirror and says, "My child, when thou lookest upon this mirror, let it be as if thou wert looking on me. Let it be with thee on thy couch and in thy hall..." (Sakamoto Tarō et al., eds., *Nihon shoki*, vol. 1, Iwanami, 1967, p. 152; W. G. Aston, tr., *Nihongi*, Tuttle, 1972, p. 83.) Ama-no-Oshihomimi, the son of the Fujiwara ancestral deity Amanokoyane, amounts to the original regent. However, the speaker here is unclear. One expects the remark to come from Go-Kōgon via Kenshun, but Yoshimoto's reaction suggests otherwise. He seems annoyed. Despite the respectful term *ōsegoto* ("utterance") associated with it, Kenshun is its more likely source. A

shirazariki narawanu yama no kage made mo
toko o naraben chigiri ari to wa
I never knew that, even below this unfamiliar hill,
I would still uphold a covenant of union.

It was surely absurd of him to have brought up that old story from the age of the gods.

Thereafter I became accustomed to being on duty all day long, just as I had been in the city. A missive arrived from the Kamakura grand counselor [Takauji], accepting an imperial invitation to call. His visit was eagerly anticipated. Meanwhile formal and informal events continued. On the 5th of the 8th month, in the rain, all received from His Majesty these topics (*dai*):

Love in terms of the skies:

omokage o noyama no sue ni nokose to ya
tsuki o katami ni chigiri okiken
When we pledged ourselves each to each by the moon,
did you wish my face to shine on every hill and moor?

Dawn while traveling:

yokogumo no nami kosu mine mo honobono to
yagate ojima ni kage zo akeyuku
Dimly, the peaks that pierce the trailing clouds
appear, and dawn breaks over Ojima.

I heard that this was the first such gathering held there. Many poems were submitted, but I have forgotten them all. In any case, some of those improvised for the occasion were dreadful, and I have omitted them. His Majesty composed some memorable ones, but I did not write them down. Others must have done so. I should look for them and add them to the ones I have.

About the 10th of the 8th month—I am not sure of the precise day—I received this through Lord [Madenokōji] Nakafusa, written on scarlet

---

comparable difficulty occurs below in connection with Takauji (presumably) refraining from music and so on while at Tarui.

143

paper and attached to a branch of autumn leaves deep red even before the start of the winter rains:[260]

> *mada shiranu miyamagakure ni tazunekite*
> *shigure mo matanu momiji o zo miru*
> Among these mountains, to me quite unknown,
> I see leaves that have colored before the winter rains.

I replied:

> *furusato ni kaeru miyuki no orikara ya*
> *momiji no nishiki katsu isoguran*
> No doubt they portend a happy progress home,
> clothed in a brocade of glory like theirs.

Thereafter rain fell day after endless day, and the mountains seemed only to grow higher. It was very dreary. Cloud and fog cloaked the eaves, wind roared through the mountain pines, and life was in all ways as bleak as it could be.

It certainly set a rare example to have built an imperial palace in such a spot, but the famous log house of old must have been very like it.[261] This imperial progress to Mino is not to be wondered at, since Empress Genshō [r. 715-724] came here repeatedly, but it felt very strange to be among these unfamiliar mountains, and I constantly missed the capital. Even the celebrated mid-autumn moon seemed to hide behind unbroken rain and clouds, and in every way I felt that I shared the feelings of the men of old, exiled two thousand leagues from home.[262]

The wind that had blown all night dropped at dawn, and the moon the next night promised to be unforgettable. His Majesty therefore gave out poem slips to everyone. This was no palace entertainment. The privy gentlemen looked thoroughly warlike in their strange, martial garb, but the contest for which each was eager, according to his own inspiration, no doubt had to do more with the flowers of

---

[260] The poem is by Go-Kōgon.
[261] Empress Saimei [r. 655-661] went to Kyushu in order to support Kudara and, at Asakura in Chikuzen, built a temporary palace of unbarked logs.
[262] *Wakan rōeishū* 242, by Bo Juyi. Genji chanted this poem at Suma.

speech. The evening breeze came up again, and soon a brilliant moon rose, illumining every nook and cranny of the mountains.

> *na ni takaki hikari o miyo no tameshi to ya*
> *monaka no aki no tsuki wa sumuran*
> That lofty radiance seems an emblem of this reign,
> tonight when the mid-autumn moon shines clear.

The arrival of the Kamakura grand counselor was expected daily, but the days went by nonetheless without any sign of him. This so worried His Majesty that he sent repeated inquiries. Letters then reached him and his officials that the waiting would soon be over. This news was a relief to everyone. The privy gentlemen from the capital gathered in groups and went around visiting one notable place or another, but I was feeling so gloomy that the days went by without a single invitation to join them. It seemed to be autumn for me alone.[263] Nothing brightened my mood. People assured me that if I went to a certain Shinnyo Yōrō Waterfall[264] and exposed myself to its waters I would feel better immediately. However, I avoid places like that. The sound of the fulling block beaten late at night let me know that the houses nearby must have been the village of Nezame.[265] No wonder that on this journey I could hardly get through the autumn nights. The palace grounds continued straight on into ricefields, and since Inaba-no-yama was not far off, I could only look forward to a quick return[266] to the capital.

> *omoiki ya omoi mo yoranu karine kana*
> *inaba no tsuki o niwa ni nagamete*

---

[263] *Waga mi hitotsu no aki*, an expression from *Kokinshū* 193 by Ōe no Chisato.

[264] Yōrō-no-taki, a famous waterfall, known for its healing powers, in the mountains south of Ojima.

[265] The village of "Lying-awake-at-night." Nezame is an old name for a locality nearby.

[266] *Ima kaerikon*, from *Kokinshū* 365 by Ariwara no Yukihira, which mentions Inaba-no-yama. At least in the present context Inaba-no-yama is a hill (an *utamakura*) within present Gifu-shi, beside the Nagara River; therefore it is indeed "not far off." By mentioning Inaba [no tsuki] in his poem, Yoshimoto assimilates himself rhetorically to Yukihira.

Never did I imagine such restless nights as these,
gazing at the moon over Inaba.

Trifles like these were my only consolation.

Late in the 8th month it was reported to His Majesty that the
Kamakura grand counselor had reached Owari. On the 25th His Majesty
therefore left the Ojima palace and repaired to Tarui. Under these
exceptional circumstances he traveled in a hand palanquin (*yōyo*). Most
unusually, people wore warrior garb rather than court dress. The hand
palanquin was hung with curtains from His Majesty's ceremonial one
(*hōren*). This had never been done, but no doubt it was proper in this
case. One recoiled at the thought of allowing the country folk actually
to see His Majesty.

[Toki] Yoriyasu, the protector (*shugo*) of the province, had under-
taken to build the provisional palace at Tarui. Made of unbarked logs
and surrounded by a low brushwood fence, it conveyed the sanctity of
the Kairyūden or the Daijōkyū.[267] A large crowd had somehow
gathered to watch his arrival. [Fujiwara no] Sanesumi carried the Sword.
Normal procedure was followed. My lodging was excessively exposed
to the wind, so I found another, where I felt quite cut off from the
world. None of the local places of note particularly inspired me, but it
is true that when the celebrated Takatsune came down here as
governor of Mino he wrote *utsureru kage wa* presumably about this
spring, Tarui.[268]

On the 26th, meanwhile, word that an evil horde from Ōmi,[269]
reportedly known as the Hachiya, would attack the province that night
provoked confusion. News that the road to the capital was already cut
off was depressing enough, and that evening there was angry turmoil
when attackers were rumored to be approaching. People gathered to
the palace, wondering loudly what would come next. It was misery to
imagine that this might mean the end. At dawn, however, it transpired

---

[267] Temporary buildings that figure in the Daijōsai.

[268] From *Shikashū* 390: *mukashi mishi/ tarui no mizu wa/ kawaranedo/ utsureru kage
zo/ toshi o henikeru* ("The Tarui spring I saw of old is unchanged, but my reflected face
betrays the passage of the years"). Fujiwara no Takatsune was governor of Mino in
1072.

[269] Go-Daigo partisans.

that there was no threat. Everyone dispersed, feeling as though awakened from a dream. Horses had been held ready, and there had been frantic discussions of where His Majesty might flee. By now, however, it is fair to call it only a memory.

On the 3rd of the 9th month the Shogun reached Tarui. His arrival was both welcome and impressive. Warriors had been streaming in and taking lodging there already for two or three days. Their copious baggage train clogged the road as unceasingly as an unbroken length of cloth. In all ways I felt greatly reassured. The Grand Counselor wore armor over a brocade battle *hitatare* and rode a chestnut steed. Yūki [Naomitsu?], Oda [Haruhisa?], Satake [Yoshiatsu?], and so on led his forward escort. The many colors of their armor and the *kuwagata* horns on their helmets, glistening like falling water, shone in the van, glittering in the late afternoon sun as though this had been the [Kamo] Festival procession. Each man made a dazzling sight. The rear guard consisted of every eastern warrior of note, such as Niki [Yoriakira] and Oyama [Tomouji?]. Before the Shogun rode Myōzurumaru,[270] dressed with indescribable brilliance and mounted on a black horse reputed to be the best in the entire Bandō region. Everything about him drew the eye. His youthful *agemaki* hair[271] was in no way discordant. He looked marvelous in a manner perfectly suited to the occasion. The ten led horses[272] were superb. I gathered that all the best-known horses from the east were there. There were many large Satake piebalds.[273]

The Shogun went straight to the palace, left his armed entourage outside, and entered alone. He went in through the main gate and stood before the middle gate. From there, through Tō-no-ben[274] he announced his arrival. The Saionji intendant of the Left Gate Watch (*saemon-no-kami*)[275] came forth and ushered him inside. The Shogun then relinquished his bow and arrows, and was conducted into the

---

[270] Aeba Ujinao, Takauji's favorite *chigo*, in his nineteenth year. He reappears in the *Gen'ishū* account of the Tōji battle (1354).

[271] Hair parted down the middle of the head and formed into a raised loop on either side, to give the effect (from the front) of horns.

[272] A normal adornment to such a warrior display.

[273] Piebalds bred by the Satake family in Hitachi.

[274] Fujiwara no (Bōjō) Toshifuyu.

[275] Saionji Sanetoshi, Hino Nako's son in his 19th year, had grown up with Go-Kōgon.

presence. He soon withdrew to his lodging in the house of the Tarui post-station madam. He had been reluctant to stay there, since His Majesty had done so first, but apparently he followed His Majesty's own urging.

Once His Majesty had reached Tarui, Takauji forsook the imperial residence (*shinden*), gave up music and other amusements, and assumed an attitude of profound respect.[276] I felt sure that, in truth, he owed his success to his grasp of benevolence and righteousness. The Kamakura right commander [Yoritomo] must have adopted the same attitude when he first went up to the capital during Kenkyū [1190-1199]. Diaries of the time note that the Emperor [Go-Toba] came out to his day room (*hiru no omashi*) while Yoritomo waited upon him in the outer aisle (*magobisashi*), seated on a round cushion (*enza*). Under the circumstances prevailing at Tarui it would hardly have been possible to do exactly that.

On the 5th of the month His Majesty received ten tribute horses. Gratifyingly, fine steeds were bestowed upon others as well. I was asked to critique poems written on the way here, on the 15th night [of the 8th month].[277] I hesitated to do so, since I lack any such authority, but I could not refuse, and reluctantly I entered my remarks. The sole pastime on this journey, day or night, had been composing poetry in Chinese or Japanese. The country folk enjoy linked verse, and I received many requests for comments on their work, but they were too much trouble, and I turned them all away. At present my time is fully taken up with preparing to return to the capital.

His Majesty distributed poem slips for the coming Chōyō gathering on the 9th of the 9th month.[278] As to poetry in Chinese, the Right Minister [Konoe Michitsugu] and those below him submitted four-rhyme (*shiin*) poems. Apparently the Chinese poems were read aloud first, then the Japanese. Since I did not attend, I asked His Majesty for them all the next day, accompanying my request with:

---

[276] A problematic sentence. Go-Kōgon reached Tarui on 8.25, and Takauji arrived on 9.3. The subject of "forsook the imperial residence" (*shinden o sarite*), and so on, is therefore unclear, but the language and circumstances fit Takauji.

[277] Of the 8th month, the great full moon night of the year.

[278] A poetry and music gathering customary at the palace.

miyabito no kotoba no tama no ika naran
kinoo o yoso ni kiku no shiratsuyu
What were the courtiers' jewels of language?
Yesterday I missed the chrysanthemum dew.[279]

I received an immediate reply. A simple parroting (*ōmugaeshi*) of the sender's poem is normal, but I particularly liked this one.[280]

That must have been the day when, suddenly, a tremendous gale set in. It grew too dark to see anything. The wind was so strong that it blew down many trees in the mountains and, needless to say, flattened the grasses in all directions. Heavy rain began to fall. Thunder boomed, and every lightning bolt seemed a direct threat. It was terrifying. The rain fell hard enough to pass straight through what it struck. Umbrellas were useless, and in the resulting confusion one could only wonder in indescribable dismay what all this could mean. Moor and mountain alike turned to swiftly running water that cut off the path even to the palace.[281]

The gale that blew on into the night was far from ordinary. Since the makeshift palace with its unbarked pillars was not sturdy enough to allow His Majesty to remain there, he moved to one Min'anji. Kenshun, who had been living there, vacated it in his favor. All this was done in a great rush. What with the wind I felt more and more desperately ill, but I steeled myself to reach His Majesty nonetheless. I have never seen such wind and rain.

I reported to him that his return progress to the capital could not be delayed. He replied that he had already gathered from the Shogun that the journey was to start immediately, the next day. His people had begun hasty preparations. This should properly have been a full-scale celebratory progress, and people had been summoned from the capital to join it. Such was the haste, however, that the plan reverted to the

---

[279] Inevitably, the second line is only a paraphrase. *Kiku* plays on "hear" and "chrysanthemum." The date corresponds to the *kiku no sekku*.

[280] Go-Kōgon had replied by repeating Yoshimoto's poem from *kinō o yoso ni* on, preceded deprecatingly by *kyō mitemo kotoba no tama no nani ka sen*, in which *kotoba no tama*, too, is repeated.

[281] Many details and expressions in this description hark back to the description of the storm at Suma in *Genji monogatari* (Tyler, *Genji*, p. 253).

original, less formal one. People rushed about in all directions, and the next morning His Majesty returned to the makeshift palace, once it had been repaired.

News arrived that the Kamakura consultant captain [Ashikaga Yoshiakira] had reached Tarui. Happily, the way to the capital was now open. That evening the Consultant Captain went straight to the palace. The procedure followed was the same as for the Shogun. The moon was especially brilliant that night, and there was no cloud in the sky. According to the onlookers, polished saddle and armor ornaments gleamed, and there were many sights to see. The next day, the Consultant Captain presented His Majesty with two horses. The departure was delayed because the Shogun was a little unwell.

The departure took place on the 19th. The senior nobles accompanied His Majesty in court dress. These were the Matsudono counselor Tadatsugi; the Shijō counselor Takamochi; Sanetoshi, the intendant of the Left Gate Watch; Nakafusa; and others. Lord Takamigi carried the Sword in full formal costume. Others joined them in all the colors of their more daily dress. The sight was one to behold. Along the way mountain folk with their loads of brushwood crowded in to see it. The provisional grand counselor [Tōin Sanenatsu?] and the Imadegawa consultant captain, still in warrior garb, did not accompany the progress but joined the company only at the halts. I traveled with the Nijō counselor, and we met the main progress that evening at Daikakuji in Ōmi. Heavy rain fell that night, and it was still raining the next morning. His Majesty's departure seemed in doubt, but it appeared that the Kamakura Consultant Captain had already set out, so the departure took place after all. That day all those accompanying the progress wore warrior garb. His Majesty spent that night at Binmanji.

The next day the sky was clear, and the escort again wore court dress. His Majesty arrived at Musadera[282] and went on from there to Ishiyama, where a residence was set up for him before the main hall. The "freshwater sea" (*shio naranu umi*), stretching away from so nearby,

---

[282] According to "The Battle of Tōji," Go-Kōgon, again in flight from Kyoto, would return to Musadera roughly a year later.

was very beautiful.[283] The beneficence of Kannon's expedient means shone more and more brightly upon this most fortunate imperial progress.

On this day the Tōin grand counselor came from the capital to join the cortège. Palace Guards officers Masatomo, Sanetoki, Takasato, and Takaie came as well, in court dress, and accompanied His Majesty's palanquin to left and right. The second- and third-ranking Palace Guards officers followed in warrior garb. Lord Yoshiakira led the way in armor. Lord Takauji, also in armor, accompanied him to the rear. I gather that his twenty or thirty thousand warriors took two days to pass by.

His Majesty went straight to his proper palace.[284] Lord Yoshiakira awaited his arrival, seated on an animal pelt.[285] The procedure for the return was the same as usual, except that the men in warrior garb came as far as the gate. The palanquin drew up to the Nanden. The senior nobles in court dress waited upon His Majesty in the court before it. Lord Masatomo carried the Sword.

The palace was just as it had been.[286] The dame of staff (*naishi-no-suke*) and the staff women (*naishi*) were on duty. Trite though the remark may be, it was a relief to see that everyone looked the same. The recent bad dream of the journey was gone, and everything promised inexpressible good fortune. The people of the capital, too, were excited about this extraordinary event, which was a wonder vouchsafed from on high. The future looked very bright.

The issue of an imperial return progress in the 9th month aroused some discussion. In Reiki 3 [717] Empress Genshō [r. 715-724] made a progress to Mino, the province in question, and among other sights viewed the Yōrō waterfall. It was so beautiful that before returning she

---

283 The expression is from a poem in the "Sekiya" chapter of *Genji monogatari*: *wakuraba ni/ yukiau michi o/ tanomishi mo/ nao kai nashi ya/ shio naranu umi* (Tyler, *Genji*, p. 316).

284 The Tsuchimikado palace.

285 Deer, bear, or perhaps even tiger.

286 According to *Entairyaku*, all the blinds and mats disappeared in 6th month, after Go-Kōgon's departure, and had to be hastily replaced.

changed the era name from Reiki to Yōrō. Tadatō no Sukune[287] declared this a happy precedent for the ninth month. That His Majesty's return followed so fortunate an example made it even more felicitous.

Thinking to pass on an account of this rare event, to feed the talk of later generations and to while away the time on the journey's sleepless nights, I wrote down rough notes, so as not to forget what had happened, on scraps torn from sheets of *tatōgami*. Difficult as the past is to forget in any case, this brief account may serve to prompt fuller memory.

---

[287] Ozuki Tadatō, a Daijōkan secretary in a hereditary line of experts in the historical records.

THE BATTLE OF TŌJI, 1355

From *Gen'ishū*

INTRODUCTION

Gen'ishū ("A Compendium of Genji Glory")[288] proudly reviews Genji (Minamoto) achievements, starting with Hachiman Daibosatsu, running through the Heian wars in the north and the triumph of Yoritomo, and ending with two eyewitness accounts. The first describes Ashikaga Takauji's drive from the Kantō toward Kyoto in Bunna 2 [1353], his call upon Emperor Go-Kōgon at Tarui in Mino, and the return from there to the capital. It is consistent with Nijō Yoshimoto's account in *Ojima no kuchizusami*.

The second, translated here and amounting to about a third of the whole, covers the battle of Tōji in 1355. Some scholars have questioned the narrator's claim to have been personally engaged in the battle, but the character of the narrative does not encourage such caution.

In his preface the anonymous author identifies Kakyō [1387-1389], roughly thirty-three years after Tōji, as his present. However, an ambiguous notation that affects one's understanding of his age when he wrote *Gen'ishū* seems to leave open the question of how old he may have been at the time. Sixty or so is one possibility. However, Kaji Hiroe's analysis suggests that in Kakyō he was looking back over the sixty years or since 1331. He would then have been in his late teens, old enough to begin fighting under Takauji. If so, he put *Gen'ishū* together roughly in his eighties. Kaji identified him as Satake Moroyoshi (?-1397), a participant in the battles of Tadarahama and Minatogawa (see *Baishōron*), and, in *Gen'ishū*, Takauji's partner in an exchange of poetic remarks made on the bank of the Seta-gawa, in the snow.[289]

Kaji Hiroe's edition of *Gen'ishū* is based on the *Satake-bon*, a manuscript originally held by the Satake house. It was presented to the

---

[288] Kaji Hiroe, ed., *Gen'ishū*, Heibonsha (Tōyō Bunko 607), 1996.
[289] Kaji, *Gen'ishū*, pp. 9-13.

Satake daimyo of Akita by one Makabe Jindayū in 1696 and is now held by the Senshū Bunko in Tokyo. The Shiryō Hensanjo at Tokyo University preserves a copy of it.

THE BATTLE OF TŌJI

Question
What is the story of the battle of Tōji?

Answer

You ask me to discuss the Tōji battle. I am not eager to do so, but naturally those born after me will wish to know about it. The full story would be too long, but I will tell you what I saw and heard during my best years, when I was among those who accompanied the Shogun from the Kantō and served him loyally in every battle. Old as I am now, and obliged to lean on a staff, I am often forgetful and repeat myself. Nonetheless, I will relate what happened.

When the Shogun led the eastern daimyo and their men up to Kyoto, his enemies along the San'indō so feared his strength that they fled the city rather than fight. On Bunna 2.9.23 [1353] the Emperor [Go-Kōgon] returned to the capital. Takauji, Yoshiakira, and the daimyo remained there in safety. The enemy was no longer an issue, having fled, and the year ended without incident. The next year, Bunna 3 [1354], brought the thirteenth anniversary of the passing of Takauji's honored mother [Uesugi Kiyoko]. The Shogun made a great vow to copy the Tripitaka and neglected no other pious Buddhist observance.

In the 11th month (I forget the day) the court held the Daijōe enthronement rite for Iyahito, in conformity with established practice, in the Great Hall of State.[290] Aeba Myōzurumaru (Takanobu) came of age at that time, so that he might take up his offices.[291] He received the fifth rank and was appointed *shōgen* and *danjō shōhitsu*.[292]

---

[290] Iyahito is Go-Kōgon's name as heir apparent. He had acceded (*sokui*) to the throne the year before (Kannō 3.17 [1352]), but to the author he remained Iyahito until his full Daijōe enthronement (*juzen*).

[291] Aeba, a favorite of Takauji and here in his 20th year, appears also in *Ojima no kuchizusami*. His formal name was Ujinao, but Takauji awarded him "Takanobu" (*taka*

The next day His Majesty was to proceed along the prescribed route via Uchino and Nijō to the purification beside the Kamo River. At Madenokōji, on the south side of Nijō, a viewing stand had been put up before the residence of the Mikohidari grand counselor Tamesada. At the same time the Shogun, at his own residence, asked an expert on viewing stands whether or not it would be rude to put one up for an imperial progress. The expert answered that there could be no objection to a viewing stand as long as the blinds were raised. The Shogun remarked, "Even so, though, there remains the possibility that the viewer might be higher than the imperial palanquin." On the morning of the day he therefore abruptly issued a strict order that all supporting posts should be removed. This was done, and as a result no viewing stand could be seen. People praised the Shogun for his grasp of etiquette.

Soon after the enthronement, news arrived that Tadafuyu (Hyōe-no-suke)[293] and Yamana Tokiuji (Izu-no-kami) were moving on the capital, the former from the central provinces and the latter from the San'indō region. Yoshiakira therefore set out [Bunna 3.10.18] to destroy them. He left from Tōji, accompanied by a large force that included Sasaki Dōyo, Akamatsu Norisuke, and others, and established himself in Harima. While the Shogun's attention was absorbed by Buddhist observances to the exclusion of all else, Momonoi Naotsune (Harima-no-kami)[294] drove out of the Southern Court-held northern provinces; subdued Etchū, Noto, and Kaga; and reached Fuchū in Echizen. News came that Tadafuyu had crossed Kibesu, followed the San'indō from Iwami to join forces with Yamana, and driven into Tanba. Some people wondered privately whether the Shogun should leave instructions

being written with the first character of Takauji's own name) with this appointment. In practice his main duties would have involved liaison with the court nobles.

[292] Respectively, a third-level officer in the Palace Guards (Konoefu) and a second-level officer in the Imperial Inspectorate (Danjōdai).

[293] A son of Takauji, adopted by Tadayoshi.

[294] With his brother Tadanobu, a faithful ally of Tadayoshi and opponent of Takauji. After Tadayoshi's death he supported the South, and together with Tadafuyu and Yamana Tokiuji strove to regain Kyoto. He submitted to the bakufu in Jōji 5 (1366) but then rebelled again. In Ōan 4 (1371) he was defeated by the bakufu in the north. What happened to him then remains unknown.

regarding his Buddhist observances with the monks at Tōji-in[295] and leave for Tōtōmi.

Despite this talk the Shogun did not budge. He said: "This problem is the work of obstructive demons. Heaven will uphold the right. Why? Because these observances are not for me: hence my great vow to copy the Tripitaka is already accomplished. This is joy heaped upon joy. I shall see the dedication services through. The enemies now threatening the capital all achieved prominence thanks to my repeated favor. If the divine gaze is upon the sinful rebels, then they will suffer the punishment of Heaven. I would still complete these services even if they were to burst into the capital." On Bunna 3.12.22 he therefore boarded a carriage to go into retreat (*shukuki*)[296] at Tōji-in.

The next day (the 13th) rare offerings were made on water and on earth.[297] The officiant (the venerable Tōryō, who lit the incense)[298] gave a sermon. Once the Tripitaka services and the matters concerning the officiating monks were completed (the hour of the monkey [4 p.m.]) the Shogun returned to his residence and the day ended. (Kashō-in dono, the daughter of Uesugi Yorishige.)[299]

Many temples coveted this Tripitaka even before it was dedicated, but the Shogun had not yet decided where it should go. At the hour of the dog [8 p.m.] on the day of the dedication, over one hundred monks from Onjōji (Miidera), some in light armor, arrived and submitted a petition to request it. The next day a letter from the temple's head monk presented a lengthy appeal, as follows:

---

[295] A Rinzai temple in northern Kyoto founded by Takauji as Tōjiji in the early 1340s; it became Tōji-in after his death in 1358. His grave is there.

[296] In Zen, the day of abstinence preceding the memorial day of a great figure's death: here, Kiyoko.

[297] A form of the Segaki-e, in which food for the starving ghosts is scattered in water and on the earth.

[298] Deng Le, a Chinese priest who reached Hakata in 1351 and joined Musō Soseki at Saihōji. Abbot successively of Tenryūji, Nanzenji, Engakuji, and Kenchōji in Kamakura, he died at Nanzenji in 1365.

[299] Kashō-in was the sister of Takauji's mother, Uesugi Kiyoko, hence his aunt. Perhaps this disconnected mention of her means that she returned with Takauji to his residence.

The history of Onjōji includes many wonders, but I will confine myself to past examples of close relations between the temple and the Minamoto house. On Kenmu 3.1.16 [1336] past, the imperial army[300] commanders Nitta Yoshisada and Kitabatake Akiie attacked us at the head of a host of rebels (*kyōto*). We sought to defend it but lacked the strength to do so, and many monks were wounded or killed. Fire reduced our sacred images and texts to ashes, and for that our tears of grief still flow. Now that the Tripitaka you vowed to complete has been dedicated, my lord, we beg to receive it at our temple for the sake of peace in the realm and the security of your house (*buke*).

The Shogun eventually heard of this and was moved. He felt that the temple's forceful appeal (*gōso*) was right and in accord with his own wishes.[301]

Now to the Shogun's removal to Ōmi. It had seemed that there would be no further trouble once the Shogun's religious observances were over. However, on the 24th, at the hour of the dragon [8 a.m.], the Emperor set forth in a hand palanquin (*yōyo, tagoshi*) with a scarlet *hitoe* stretched over him to shield him from the sun.[302] Takeda Nobutake (Izu-no-kami), who had been appointed to oversee this emergency progress (*rinkō*), guarded the palanquin front and rear. The senior nobles, privy gentlemen, and other officials accompanied him, irregular in costume and headdress. Bōjō Toshifuyu[303] wore armor (*haramaki*) and a sword. Atsuta no Tayū Hōgan Akiyori, of the imperial police, wore a folded eboshi (*hire eboshi*) and a white robe under his armor. The rank-and-file bore plain arrows (*hiraya*). The heavily bearded squad commander (*kachō*) and his men had bows and arrows. They looked impressively competent.[304] His Majesty traveled from

---

300 *Kangun*, the army of Go-Daigo.

301 Miidera still has this Tripitaka.

302 The Southern army under Ashikaga Tadafuyu and Momonoi Naotsune had taken Kyoto that day (Bunna 3.12.24).

303 Mentioned in *Ojima*. He announced Takauji's arrival at the Mino palace. Such a noble would wear armor only in dire circumstances.

304 Particularly since they were nobles and shrine attendants, not hereditary warriors. The meaning of *hiraya* is uncertain.

Tsuchimikado down Nishinotōin to Nijō, then eastward to Awataguchi, where he arrived just as the Shogun's banners reached the Kamo riverbank.

As usual the Shogun wore black armor and carried sword, bow, and war arrows (*soya*). Around his mount rode Satake Yoshiatsu (the battlefield adjudicator)[305] and his brothers; Yūki Naomitsu; Jōei; Nasu Suketō (Bizen-no-kami); Yūki Shigetomo; and a thousand mounted warriors. Behind him also rode Oda Takatomo (Sanuki-no-kami) and Koyama Ujimasa.

When the Shogun reached Seta the Emperor's palanquin crossed the river. Sasaki no Gorō and Toki Yoriyasu then came forward to meet him. His men crossed on a pontoon bridge (*ukihashi*) and on boats. Once all had done so, the Shogun dismounted so as to cross the bridge. Sasaki no Gorō then came over from the far bank with a bearer who carried a large bamboo tube of wine. Sasaki personally placed before the Shogun a wine cup accompanied by strips of dried abalone. It was snowing, and a hard north wind was blowing. The Shogun gazed at the lake and smiled as though a poem had come to mind. Satake Moroyoshi met his eyes and recited *Yuki o hana*.[306] "There that scene is, right before us," he said. "Yes," the Shogun replied, "and also the one about the boats rowing across the lake and the petals on the wind over the Shiga hills."[307] He must have appreciated Moroyoshi's quickness to catch the mood of the moment and seen that he was a man of taste (*sukimono*).

Through Takanobu, the Shogun then suggested to Toshifuyu offering the Emperor, too, wine and refreshments. Toshifuyu asked His Majesty whether he would like that, in the snow. His Majesty said yes.

Toshifuyu therefore ordered wine and so on from the temple at Ishiyama. Feeling that an old wine jug (*chōshi*) would not do, he laid two

---

[305] *Samuraidokoro*. This admininstrative unit was responsible for deciding rewards. Yoshiatsu is responsible for recording meritorious deeds on the battlefield.

[306] *Gosenshū* 485: "Snow at my old home has piled up like blossoms, and I, too, watching, feel my cares slip away" (*furusato no/ yuki wa hana to zo/ furitsumoru/ nagamuru ware mo/ omoi kietsutsu*).

[307] *Shinkokinshū* 128: "The mountain wind from Hira has so swept away the petals that boats rowing across the lake cut a clear track through them (*hana sasou/ hira no yamakaze/ fukinikeri/ kogiyuku fune no/ ato miyuru made*).

or three sheets of paper one over the other and thrust his hand in down to the bottom.[308] He then poured wine into the *chōshi* from the bamboo tube; opened a scarlet, imperial fan; placed the cup and the abalone on it; and had Takanobu present it. Toshifuyu took it and, stationed before the palanquin, offered the wine to His Majesty, who drank three times and declared that the Shogun must have the cup. Toshifuyu and Takanobu came together before him and reported on the weather. His Majesty called Toshifuyu closer. Toshifuyu knelt; reverently took the cup; received the wine; poured it into a separate vessel; and drank three times. With the cup he then withdrew. Those in attendance were ordered to warm the wine at the large fire then burning, after which the Shogun was to receive it. Takanobu returned to the Shogun and waited there to take it. All this struck me as conforming to proper protocol.

The Shogun, in his palanquin, allowed the bulk of his men to cross before doing so himself. At the hour of the rat [12 a.m.] he and the Emperor lodged at Moruyama, himself in the abbot's quarters and His Majesty in Musadera (Chōkōji) proper.[309] The army lodged at Echigawa and Shijūku-in.[310] The righteous force (*gisei*) in Ōmi allowed the rebels from the central and northern provinces into the capital. From the west, Yoshiakira, the Hosokawa men from Shikoku, Sasaki Dōyo, Akamatsu Norisuke and others, as well as a contingent from the south (*nankai*), seem to have led the way from Yamazaki to positions in the Western Hills (*nishiyama*). Toki and Sasaki followed the daimyo from the eastern provinces along the Tōkaidō through Mino and Ōmi, while Yoshiakira established himself in Harima, the plan being no doubt to attack from both east and west. Yoshiakira sent a fast courier to urge those in the east to have the Shogun go down to Kamakura; or at least so it was the rumored.

---

[308] Apparently he puts sheets of clean paper over the mouth of the *chōshi* and then pushes them in, to line the vessel so that the emperor's wine should not actually touch its walls.

[309] A temple named Kōsaiji now calls itself Musadera (Musa being name of the area) and claims the honor of Go-Kōgon's visit in 1354, but there is a Chōkōji nearby. Go-Kōgon had stayed there already a year earlier, on the way back to Kyoto from Mino.

[310] Echigawa is a post station on the Tōsandō. Shijūku-in is a temple with forty-nine (*shijūku*) buildings, dedicated to Miroku.

In Ōmi, meanwhile, the New Year came. Early in the first month of Bunna 4 [1355], Momonoi Naritsune, with a thousand mounted men, was the first to enter the capital from the north. However, Tadafuyu remained behind in Tanba. Momonoi hastily appealed to him to come soon, on the grounds that he could not hold the capital solely with his own forces. Therefore Tadafuyu entered the capital on 1.15. In Ōmi, all those who looked to the Shogun—housemen (*kenin*) and protectors (*bunkoku=shugo*) alike—rushed to join him. Niki Yoshinaga (Echigo-no-kami) arrived in haste at the head of the men from his provinces of Iga and Ise. Soon the Shogun's forces were beyond counting.

This situation encouraged an advance on the capital, and on 1.19 the warriors set out. The next day, 1.20, they camped at Seta. The Shogun had already ordered Sasaki Dōyo to see to installing a pontoon bridge, and Sasaki had the work under way. By the hour of the monkey [4 p.m.] on 1.21 planks already covered most of the bridge, the greater number having been provided by the abbot of Ishiyama.

When ten boatmen and more crossed the river and attached both ropes to posts, some men objected that it would take only a concealed enemy band to cut them, with disastrous consequences. From morning on, therefore, two warriors were stationed on the bridge to forestall any such thing. They looked as though they were waiting for the rest of the planks to be laid. When only two spans at the end of the bridge remained uncovered, the two rose to their feet; took up black-laced armor and spears; donned brightly trimmed, smoked-leather armor; seized halberds; tied on their helmets; and leaped lightly across to the other side. There they opened their fans and beckoned with them to those left behind.

The warriors crowded together at the east end of the bridge almost pushed one another into the river in their commendable eagerness to cross. The first to do so were Hosokawa Kiyouji (Sagami-no-kami) and his younger brother, Yorikazu. They naturally looked very brave. Those who dashed after them included Imagawa Sadayo (Sakyō-no-suke),[311] Yūki Naomitsu, Ōuchi Shigetomo, Takamiki, and Sasaki Ujiyori.

---

[311] The author of *Michiyukiburi* and *Nantaiheiki*.

All raced after Kiyouji. The mass of the Shogun's warriors then camped three *ri* further on, in the pine wood of Awazu.

The Shogun crossed the river and lodged in the abbot's quarters at Ishiyama. Some reminded him that he should assign Sasaki, who had been responsible earlier for guarding the bridge, to do so again that night. The Shogun replied, "As long as the bridge is there, it could actually harm the frightened men if the battle were to go badly. However well guarded it might be, if the enemy nonetheless managed by stealth to cut the ropes, the censure of the world at large would be intolerable. It would be inadmissible for the army to retreat across this bridge after losing a battle, and the bridge is therefore useless. Return the planks to Ishiyama and during the night cut the ropes." Such was his stern command. The battlefield adjudicator (*bugyō*) Saitō Shirō Hyōe-no-jō executed it. All agreed that the Shogun was a wise commander indeed.

Now I have an old story to tell about another bridge.[312]

In Kenmu 2 [1335] discord arose between sovereign and subject,[313] and armed conflict broke out on the Yahagi-gawa in Mikawa.[314] The imperial army under Nitta Yoshisada moved to attack. The eastern warriors lost the advantage and cut the road with a trench at Mizunomi in the Hakone mountains.[315] Tadayoshi was in command there. Kō no Moronao and Moroyasu, the Niki and Hosokawa men, Soga Morosuke, Shimazu Sadahisa, Iwato, and others, fewer than three hundred mounted warriors in all, stood against a great army.

At this point the Shogun abandoned the Hakone mountains and during the night of 12.10 crossed the Ashigara pass, preceded by a force under Satake and Yūki. On 12.11 (the hour of the dragon [8 a.m.]), at Takenoshita Aizawahara, they won two battles. The next day, 12.12, at the battle of Sano-yama, Ōtomo Sadanori arrived with more than

---

312 *Baishōron* ("The Bridge over the Tenryū River") tells the same story more briefly.

313 Emperor and shogun. The "imperial army," below, is Go-Daigo's.

314 Takauji had been in the capital but left for Kamakura without permission in 1335 so as to aid his brother Tadayoshi. Tadayoshi was initially in Kamakura but then fled to Hakone.

315 Mizunomi was a barrier (*sekisho*) in the mountains on the Tōkaidō, southwest of Ashinoko. It appears also in *Baishōron* ("The Battle between Yoshisada and Takauji.")

five hundred mounted men, and they won again. That night heavy rain fell. Yoshisada lifted the guard on Mizunomi, and the great army retreated. The Shogun attacked fiercely. At dawn on 12.13, in the rain, he attacked at Izu-no-Kofu Obama. Yoshisada headed in defeat for the coast road. Meanwhile the force at Mizunomi came down, and the two commanders met at Fuchū. Such was the result of the Shogun's strategy.

Yoshisada remained several days beside the Tenryū-gawa in Tōtōmi, then threw a pontoon bridge across it. His whole army crossed. When the last of his men had done so he ordered the watch on the crossing not to cut the ropes, ignoble though the bridge might be, but to guard it well, so as to give passage to the men of the east. All, high and low, felt as though they were back in the capital.

This time, at Seta, the Shogun's decision to cut the bridge revealed his martial resolve and skill. Considering now both examples, Yoshisada in Kenmu and the Shogun in Bunna both won martial fame thanks to a bridge. The principle in each case was the same. Do not both examples demonstrate Genji valor?

The Shogun set out the following night, on 1.22, and chose to stop that evening at Higashi Sakamoto. Toki and his men went ahead to lead the way. They had divided into two corps, one to follow the main road and the other the fields along the shore, when a messenger arrived from Miidera, near Ōtsu, with an urgent report to the effect that Momonoi Naotsune had taken up a position with a thousand men on Nyoi-ga-mine. Would the Shogun's force confront them?

In haste the Shogun answered the messenger: "This is why I have been slow to raise my banners. Hosokawa Kiyouji has been stationed on Awazu-yama since yesterday. The further he advances, the more I will reinforce him. We will then break into the city. He talked about taking up position on the Ōsaka pass (*sekiyama*), but he should divide his men into two corps at Higashi Sakamoto and report to me at once."

The path was narrow, however, and the men many. The Shogun reached Sakamoto at nightfall. The local people reported that an imperial force had been there until midday, but that, seeing the Shogun's strength, over three hundred had fled to the mountaintop and would now be reaching Nishi Sakamoto.

Meanwhile, the Shogun was at the Higanjo of the Great Shrine,[316] where the monks and elders of the mountain paid him homage. The disciples resident in the Gachirin-bō and Gachizō-bō, the Kongō-in, the Chishō-in, the Saishō-in, the Kaizō-bō, the Enmei-bō, the Sugiū-bō, and the Yamamoto-bō all wore armor (*haramaki*) under their robes, carried halberds, and wore lacquered *ashida* clogs.

The Ajari of Yamamoto-bō, the leader of them all, stepped forward and said: "Your arrival here, my lord, confers new glory upon the Dharma taught on our Mountain. Our three thousand monks (*shuto*) are therefore unanimous in welcoming you. They are so many, however, that if any among them were by chance to entertain dissenting ambitions of his own, and if fire were unfortunately to break out among the lodges on the mountain, the result would be turmoil in Sakamoto.[317] You need not worry if only your force will guard the Mountain."

His remarks made sense, but the Shogun's men were ill at ease there, and the Shogun seemed unsure to whom to entrust this duty. At this point Toki Naouji (Kunai-no-shō), present in the Shogun's service bearing his elder brother's sword, said: "My lord, someone among your many men must know the Mountain. You are bringing the easterners with you, but the housemen and protectors hurrying with their men to join them will not arrive in time. One corps from among us should be sent up the Mountain."

The Shogun was impressed. The whole Toki force consisted of the Gomontsuki squad (*ikki*), the Matsu squad, the Toki Kunai-no-shō squad, and the Umamawari: four in all, for a total of over two thousand riders. "At any rate," Naouji continued, "I will take my own contingent up the Mountain." He removed his body armor (*yoroi*) and, wearing only light armor (*kogusoku*), took off his shin guards (*sune-ate*), personally lit a great torch, and set out. The Shogun called him back, served him three cups of wine, and gave him a sword. Naouji withdrew at the hour of the rat [12 a.m.]. His five hundred men climbed the steep slope, each

316 The Hie Shrine. The Higanjo was a shrine building where a Buddhist service called Higan-e was held at the spring and autumn equinox (*higan*).
317 Takauji was staying in (Higashi) Sakamoto. Go-Kōgon may have been there, too. He was present there at least on Bunna 3.14 (1355), before his return to Kyoto on 3.28.

with a torch. In speech and manner he seemed worthy to confront alone a thousand men. When dawn came the rest of the force climbed the Mountain and stationed themselves there.

The Shogun remained at Sakamoto from 1.22 to 1.28. Meanwhile, the three thousand monks presented him with a petition, the burden of which was this:

What do we ask? We request authority over the province of Ōmi and proprietary rights to three estates: those of Iwaki, of Hyōzu (which supports the Heir Apparent), and of Harimada, with a combined yield of over 20,000 *koku*. This Mountain served Emperor Go-Daigo loyally when he made an emergency progress here on Kenmu 3.1.5 [1336], and again later.[318] Such was the difficulty involved that he gave this Mountain authority over the province. As to the three estates, we received no formal decision. Properly speaking, however, the land itself is not ours.

Now the Shogun has honored us with this visit. This Mountain has enjoyed a long friendship with the Genji. Eryō of Mudōji prayed intently before his sacred image of Fudō in order to achieve the enthronement of Emperor Seiwa (Korehito).[319] Moreover, the resident monk Tada no Hōgen Genken was the elder brother of Raikō, Manjū's eldest son.[320] Again, in the summer of Juei 3 [1184, actually Juei 2] Kiso no Yoshinaka, a Genji, fought repeatedly and victoriously in the north, overthrew the Heike, and attacked this province. However, because of reservations about him this Mountain did not allow him to approach. When his letter came,[321] the whole Mountain met in council and, in conformity with the will of the divinities Iō and Sannō, responded with a letter of

---

[318] Actually, Kenmu 3.1.10 and 5.27: the first time to escape Takauji's attack from the Kantō and the second to escape his attack after his return from Kyushu.

[319] See *Heike monogatari* 8 ("Natora"); Tyler, *Heike*, pp. 412ff, especially p. 425. Seiwa, who succeeded to Montoku in 858, started a major Genji line.

[320] A half-brother: a son of Minamoto no Raikō's mother but apparently not of Manjū. He lived 981-1020 and was a disciple of Genshin.

[321] Yoshinaka's appeal to Hiei for support and cooperation (*Heike* 7; Tyler, *Heike*, pp. 374-276).

assent. Yoshinaka was pleased and came up the Mountain. The Heike set fire to the capital, fled, and were destroyed.

In the spring and summer of Kenmu 3 [1336] the Emperor twice came to the Mountain, by no means at our invitation. Rather, he insisted. Many monks lost their lives, and in recompense he should have thanked us. However, our bitter entreaty did not reach him, and since then many years have passed in sorrow. Now the Shogun means to enter the capital, and on this battle will hang the fate of the realm. Peace or peril for the land will be at stake. The monks therefore are unanimous in praying for his safety and in urging him on to victory. For this reason, before life or death are decided for them, they beg to be granted control over the province and proprietary rights to the three estates. If it pleases you to decide in our favor and grant us all that we wish, then the whole Mountain will be grateful and serve you loyally.

Meanwhile, the Southern rebels—Kusunoki and the rest—had remained as active as ever since Tadafuyu took Kyoto. On 1.28, in the snow, the Shogun's full army ascended the Mountain and lodged there either in the monks' quarters or in the open. At this point a courier brought this message from Yoshiakira: "My men will move up from Yamazaki to take positions at Yoshimine, Enmyōji, Ōharano, and Oi-no-yama.[322] I will inform you when these positions are secured."

On 2.3 the Shogun camped at Hachibuse in Nishi Sakamoto. His army occupied the area all the way from the Sekizan Shrine at Nishi Sakamoto to the bank of the Kamo River. That evening another courier arrived from Yoshiakira: "I have moved to Sakura-yama.[323] My men swarm like clouds and mists. As I have said before, I understand that once I move to the Western Hills, there will be simultaneous fighting on both sides of the city, east and west. I will be ready for it."

Yamana Tokiuji (Izu-no-kami) and his eldest son Moroyoshi had previously led a force up the San'indō to Yamazaki. On 2.6, at the hour of the dragon [8 a.m.], that force moved out and attacked Yoshiakira's.

---

[322] All locations along the western edge of Kyoto.
[323] Southwest of Yamazaki, in present Takatsuki-shi (Ōsaka-fu).

The battle of Sakura-yama scattered the blossoms from the trees. The Shogun's allies, ranged over thirty *chō* [3 km.] of the mountains stretching up from Kawachi were defeated, and the attackers came close to where Yoshiakira sat on an animal hide (*shikikawa*), his banner flying. Sasaki Dōyo and Akamatsu Norisuke attended him. When the attack came, some urged him to mount. He said, "I will not move a step. I need no horse. Remove mine immediately." The Hosokawa Yoriyuki brothers and Hosokawa Shigeuji brothers linked arms, charged into the foe and scattered fire. At the sight, half a dozen men, relatives, charged into the Susugo squad of Akamatsu's force. Four were killed, and two suffered many wounds. Repulsed, the enemy [the Southern army] withdrew. Yamana Moroyoshi Kingo was gravely wounded during the battle, which started in the morning and lasted all day. The evil horde therefore capitulated and withdrew to their base position at Yamazaki.

The position being secure, Yamana Tokiuji went into seclusion at the nearby shrine of the Yodo Deity. That day the Hosokawa men from the San'yōdō and Shikoku sustained many deaths and wounds. The Shogun, who was at Nishi Sakamoto, knew nothing of this encounter. At the hour of the boar [10 p.m.], over two hundred of Momonoi's men surrendered to Toki's contingent and the one from Etchū. The Shogun heard of it only when they explained what had happened.

The next day, 2.7, at dawn, Hosokawa Kiyouji moved out and took positions at Imahie and Amida-ga-mine.[324] Imagawa Sadayo and Niki Yoshinaga (Echigo-no-kami) led a force from Iga and Ise, and Koyama Ujimasa positioned himself with his contingent on the southern slope below Kiyomizu. Satake (then the battlefield adjudicator), Oda, and their men took up position at Gion. Nasu Suketō (Bizen-no-kami) and Ebashi raised their banners side by side.

On 2.8 Hosokawa Kiyouji attacked the capital, but the enemy did not advance to meet him. He therefore set fires and returned to his position.

---

[324] Imahie (now Imahie Jingū) is on the furthest eastward extension of Shichijō, at the foot of Amida-ga-mine (196 m.), not far beyond the present Kyoto National Museum.

On 2.9 the Shogun moved his position from Hachibuse at Nishi Sakamoto to Ryōzan[325] beside Shirakawa. Then on 2.13 he moved from Ryōzan to Jūjūshin-in on Kiyomizu-zaka.

2.15 was the day of the Nehan-e. The enemy, stationed at Tōji, sent a contingent out along the streets and avenues, and clashes occurred here and there. All strove to display martial valor (the Oda and Satake forces before the Kokufu Shrine at Higuchi-Kyōgoku, Hosokawa Kiyouji at Rokujō-Muromachi, the Toki men at Shichijō-Bōmon, and Niki Koshichirō), and in the end they kept the enemy back from the riverbank. They killed or captured many and remained ready where they were, uttering battle cries. Seeing the strength of his allies, the Shogun sent a messenger to each with an expression of his satisfaction.

All this was happening right in the city, and people stood on the Gojō bridge to watch. Despite the victory many men were wounded or killed, and their fellows mourned them deeply. Curiously enough, throughout the following night streetwalkers (*tachigimi*) stood sleeve to sleeve on Kiyomizuzaka, while *zatō* played the biwa and some fools even sang *Heike*. More curious still were the characters known as "old-needle buyers" (*furuhari-kai*), presumably dealers in used goods (*tsukawashimono-kai*), who, on days without fighting, roamed the bathhouses of the city, frequented either by our side or the other, crying, "Old wares! I buy old wares!" They often paused to chat and suffered no harm. They never turned up for conflict in the countryside. This was the capital, after all.

At this juncture over three thousand mounted men reached the capital, sent by Ashikaga Motouji[326] in the Kantō and commanded by Hatakeyama Yoshifuka (Owari-no-kami) and his younger brother Yoshiteru: the Hei squad (*hei ikki*),[327] which included Takasaka, Furuya, Doi, and Tsuchiya, and the Shirahata squad,[328] including Kodama, Inomata, and Murayama. They stationed themselves before Hosshōji.

---

[325] Now read Ryōzen, a peak in the Eastern Hills.

[326] Takauji's second son, hence Yoshiakira's younger brother. He was Takauji's permanent representative in Kamakura. His ambition to succeed to Takauji as shogun is an issue in *Nantaiheiki*.

[327] A league of Musashi and Sagami lineages descended from the Kanmu Heiji.

[328] A league of lineages descended from the Musashi Shichitō.

The army to the west had taken positions on the hills from Yamazaki to Yoshimine, Enmeiji, Ōharano, and Oi-no-yama. The strategy was that the armies should attack from east and west, then station themselves close to Tōji. On 3.8 the western force moved out, crossed the Katsura-gawa, advanced along Shijō and Rokujō, and took up position to the west of Ōmiya. Akiba from Bitchū was the first to attack, at Rokujō-Ōmiya, where many of his relatives and housemen were wounded or killed. On this day the Shogun joined Hosokawa Kiyouji's position at Imahie, and, in obedience to his command, Takeda Nobutake (Mutsu-no-kami) led the Kai squad to a position on Amida-ga-mine. Hosokawa Kiyouji moved out, hurried to where Akamatsu was at Shichijō-Higashinotōin; put up a tower (*yagura*); daubed its walls;[329] joined forces with the Niki Yoshinaga and Oyama contingents before the Chōkōdō, at Rokujō-Nishinotōin; and from Shiokōji to the Kusai-in precincts at Hachijō-Higashinotōin the Toki force built towers, and reinforced their walls and fences.

At dawn on 2.12 the Hatakeyama brothers, each with his own squad and reinforced by men from the east, set out on foot down Nishinotōin from the Sameushi Shrine. A large force issued from Tōji to meet them. Meanwhile, during the hours of the serpent [10 a.m.] and horse [midday] they set fires at the end of the bridge at Shichijō-Nishinotōin. Inomata (Echizen-no-kami) was the first easterner to die in battle. Hatakeyama Yoshifuka's houseman Ogawasawara Yajirō also died, as well as Hosokawa Shigeuji's man Watanabe Rengeji.

The battle was raging when Sasaki Dōyo raced in from Higashi Sakamoto. His Majesty had chosen to reside in the quarters of the Hiyoshi Shrine priests, guarded by Sasaki, but with the battle in Kyoto at a critical stage Sasaki rushed to a temple at the foot of the mountain, took up position there, and personally raised his banners. The enemy did its utmost to dislodge him. Hosokawa Kiyouji saw this and joined forces with Sasaki to attack. They were wounded while fighting at the Shichijō and Aburanokōji crossing. The men of their contingents exerted themselves with might and main. Hatakeyama Yoshifuka

---

[329] Perhaps with earth or mud, to ward off fire.

relieved them and pursued the enemy to Shichijō Horikawa, where he, too, was wounded.

The Shogun's men faced Nishinotōin, and the enemy Horikawa. Aburanokōji ran between them as they repeatedly advanced and retreated. Sasaki took this opportunity to reinforce his position and put up many towers. Meanwhile, despite the substantial size of his force, the warriors rushing up in fives and tens to join him in the fight were driven eastward along Aburanokōji.

The sight enraged Hosokawa Kiyouji. He dismounted, removed his armor, revealed his red *kosode*,[330] secured his wounded left arm around his neck, and girded only with a sword, opened his scarlet fan and rebuked them: "For shame! Turn back! Come back!" However, not one man stopped. Edo Takayoshi (Tōtōmi-no-kami) and Edo Fuyunaga (Tarō, later Shimōsa-no-kami), uncle and nephew, linked arms and stood together on Aburanokōji, heedless of their rear; whereupon fourteen more of their relatives lined up with them, sporting the Ōgasa helmet badge. They clashed violently with the attackers, captured some, and drove the rest westward along Aburanokōji. Kiyouji fought together with them. Edo Takayoshi and Tarō belabored the stragglers, each hilariously praising the other. Edo the uncle proclaimed his nephew the mightiest warrior in Japan.

While the Shichijō battle hung in the balance, at Imahie the Shogun learned that both Hosokawa Kiyouji and Hatakeyama Yoshifuka had been wounded. He immediately donned his armor, demanded his horse, mounted, girded on his sword, and with Aeba Myōzurumaru and Aeba's men—twenty riders in all—raced straight to and across the Kamo river. He did not remove his armor until he reached the tall tower at Kiyouji's Shichijō-Higashinotōin position. He was impossible to miss, dressed as he was that day in a red *hososode* with two stripes of applied gold foil.

Kiyouji and the other Hosokawas, Toki, and Sasaki, worried to see the Shogun there in the midst of the battle. He smiled his usual smile. "If we lose, we will all die together," he said. "There would be no point in arriving *after* this position falls." Wine cup in hand, he continued,

---

[330] A guess at the meaning of *aka kosode wo setawori*.

"Each of us will fight when the enemy approaches, and when the time comes for me to kill myself I will let you know." His looked so composed that, obviously, he would flinch before no attacking god or demon. His poise and dignity struck me as extraordinary. Victory or defeat in battle may depend on fate, but everyone calmed down once the Shogun had joined Kiyouji's position.

Nonetheless, the Shichijō battle was still raging. The easterners and the Shirahata squad relayed each other all day in the fighting, and many were killed or wounded. The Shogun's forces fought to exhaustion. At the hour of the bird [6 p.m.] Kiyouji requested reinforcements. The Shogun agreed that he needed them but stipulated that they were not to be deployed without his express order. He then summoned Nasu Suketō (Bizen-no-kami), who had dismounted on the Shichijō riverbank and remained there without loosing a single arrow, and gave him the order personally—with regret, since he so counted on the man.

Suketō saw that the battle on Shichijō had reached a critical point. "Soon it will be dark," he said. "Little daylight remains. I will now withdraw in haste from your presence and do my duty." His hot-blooded relatives and housemen, who in obedience to the Shogun's command had spent the day chafing over having merely to watch the battle, now advanced.

Suketō wore that day armor inherited through the generations from his ancestor Shuketada, who had worn it during the Mutsu wars:[331] black-laced and silver-trimmed with a sagittaria-leaf pattern. He wore two swords and carried a black-lacquered, rattan-wrapped bow with, at his back, twenty-five *soya* arrows fletched with eagle feathers in an *ōnakaguro* pattern.[332] He declared upon withdrawing, "If the enemy is too strong I will die in your service. If defeated, I will not return." He took from his side an old *horo* and put it on, tied his helmet cord, drew his horse to him, mounted, and set out westward along Shichijō.

---

[331] Suketada is the name of Shigetō's father. No Suektada fought with Yoriyoshi in the Early Nine Years War.

[332] A broad, black band flanked on either side by white.

Behind him came his uncle, Nasu Tadasuke, and other such men of his as Iono, Ashino, Fukuhara, and Inazawa—a total of over two hundred. The enemy army was waiting beyond Shichijō-Higashinotōin, east of Aburanokōji. His fiery young men urged a mass, mounted charge to trample and scatter them, but Shigetō issued this order: "A mounted charge against warriors on foot is all very well on otherwise unoccupied terrain in the wilds, but against an army on foot with Tōji at their back it is out of the question."

At the east end of the bridge over the Nishinotōin brook he dismounted, released the strap of the *horo*, and charged with a sword blade pressed to his forehead. The band of young relatives shielding him charged pell-mell to clash with the enemy, who buckled for a moment and fell back. His men killed or captured a few and drove them along Aburanokōji and Horikawa to Nishi-no-hata. There they raised a battle cry and sent a man with this message: "We have driven the enemy on Shichijō back to his main position on Horikawa. So many of us have been killed or wounded that our contingent is badly depleted. Please send reinforcements." They raised their banners between Aburanokōji and the burnt-out southwest corner of Shichijō.

The Shogun sent a reminder that daylight would not last much longer. Accordingly they decided to continue fighting until dark and only then to return to their position. Shigetō's personal band (*tezei*) remained alone, side by side, their neckplates low, when one contingent emerged from Aburanokōji and another from Shiokōji, and came down on them in great numbers. Although isolated, they scattered fire around them and retreated not one step. Shigetō and his nephew Tadasuke lost many relatives and housemen to death and wounds. The enemy fought mightily and suffered similarly. At last the enemy fell back to his base position (*honjin*), the battle of Shichijō lost.

Breathing weakly, still in armor and *horo*, Shigetō was lifted onto Hiroto[333] and went to appear before the Shogun. The Shogun saw his many wounds and expressed wonder at the greatness of what he had done. Shigetō seemed to hear his gracious words. He opened his eyes wide, pressed his bloody hands to his chest, nodded repeatedly in an

---

[333] Apparently the name of his horse. A powerful wind known in his home area of what is now Okayama-ken is called *hiroto kaze*.

attitude of profound respect, and breathed his last. The Shogun's eyes filled with tears. He remarked that in Kenmu 3, when he retreated to Kyushu, he had not had a single ally in the East. Only this Shigetō's father, Suketada, had confined himself in the fortress of Takadate and performed his loyal duty.[334]

Each contingent fought all day. The Toki, Satake, and Oda men headed for Kaikōji at Hachijō-Horikawa, where Momonoi Naotsune had fortified himself. All were on foot. It must have been early in the hour of the bird [6 p.m.], when the Shichijō battle was going badly and the enemy had the advantage, that the three commanders joined forces to attack, and Satake Kaneyoshi (Shimōsa-no-kami) was killed. All fought without a thought for their lives.

When the Shogun's men won and drove the enemy into Kaikōji, the enemy withdrew from Tōji and set out along the Tsukurimichi.[335] I gathered that Kusunoki was in command of the Southern army. At nightfall he was defeated, and that night, in the rain, the evildoers fled Tōji. I heard that the next day they occupied Tennōji and Sumiyoshi.

In the meantime, both commanders, east and west [Takauji and Yoshiakira], repaired to the palace, and the Emperor returned from Higashi Sakamoto [Bunna 4.3.28]. High and low in the capital rejoiced in peace at last, and the Shogun's glory swept the evildoers' dust from the city. This was further evidence of Genji might. The men of every house enjoyed the rewards of their signal deeds. Those led from the Kantō by Hatakeyama Yoshifuka and Yoshiteru to join the fray received the Shogun's heartfelt thanks. He then dismissed them to return home.

Such was the Bunna battle of Tōji.

---

334 This incident is otherwise unknown.

335 An important road from the site of the ancient Rajōmon directly southward to Toba.

RETIRED EMPEROR KŌGON'S LAST YEARS

From *Taiheiki* 39
"Kōgon-in Zenjō Hōō angya no koto"

INTRODUCTION

No document confirms the *Taiheiki* narrative of Kōgon's last years, but the account of his death matches this entry in *Moromori ki*, dated Jōji 3.7.7 (1364):[336]

> Last night at the hour of the ox the Cloistered Emperor (*daijō hōō*) passed away in his fifty-second year, having renounced the world years ago....He breathed his last in a grass hut in Tanba. Since the 4th month he had suffered three times from a common malady, and thereafter apparently refused further nourishment. The realm will of course be in mourning (*ryōan*).

RETIRED EMPEROR KŌGON'S LAST YEARS

In Enbun 2.2 [1357] Cloistered Emperor Kōgon was released from captivity at Anō, in the Yoshino mountains, and returned to the capital.[337] So compelling then grew his distaste for the world that, wishing to reduce his presence in it, he repudiated the clouds of Guyeshan and renounced the blossoms of Fenshuiyang.[338] He donned religious robes, shaved his head, joined those who had likewise

---

[336] Quoted in Yamashita Hiroaki, ed., *Taiheiki* (5 vols.) Shinchōsha (Shinchō Nihon koten shūsei), vol. 5, 1988, p. 465, n. 20. *Moromori ki*, the diary of the Northern Court official Nakahara Moromori, covers, with gaps, the years 1339-1374.

[337] Kōgon's full title here, Kōgon-in Zenjō Hōō, anticipates his renouncing the world. The text erroneously gives the year of his return to Kyoto as Shōhei 2 (1352, Shōhei being a Southern Court *nengō*). The translation supplies the correct date. Enbun is a Northern Court *nengō*.

[338] Decorative references to Chinese lore. Guyeshan means a retired emperor's palace.

rejected the common dust, and moved to a quiet spot, known as Kōgon-in,[339] behind the village of Fushimi.

The place was still so near the capital that, to his distress, visits from former subjects were all too common. He detested any news of worldly cares.

> Coming, there is nowhere to stay.
>
> Leaving, there is nowhere to go.[340]

"Before the staff runs the living path,"[341] Abbot Zhongfeng wrote when he left on his wanderings. Impressed by the power of his words, Kōgon gathered no acolytes to accompany him, only a certain Jungaku, with whom he set out on pilgrimage through mountains and forests.

He decided first to see the West. Passing along the Naniwa coast in Settsu, he found the pines along the shore swathed in mist. The dawn scene so moved him as he gazed on it from afar that with tears in his eyes he made this poem:

> *tare machite mitsu no hamamatsu kasumuran*
> *waga hinomoto no haru naranu yo ni*
> For whom does mist shroud the pines I see on Mitsu shore,
> when in my sunrise land there is no spring for me?

He lingered on the coast, far from the mountains, until the sun began to sink into the waves; and so loath was he to leave that he stayed on even then to contemplate the view. The moment was just the one evoked by the couplet about never tiring of seeing sunlit mountains reflected in water stained by the setting sun.[342] With a pang he noted that only renouncing the world had afforded him such a sight.

From there he went on to Kōyasan. He crossed Uryūno at Sumiyoshi. Green shoots were sprouting in the burnt-over fields, for spring had already come. The westering sun reddened the pines. The ocean vista before him, and the novelty of all that he saw, so stirred him that he felt no fatigue. Of old his feet had touched only gilded silk

---

339 Otherwise unknown.

340 No source for this verse has been identified.

341 A line by the Yuan-dynasty Rinzai monk Zhongfeng Minben (J. Chūhō Myōhon, 1263-1323).

342 Clearly from a couplet in Chinese, but unidentified.

cushions, but now he soiled them in deep mud and damp earth. His companion monk held under his arm not the imperial seal, but a begging bowl.

That night they walked as far as the shore at Sakai. Fisherfolk clustered on the tidal strand, gathering seaweed and sea greens, wore boxwood combs in their hair. Watching them appear and disappear again among the reeds, he saw that he had never realized how the common people labor to send tribute to their sovereign, and he could hardly believe it.

To the east he saw a cloud-topped mountain shrouded in mist and asked a woodcutter resting on the path for its name. "That is the celebrated fortress of Kongōsen,"[343] the man answered, "where so many warriors of Japan died in battle." "How awful!" Kōgon thought. "Those battles were fought to defend my own imperial line. Those warriors' endless kalpas of suffering in the Evil Realms are my fault!" He bitterly rued his past misdeeds.

Late that day he crossed Ki-no-kawa.[344] The pillars of the flimsy bridge were visibly rotten and dangerous, and he was so afraid that he could only barely bring himself to step onto it. He was frozen in the middle when seven or eight burly warriors arrived and saw him there. "What a miserable coward you are, you monk!" they said. "We're in a hurry, and there's no other bridge. If you mean to cross now, get on with it! If not, then cross after us!" They shoved the Cloistered Emperor out of the way, and he fell off into the water.

"How awful!" Jungaku cried. Still clothed, he dove in and pulled him out. Kōgon was soaked through, and his knee was bleeding where it had hit a rock. Weeping, he entered a wayside chapel and changed robes. Sovereign and subject could not help thinking back to the world they had renounced and reflecting that similar incidents must have occurred in times gone by. The tears that fell on their sleeves never left them dry.

Kōgon followed a narrow, newly cut trail over mountain after mountain, stream after stream, looking endlessly down, day after day, from towering heights and feeling utterly spent. "Once," he reflected,

---

343 Now read Kongōzan, the fortress mountain of Kusunoki Masashige.
344 The river that flows through Wakayama. Upstream, it becomes the Yoshino-gawa.

"the Daikakuji Cloistered Majesty [Go-Uda] traveled to Kōyasan, and with him a throng of senior nobles and privy gentlemen who, in ardent faith, prostrated themselves thrice each *chō* until their foreheads touched the ground, so rare was their sovereign's piety. I might well have followed his example, if only the world had been at peace during my reign."

Upon reaching Kōyasan he opened the doors of the Great Pagoda and saluted the Twin Mandalas. The Novice and Chancellor Kiyomori had personally painted the more than 700 divinities in the Taizōkai and the over 500 in the Kongōkai.[345] What long stored-up good karma could have inspired so meritorious a deed in so inveterately evil a man? At times the moon of the Six Elements Unimpeded shines clear, and one awaits the spring blossoms of the Four Interpenetrating Mandalas. Kōgon realized that Kiyomori had not been solely evil. Petals may fall like snow yet not weigh down a *kasa* hat. Though darkness gathers beneath new leaves, the sun is still in the sky.

That day he repaired to the Oku-no-in, where he opened the door of the Great Teacher's nirvana cave. Wind through the pines on the peak proclaimed the truth of the Teaching's salvific beneficence, while cloud-hidden mountain blossoms concealed the figure on the central throne.[346] Although the past Buddha's [Shaka] transformative presence is gone, his teaching seemed still to resound in Kōgon's ears. The Lord of Compassion's [Miroku] descent into the world lies far in the future, but the vista of the Three Assemblies seemed already present before his eyes. For three nights he kept vigil at the Oku-no-in, and at dawn, when he withdrew, he composed this poem:

> *takanoyama mayoi no yume mo samuru ya to*
> *sono akatsuki o matanu yo zo naki*
> Takano-yama: each night, I know, may bring
> the dawn that dispels illusion's dreams.[347]

---

[345] *Heike* 3 tells how Taira no Kiyomori rebuilt the Great Pagoda and painted the mandalas.

[346] The Dainichi of the Taizōkai mandala.

[347] "Takano-yama" is the "Japanese" reading of the name Kōyasan.

He decided to spend the summer retreat quietly among these mountains and undertook a round of the halls. He was so engaged when two black-robed figures who seemed only just to have renounced the world bowed low before him in silence, weeping bitterly. He stared at them, perplexed as to who they might be. They had been among the men who pushed him off the bridge into the river.

He was about to pass by, astonished that such shameless characters had renounced the world and wondering why they had done so, when they turned to follow him and in tears said to Jungaku: "We had no idea how exalted a personage His Cloistered Majesty was when he crossed the river and we abused the Jade Body.[348] In horror of this deed, we became what you now see before you. The seed of enlightenment arises, they say, from contingent causes, so that if we now devote ourselves to gathering firewood and drawing water, and in this way serve His Cloistered Majesty perpetually for three years, the Buddhas, the Gods, and the Three Treasures may forgive us."

Kōgon replied, "Enough! The Buddha once trod the path of the Bodhisattva Never-Despise,[349] reproved none who cursed him, and respected those who beat and trampled him. Still less do I now, in renunciate guise, care a whit about anyone's past. Why should a fleeting error trouble me? It is certainly a fine thing that you have renounced the world, but no, there is no question of your placing yourselves at my service." The men refused to leave them for a moment, and Kōgon therefore chose a moment when they had left to draw holy water, to summon Jungaku and, with him, steal away from Kōyasan.

Since his path led him toward Yamato, he visited on the way the Southern Emperor's palace at Yoshino. Until three or four years earlier the two imperial lines had been divided into North and South, and had fought hither and yon. Beyond even Wu's plan to overcome Yue at Kuai Qi, or Han's against Chu when they fought beside the Ba river,[350] Kōgon had become a wandering monk in hempen robe and straw sandals;

---

348 The imperial person.
349 A fugure in the Lotus Sutra.
350 The plans of Wu and Han to redress in the fullness of time the shame of temporary defeat.

had exchanged his imperial palanquin for walking; and in this guise had come far across the mountains. The visitor had not yet been announced when Go-Murakami moistened the sleeves of his robe, and his tears were flowing before the visitor even entered his presence.

The two Emperors spent a day and a night together, and they talked of many things. "You know," Go-Murakami said, "I cannot make out whether your gracious visit is a waking dream or a confused real one. You have relinquished the residence of a Retired Emperor to set out on the Buddha's true path, but whereas you might have followed the Kanpei example and emulated Kasan,[351] you wander like a drifting waterweed and follow the dead-wood adherents of Zen. What so inspired you to seek enlightenment? I envy you."

Choked with tears, Kōgon could not immediately reply. In time he said, "Complete as you are in wisdom and virtue, you have no doubt divined my answer without a word from me. Subject for eons to every passion, I had no wish to drift like a dust mote through the void, but I could not free myself from the bonds of old karma. The temple where I would have so much preferred to live remained in my heart, but I could not halt the approach of old age.

"Meanwhile no day went by without disorder in the realm. Early in Genkō [1331-1334] I fled to Banba in Ōmi,[352] and I was there when over 500 men took their lives. The blood set my mind reeling. Late in Shōhei [1347-1370][353] I was imprisoned in these mountains and for two years experienced the miseries of captivity. I realized then just how hateful the world is. I had no wish to regain the throne or to take up the reins of government. However, one of the warring sides insisted on

---

[351] In 897 Uda abdicated in favor of Daigo and founded Ninnaji. Kazan (as the name is now read; r. 984-986) renounced the world and became a religious wanderer. Perhaps Go-Murakami means that rather than follow Shingon, like Kazan, Kōgon is a devotee of Zen.

[352] Actually, late in Genkō: Genkō 3.5.9 (1333). *Baishōron* covers this moment in its account of Ashikaga Takauji's destruction of the Hōjō. Hino Nako's father and one of her brothers accompanied Kōgon in his flight (*Takemuki-ga-ki* 30-34). According to *Taiheiki* 9 ("Shushō, shōkō go-chinraku no koto"), a stray arrow lodged in Kōgon's left arm at Shinomiya-no-kawara (the Ōsaka barrier) and was extracted by Suyama Bitchū-no-kami.

[353] "Late in Shōhei" cannot possibly be right.

184

looking to me to lead them, and I had no escape. I could only long for the day when I might live deep in the mountains, among clouds and pines. Then heaven and earth issued a new mandate,[354] and allowed me to abdicate. My troubles gone, I assumed my present guise." So he spoke, weeping. Go-Murakami and his courtiers wrung tears from their sleeves.

The time had come for Kōgon to leave. His host offered him a horse, but he steadfastly declined to accept it. Despite his fatigue, he bound worn-out straw sandals over his snow-white feet and set out. Go-Murakami accompanied him as far as the guardhouse (*mushadokoro*). The blinds were lifted, and the courtiers saw him off to the edge of the palace grounds, where they stood, weeping. Each mountain cabin or rustic lodge on his way reminded him painfully of the pine-wood gate and rush-thatched shelter where, just a few years ago, imprisonment had rendered unbearable every moment of every day. Had the fortunes of war had not swept him into these mountains he would never have lived among them or had occasion now to think back to those terrible times.

His wandering through the provinces over, he returned for a time to Kōgon-in, but palace messengers kept coming to interrupt the pines' tranquil voice, and visits from former courtiers constantly obstructed the moonlight filtering through the leaves of the vines; so much so that he preferred no longer to live there, either. He therefore stole away to a spot named Yamakuni[355] in Tanba. Mountain fruits and nuts fell around his dwelling, and on these, in the morning, he broke his fast in the cruel autumn wind; while at night, clad in one thin robe against the cold, he hugged a brushwood fire. Emaciated by the elegant austerity of his life, he sometimes felt too weak to carry water from the spring. He then melted snow in a stone urn and sipped tea, hearkening the while to the unsullied wind. When weary of picking bracken shoots with tottering steps on the steep hillside, he ate *ume* from among the

---

[354] The accession (*sokui*) of Go-Kōgon in 1352.

[355] Jōshōji, a Rinzai (Tenryūji-ha) temple in Kyōto-fu, present Kitakuwata-gun. At the time it was uninhabited (*mujū*). Kōgon rebuilt a small hall there. Now named Jōshōkōji (the *kō* means "imperial"), the temple is known for a venerable weeping cherry tree allegedly planted by Kōgon himself.

rocks and serenely savored a few lines of verse. Renunciation of physical comfort filled his heart with peace. Far off there were rivers and lakes, and nearby mountain streams. Time went by. While he lay on worn-out bedding, his spirit roamed beyond heaven and earth. In the summer of the following year he suddenly felt unwell. At last, on the 7th of the 7th month, he passed away.

Notes from a Journey to Kyushu:

MICHIYUKIBURI

Imagawa Ryōshun

INTRODUCTION

Imagawa Ryōshun (1326-1414?), born roughly sixteen years after Hino Nako and six after Nijō Yoshimoto, was a prominent poet and warrior. Originally named Sadayo, he took the religious name Ryōshun after the death of Yoshiakira, the second Ashikaga shogun, in 1367.

In Ōan 3 (1370) the third shogun, Yoshimitsu, named Ryōshun his administrator (*tandai*) in Kyushu, a vital office that amounted to shogunal viceroy. His mission was to rid Kyushu of Southern Court partisans, end decades of fighting between local warlords, and impose Ashikaga authority throughout the island. In *Michiyukiburi* he described his journey there. A good many manuscripts of it survive. This translation relies on the one published by Shōgakukan.[356]

Ryōshun set out on Ōan 4.2.20 (1371), traveling down the coast on land while his men followed by sea. Over nine months later (11.29) he reached Nagato, where *Michiyukiburi* stops. His journey was probably not as leisurely as it often sounds. He was clearly anxious about the success of his mission, and he no doubt took the trouble to cultivate the good will of the daimyo along the way. In Kyushu his first task was to take Dazaifu, which he did the following year, supported by (among others) the Suō daimyo Ōuchi Hiroyo and his son Yoshihiro. Yoshihiro figures prominently in *Nantaiheiki*.

The title *Michiyukiburi* means something like "taking in the sights along the way." Ryōshun filled his account, as travelers did then, with poems about the places that he passed, and he wrote in an elegant style very different from the one he adopted in *Nantaiheiki*. With him he took, no doubt among other works, Reizei-school treatises on poetry and a still-extant copy of *Roppyakuban uta awase* (1194).[357]

Ryōshun first studied waka formally in his early twenties under Reizei Tamehide (?-1372). His distinguished student Shōtetsu (1381-

---

[356] Nagasaki Takeshi, Iwasa Miyoko, et al., eds., *Chūsei nikki kikō shū* (Shinpen Nihon koten bungaku zenshū, vol. 48), Shōgakukan, 1994.

[357] Kawazoe Shōji, *Imagawa Ryōshun*, Yoshikawa Kōbunkan, 1964, p. 96.

1459) wrote in *Shōtetsu monogatari* (ca. 1450) that Ryōshun was inspired to do so by Tamehide's poem:

> nasake aru tomo koso kataki yo narikere
> hitori ame kiku aki no yo sugara
> A true friend in this life is hard to find.
> Alone, through the autumn night I listen to the rain.

Ryōshun also studied renga, first under Kyūsei (1284-ca. 1378) and others, then under Nijō Yoshimoto. Yoshimoto's renga treatise *Kyūshū mondō* (1378) answers questions that Ryōshun sent him from Kyushu.

Late in life Ryōshun still counted himself formally as a waka disciple of Tamehide's grandson Tamemasa (1361-1417), but by then he was an authority himself. His treatise *Imagawa Ryōshun kaishi shiki* (1392) dates from near the end of his time in Kyushu (1395), and he devoted himself further to poetry after the collapse of his other hopes in the aftermath of the Ōei Disturbance (Ōei no ran, 1399). The introduction to *Nantaiheiki* covers that subject.

In the colophon to the source manuscript of *Michiyukiburi*, Ryōshun wrote of deteriorating handwriting and loss of control over his brush, just as in 1402 he closed *Nantaiheiki* with these words:

> This year I suffer so from palsy that at times I cannot control my wandering brush. My writing is becoming worse and worse. I skip characters or kana. Such are the ravages of age, for which I beg the reader's indulgence.

He was then in his seventy-eighth year. The source manuscript must date from about the same time.

Nonetheless, Ryōshun went on writing. His *Nigonshū* (1409), for example, opposes the Nijō school insistence on banning from waka any word not present in the first three imperial anthologies (*Sandaishū*). *Rakusho roken*, written in his eighty-seventh year, is a summation of his teaching. He also left *Rokuon-in-dono Itsukushima mōde no ki* (1389) an account of a pilgrimage to Itsukushima with Yoshimitsu. Finally, a letter of advice believed to have been addressed by him to

Nakaaki, a younger brother whom he had adopted as a son, was widely read in the Edo period and influential in education.[358]

---

[358] Carl Steenstrup, "The Imagawa Letter: A Muromachi Warrior's Code of Conduct Which Became a Tokugawa Schoolbook, *Monumenta Nipponica* 28:3 (Autumn 1973).

MICHIYUKIBURI

Late at night on the 20th of the 2nd month [Ōan 4, 1371], by the light of a misty moon shining from the edge of the hills, I crossed the Katsura-gawa. A shower of drops wetted my traveler's sleeves. Wilted as they were by this early dawn departure, it was all the easier to imagine what drops from the oar would soak them on the sea-lanes toward my destination. That day I reached Yamazaki. I knew the place well, but perhaps it was regret at setting off on this journey that lent an air of sorrow there to the most commonplace grasses and trees.

Upon reaching the Akuta-gawa in the province of Tsu, I wondered anxiously what fate awaited my worthless self (*chiri no mi*).[359] The local folk of Segawa and Koyano watched my train go by, and whatever I may have thought of them in the past, I now envied their carefree air.

> *kaku bakari kurushikarazu wa ashibi taku*
> *koya no naka ni mo yo o yatsusan*
> Were it not impossible, I would gladly live
> unknown at Koyano,
> in a hut where a rush fire burns.[360]

Along the river there rose an ancient, thickly-wooded hill. A torii stood there. Upon questioning the local people I learned that when Tarashi-hime [Jingū Kōgō] returned from conquering the Three Koreas she buried her armor and helmet on this hill, which has been known ever since as Muko-no-yama.

> *kono tabi mo araki namiji no sawari naku*
> *nao fukiokure muko no yamakaze*
> On this journey, O wind down Muko-yama,
> speed me, too, safely across the waves.

---

[359] *Chiri*, like the *akuta* of Akuta-gawa, means "refuse," "rubbish."
[360] The "rush fire" (*ashibi*) draws on *Manyōshū* 2651. *Koya no naka* ("in a hut") plays on the place name Koyano.

A poem in an old collection, too, mentions *irie no sudori*[361] on the shore below Muko-yama:

> *muko no ura no irie no sudori ika ni shite*
> *tatsu ato ni shimo tomaru kokoro zo*
> O birds on the sandbars, in the inlet along Muko shore,
> how, even after you have taken flight,
> can your footprints remain, just as I long to stay?

After passing Uchide-no-hama [362] I reached the Ashiya-no-sato mentioned as "where I live" by Narihira in his poem:

> *haruru yo no hoshi ka kahabe no hotaru ka mo*
> *waga sumu kata no ama no taku hi ka*
> Are those, I wonder, stars on a cloudless night,
> fireflies by a stream, or the fires that fishermen
> light at sea off my home shore?[363]

Between there and where I was, under the pines near the rocky shore, stood a sacred fence and a torii. The place seems to have been known as Mikage-no-matsubara ever since the Kitano Shrine manifested itself (*yōgō*) at the spot.[364]

> *kimi ga tame kurakarumajiki kokoro ni wa*
> *kami mo mikage o utsusazarame ya*
> Within my heart, bright with my sovereign's light,
> surely the deity, too, will wish to reside.

Soon I reached the Ikuta-gawa. The burial mounds of the young men who shot the bird on the river here stand beside the path.[365] The breeze sighed through the pine grove, and I wished that I could stay and listen to it forever.

---

[361] "Birds on the sandbars," in *Man'yōshū* 3578.

[362] Hyogo-ken, Ashiya-shi

[363] *Ise monogatari* 87. Translation from Joshua S. Mostow and Royall Tyler, *The Ise Stories*, University of Hawai'i Press, p. 189.

[364] The name means "Pine Wood of the Sacred Presence."

[365] The graves (*tsuka*) of the maiden Unai and her two suitors, a story told in the *Manyōshū*, in *Yamato monogatari*, and elsewhere, and dramatized in the Noh play *Motomezuka*.

I then spent a night at Minato-gawa, and the next day one or two friends came from the capital to visit me. I felt more forlorn than ever when the time came for them to leave. "Reluctant to go on" (*yukiushi*) described my feelings perfectly.[366]

> *tabigoromo asa tatsu sode no minatogawa*
> *kawaranu se ni to nao ya tanoman*[367]
> This morning, bound in travel dress,
> with dripping sleeves, past Minato-gawa,
> I still hope that her promise for the future holds.

I came to Suma. There was nothing especially memorable about the place,[368] but the very dreariness of the frail-looking houses huddled under the hill, with their fences of brushwood or sparsely woven bamboo, brought to mind the picture of *his* dwelling[369] there, of old. This is where the barrier hut used to be, but these days there is no longer even a board-roofed hut, still less any barrier guard. I saw fishing boats roaming about near the shingle beach. This must be where the journey along the shore to the Akashi Novice's residence began.

Further on, between the sea and foot of the hills, I came to a place named Ōkuradani. The pine grove and the white sand invited me to linger, but I somehow disliked the menacing overtones of the name.[370] Moreover, in fear of the many pirate boats said to threaten travelers in those waters, I passed on in haste. What a shame that such danger should lurk in so lovely a place!

White sand above all, it seemed to me, sets the Akashi beach apart: white as an expanse of snow and backed by the green of ancient pines, grove after grove, bent by the wind across the shore, their branches hung with trailing moss. There were houses here and there, up against

---

[366] From *Kokinshū* 388, by Minamoto no Sane.

[367] Especially elaborate word plays make this poem difficult to translate meaningfully. One (*sode no minato[gawa]*) draws on Ise monogatari 26 (*The Ise Stories*, p. 76).

[368] As Yoshikiyo said of Akashi to Genji in the "Wakamurasaki" chapter of *Genji monogatari*.

[369] Genji's.

[370] Ōkura ("big storehouse") can sound, to one so inclined, like "great darkness."

the hill.[371] Awaji, which from Sumiyoshi had been veiled by mist, looked very close. The view was especially beautiful.

Everything I saw on the way through Harima impressed me deeply. Inamino spread, unbroken, to the four quarters, its vast expanse of sparse *chigaya* grass dead and brown above, but with green shoots emerging from below. It made a remarkable sight.

> *choku nareba kuniosame ni to inamino no*
> *asajiu no michi mo mayowazaranan*
> By my sovereign's command I pass Inamino,
> on a mission to impose peace.
> May I not lose my way among its wastes of sedge!

Upon passing Shimizu and Kanagasaki I asked what lay further south. It turned out to be the village of Shikama. The route on foot was a little longer, but the vast, open view where the river emptied into the sea had a beauty of it own.

A little further on, a rock barrow[372] stood beside a river, inhabited by a divine presence. I saw there several of the shapes visible before the Izumoji Shrine and asked what they meant. I received this answer: "Upon first passing this way, every traveler, high or low, takes one and carries it around the barrow, making the motions of congress between man and woman." What a terribly embarrassing thing to do!

Oh yes: this sanctuary's main shrine stands in the sea not far away, and I was told that whenever anyone does so the shrine shakes. No doubt this is a divine manifestation.

> *tsutaekiku kamiyo no mito no maguai o*
> *utsusu chikai no hodo mo kashikoshi*
> That fabled congress in the age of the gods:
> how awesome to find it shifted to this place!

The place is called Isozaki or Iso-no-watari.

---

[371] *Okabe no ie*, the expression for the Akashi Lady's house in the "Akashi" chapter.
[372] A heap of stones, perhaps the base for a *dōsojin* altar. The shapes mentioned below are phalluses. The Izumoji Shrine, in Kyoto, was an ancient *dōsojin* shrine.

> *tabi nareba tokete mo nenu o haru no yo no*
> *iso no watari no tooku mo aru kana*[373]
>
> Travel allows no time for restful sleep.
> Haste, this spring night, over Iso-no-watari
> still leaves such a long way to go!

Further on there is a village called Koi-no-maru. I wondered what lovesick fellow could possibly have given it so amusing a name.[374]

> *yume tote mo imo ya wa miyuru tabigoromo*
> *himo dani tokanu koi no marone ni*
>
> Not even dreams give me a glimpse of my love:
> sleeping alone, I do not even untie my travel robe.

The name instantly called a certain someone to mind.

In the village of Kagatsu[375] every household made objects known as jewel-drop jars (*tamadare no kobin*). Through the pines, beyond the top of the hill, you could just glimpse the glittering sea. It was a pretty view.

That day I reached Fukuoka. The houses were lined up side by side, and the people's cooking hearths were burning merrily. The place nicely matched its name.[376]

Further on there was a river with a ford called Mino-no-watari.

> *furusato mo koishikarame ya azumaji no*
> *mino no watari to omowamashikaba*
>
> I would have missed home sharply, had I recalled
> the Mino-no-watari on the road to the east!

I stayed somewhere called, I believe, Karakawa. Early the next morning, a row of shrine priests in dark yellow stood under the torii near the path to the Kibitsu Shrine, apparently offering sacred streamers to assure me a safe journey.

Kibi-no-Nakayama[377] must be called that because it rises between two shrines, one in Bitchū and the other in Bizen.[378] The brook there

---

373 The syllables *iso* play in the place name and on the word *isogi* ("haste").

374 Taking *maru* to be the first-person pronoun *maro*: "lovelorn me."

375 Kakato in Bizen-shi, Okayama-ken, a pottery center (Bizen-yaki). The jars mentioned are for saké and so on.

376 This Fukuoka is in Okayama-ken. Ryōshun plays upon the *fuku* (good fortune) in the name.

sounded surprisingly forlorn.[379] The sacred fence that came down to it looked impressively holy. I offered an *uwaya* arrow at each of these shrines.

Next, I next crossed the Karube-gawa,[380] then Sei-yama, to lodge at the village of Yakage.

> *mononofu no takeki na nareba azusayumi*
> *yakage ni tare ka nabikazarubeki*
> So warlike, this name that evokes the catalpa bow,
> who would not yield to the threat of its arrows? [381]

In Bingo I found more intriguing places than famous ones. A series of inlets obliged me to make long detours. The seafolk's dwellings huddled against the hills. I struggled down a steep slope to reach the shore at Onomichi. Northward from there an expanse of tall *chigaya* grass extends below a rocky hill. Along its base the houses are too crowded together to leave room even for drying fishing nets. An arm of the sea stretches far from west to east, and the flood or ebb tides rush along it all day. The sails of the ships passing back and forth, as the wind rises or drops, make a lovely picture. Many ships from distant Michinoku or Kyushu lie rocking at anchor, while tiny boats, like little birds, ferry back and forth from shore the women who bring the sailors a single night of love.

Directly across this water lies a hilly island. The man who owned this island long ago was so deeply devoted to poetry that he indulged in composing poems about laborers in the ricefields or seafolk diving into the sea—so much so, they say, that the island soon became known as Uta no Shima ["Poem Island"]. You can just make out the salt huts and the smoke that rises so touchingly from them. There is a saying that it always rains a day or two after the salt fires have burned there, and no doubt it does. Further south there are more pretty

---

[377] A hill on the border between Bizen and Bitchū.

[378] Kibitsuhiko Jinja to the east and Kibitsu Jinja to the west.

[379] An allusion to *Kokinshū* 1082, which mentions the bright clarity (*sayakesa*) of the brook's sound.

[380] Now the Takahashi-gawa in Okayama-ken.

[381] The *ya* in the place name Yakage sounds like either "arrow" or "dwelling." Ryōshun plays on the former.

islands to be seen. The whole area resembles Shiogama in Michinoku, and seafolk sensitive to beauty must inhabit these islands, too.[382]

I brought together the seaweed scribblings that had come to mind during my busy journey so far.

> *uchikawasu tomone nariseba kusamakura*
> *tabi no umibe mo nani ka ukaran*
> If only my love and I slept sleeve over sleeve,
> pillowed upon grass,
> no journey beside the sea could be melancholy.

> *imasara ni shiranu inochi o nageku kana*
> *kawaranu yoyo to iishi chigiri ni*
> Ah, how I deplore the uncertainty of life,
> after swearing constancy through all ages to come!

> *nakanaka ni wakare no kiwa wa to mo kaku mo*
> *iwarezarishi zo ima wa kanashiki*
> I left her no word of comfort when we parted,
> and how bitterly I regret that now!

Now, in Bingo there are few examples of respectable writing, and even if some official document should turn up from time to time among the silverfish, no one is competent to make sense of it. Even I, ignorant as I am, go astray. Things could hardly have been this bad even in the days when writings were secreted in walls and in stone containers.[383] I was shocked, and these poems came to mind.

> *ika ni shite yomogi no naka no yomogi dani*
> *asa ni nitaru wa sukunakaruran*
> How can it be that, amid the wormwood stalks,
> so few should follow the example of hemp?[384]

---

[382] The seafolk (*ama*) of Shiogama are famous in poetry for enjoying, despite their labors, the beauty of where they live.

[383] An allusion to the Confucian classics, hidden to save them from the First Emperor's burning of the books.

[384] The wormwood (*yomogi*) stalks, which normally grow crooked, are those who know nothing of letters. The hemp (*asa*), which naturally grows straight, seems to be those who acquire learning. The motif is from Xun Zi.

> *tsukuzuku to midori no sora ni aogazu wa*
> *yo no uki tabi ni ikade sugusan*
> If we do not lift our gaze to the blue heavens,
> how can we survive the sad journey of life?

> *oimagaru maki no maroki no yumitori wa*
> *sugunaru yori mo chikara koso are*
> The warrior with a bow of naturally bent wood
> surpasses him with one of wood worked straight.[385]

People call it shameful to be wealthy in troubled times, and I have come lately to see how right they are.

On the 19th of the 5th month I moved from Onomichi in Bingo to Nuta in Aki. On the way I encountered a mountain jutting southeastward, beyond a dry stretch of beach. I followed the shore path northwest all the way to a place called Yoshiwa. Soon darkness fell.

> *hi mo kurenu yūshio tooku nagare ashi no*
> *yoshiwa no iso ni yado ya karamashi*
> The sun is down, and rushes run far out on the tide;
> but not I, who would gladly lodge on Yoshiwa beach.[386]

Two thickly wooded islands stand side by side there, in the sea. They are called Kujirajima ["Whale Islands"]. In the last month of every year many fish known as *kujira* gather there. In the first month of the next year they apparently leave again. "They do this because of the vow made by our local deity," the fishermen say. Southward from there, where the open ocean begins, is Mekari-no-ura.[387]

> *tabigoromo sode mo nurekeri ama otome*
> *mekari no ura no nami no tayori ni*

---

[385] The intent of this poem is unclear.

[386] A play on the *yoshi* (rushes) of the name Yoshiwa.

[387] Perhaps the sea passage between Mukō-jima and In-no-shima. Here and often elsewhere in *Michiyukiburi*, not to mention classical literature in general (for ex., Suma-no-ura in *Genji*), an *ura* is a stretch of shore over which the local community claims exclusive fishing and other marine harvesting rights.

Waves on Mekari shore,
where seafolk maidens gather seaweed,
start tears that wet the sleeves of my travel robe.[388]

A steep promontory jutting southward from the coast, thickly wooded with pine and cypress, makes a handsome sight. Its name is Ito-saki.[389]

> *kazuki suru ama no tebiki no itosaki wa*
> *shio taregoromo oru ni zo arikeru*
> At Itosaki the diver women spin the thread
> they weave into their brine-dripping robes.[390]

Across from it, beyond a stretch of dry beach, lies In-no-shima. Further on I came to the border between Bingo and Aki. Among those hills there is a thatched chapel. The Nuta-gawa flows below it into an arm of the sea. I was out on this river in a boat when the sun went down and darkness gradually swallowed the slopes nearby. Fireflies flitted dimly back and forth. I was feeling somehow downcast when pine torches approached the village, their flames brightly reflected in the river's waves. The scene reminded me of cormorant fishing.

Until Juei [1182-1184] this place was apparently under the sea, and oysters clung to the rocks. The hills some distance away were thickly wooded and made a very pretty scene.

A shrine called Koshiki-no-Tenjin stood on the west side of the river, in a hillside grove of ancient pines. When that divinity [Michizane] was sent down to Kyushu, he ate parched rice here on the way, and his *koshiki* ["rice steamer"] remained at the spot. It is said still to be here. It was immediately presented to the shrine and placed beside the shrine's most sacred object. There is also a miraculous spring. They say that Tenjin dug it with his own hands.

> *waga inoru tanomi mo koto ni mashimizu no*
> *asakarimajiki megumi o zo matsu*
> My prayers are many, and this pristine spring deep;
> I know that I can count on great blessings.

---

[388] The sound makes him think of his love at home, and how far away she is.
[389] A shallow promontory, east of Mihara-shi, that rises steeply to 430 m.
[390] The poem plays on the *ito* ("thread") in the name Ito-saki.

Next to this hill, on a slope far along a path through the ricefields, a grass-thatched chapel stands in a dense thicket of pine and bamboo. Apparently this is where, in the days of the Heike, the Nuta lord[391] fortified his position, and where Lord Noritsune[392] attacked him and reduced his fortress. Even now, peasants plowing their fields sometimes turn up an old skeleton with an arrow or dagger hole in it. Nearby there were many people at work, weeding the paddies.

> *sode nurasu narai mo kanashi ayame karu*
> *nuta no ta no kusa kyoo wa toritsutsu*
> How touching that they wet their sleeves at Nuta,
> where sweet flag grows,
> gathering today grasses in the ricefields.

Southward from there many deities are worshiped, and Otoko-yama seems to be among them.

> *tanomu zo yo koko mo minami no otokoyama*
> *onaji miyai ni kakeshi inori wa*
> Here, too, at this southern Otoko-yama
> my prayers go forth, as once at your great shrine.

Why should the oracle "Above all other men, my own" not cover even my foolish self?[393] A spirit may soar through the heavens, but the deity discerns its flight, and I would gladly discover how to cleanse my heart so as to match the light that he shines upon me.

I wrote these seven poems on paper mulberry leaves as offerings for the seventh night of the seventh month.

> *momijiba no nishiki no hashi ya watasuran*
> *tanabata-tsu-me no mare no ōse ni*

---

[391] The Nuta no Jirō (Tarō in the *Enkyō-bon*) of *Heike monogatari* 9.

[392] Noto-no-kami, the son of Taira no Kiyomori's brother, Norimori.

[393] From a Hachiman oracle dated Tenpyō Shōhō 7 (756) and recorded in *Hachiman Gudōkun* (Sakurai Tokutarō et al., eds., *Jisha engi* [Nihon shisō taikei 20], Iwanami Shoten, 1975, p. 263) and related documents: "Above all other lands, my land; above all other men, my own; so that no ax should fell a sacred tree and nor any sickle cut sedge....Should a single one of mine (*ujibito*) suffer an injustice, I will quit my shrine, ascend to the void, and thence rain disaster upon the realm." Ryōshun, like the Ashikaga, could claim the favor of Hachiman.

A brocade bridge of autumn leaves may well give passage
toward that rare meeting with the Weaver Maid.

> *nishi no umi ya ware koso tanome tanabata no*
> *kyō wataru se no sawari nakereba*

O western seas, I, too, beg safe passage,
if only nothing hinders the crossing today.

> *waga inoru kokoro no sue mo tōranan*
> *kyō no tamuke no moji no sekimori*

May my fondest prayers be heard and answered,
O Moji barrier guard to whom in offering
I address my poems today!

> *kyō yori ya nao tanomamashi tsukushibune*
> *kaji no nanaha no kami ni makasete*

Today and henceforth my faith will grow
that my ships, by divine grace, will reach Kyushu safely.

> *toki kinu to haya machiwatase hikoboshi no*
> *iohata oreru ito no shimabito*

Yes, the time has come: swiftly assure our passage,
you with the Oxherd's many looms, you men of Ito Isle!

> *aimimaku hoshi ni ya itodo inoramashi*
> *aki wa hana saku kiku no takahama*

I shall pray still harder to the lover-stars,
to see, this autumn, chrysanthemums
bloom at Kiku no Takahama.

> *chigiri arite aki wa kanarazu tanabata no*
> *matsura no kawa o watarubeki kana*

As the stars are pledged to meet each autumn,
so I, too, this autumn shall cross the Matsura-gawa.

I worked the names of some well known Kyushu places into them.

On the 29th of the 8th month I left Nuta in Aki and passed through
the mountain village of Nyūno. Ono no Takamura once lived here, and
apparently it soon became known as Takamura or as Ono. There is a
large mountain temple. I spent that night at the village of Takaya.

The next day I took the Ōyama road over the mountains. The autumn leaves were turning everywhere, and the *hahaso* and *kashiwa* oaks were in full color. Brooks and rills flowed on every side, under mountain shade impenetrable even to the sun, and the sound of water beating against rocks troubled me. Trees fallen across deep ravines here and there became, themselves, the trail.

> *momijiba no ake no magaki ni shiruki kana*
> *ōyamahime no aki no miyai wa*
> How bright it is, the sacred fence of autumn leaves
> around the Lady of the Mountain's shrine!

I came down from the mountains at the village of Seno. Here, too, the slender trails ran through steep gorges. I was reminded of Utsu-no-yama in Suruga.

On the last day of the month I reached the shore at the village of Kaita. High mountains rose toward the south. Below them, dry beach stretched far away along a bay, and to the north houses stood up against the mountains. After twenty days here I left on the 19th of the 9th month, with the dawn moon still in the sky. There was something lovely about my journey along the tidal shore.

I next reached the shore at Sasai. On the 20th I made a pilgrimage to Itsukushima. Three or four peaks rise from the island. Among the ancient forest trees on their slopes, venerable pines lean from rocks and grow vigorously even to the water's edge.

Between this island and a high promontory[394] that juts out toward the east—a distance of some twenty *chō*—there is another small one, apparently inhabited. It seems to be the one called Koguro-jima. The area nearby is apparently called Atato.

> *shimamori ni iza koto towan ta ga tame ni*
> *nan no atato to na ni shi oiken*
> O island guardian, I have a question for you:
> what enemy, and whose, gave your island its name? [395]

---

[394] Perhaps the northwest tip of Nishinoumi-jima, east of Itsukushima.
[395] Ryōshun takes the *ata* in the island's name as meaning "enemy" (*ada*). His poem draws on the last one in *Ise monogatari* 9.

Further south, more islands show through the mist. That stretch of sea is called Masakari-no-seto. I gather that it separates this province from Iyo. It is unusual that the boundary between two provinces should lie in the sea.

The shrine just mentioned faces roughly northwest. At high tide the sea comes in under the shrine's gallery. The torii stands in the sea. The gulfs and bays around the island present countless beautiful views. There are said to be a hundred fishing hamlets (*ura*). Alas, while rowing quietly around the island I could not help missing friends from the capital and family from home, and I wished only for the company of those dear to me. I had yet to see Misen and Takimoto,[396] but I was warned to hurry back because the sun was going down, and I never saw them at all.

I therefore turned back, rowed to the beach in front of the shrine, and dropped two relic grains (one from Tōji, one from Hamuro[397]) into the sea. This was to pray for a safe journey onward.

The men rowing my boat into the setting sun, remarked that rowing against the ebb tide slowed the boat so much that they were aiming for the inshore *nurumi*. "Why is that?" I asked. They explained, "When the tide runs fast, the inshore current flows in the opposite direction, which makes rowing easier. *Nurumi* means a back-current."

> *isogiwa no nurumi ni kakete ideshi fune no*
> *hayashio michi ni mukau hodo nasa*
> The boat that rides the back-current, close-in,
> follows all the more swiftly the rising tide.

Mountains surround this stretch of shore on all four sides, and it is as difficult as on the open sea to tell how the flood or ebb tide runs; such is the island's situation. The place could be the sea lord's palace, it is so far removed from the common world. It is almost frightening.

On the 21st I left Sasai, passed along the dry beach to the west of the Chi-no-Gozen shrine,[398] and took the path through the mountains. Eventually I came to the place known as Ōno-yamanaka.

---

[396] Misen is the highest peak on the island of Itsukushima. The place name Takimoto is unknown, but there is a Taki-no-miya shrine on the slopes of Misen.
[397] Hamuro Jōjūji.

The daybreak moon of the ninth month still hung, pale, in the sky, and such heavy dew dripped from the trees that one needed an umbrella. Amid the thick, deep-hued autumn foliage, the wind-blown chinquapin leaves fluttered white.[399] The sound of wind in the pines mingled with the babbling of mountain streams in an entrancing dawn.

> *to ni kaku ni shiranu inochi o omou kana*
> *waga mi isoji ni ōno nakayama*
> My thoughts run to the unknown that awaits me,
> now that, at fifty, I hasten down the shore
> to Ōno Nakayama.[400]

> *mukashi tare kage ni mo sen to maku shii no*
> *ōno nakayama kaku shigururan*
> Who of old, for shelter, planted these *shii* trees,
> that such chilly drops should fall at Ōno Nakayama?

I wrote this one when the expression *mukai no oka ni shii makite*, from an old collection,[401] suddenly came to mind.

After making my way through the mountains I came down again to a shore similarly named Ōno-no-ura. The hills across the water were the southern end of Itsukushima. I had gone all the way round and come out at the same place. My men's larger ships, which had set out that morning from Sasai, were visible under sail in a following breeze. Those aboard must have been gazing curiously in my direction.

> *ōno ura o kore ka to toeba yamanashi no*
> *katae no momiji iro ni idetsutsu*
> Is this, I asked, Ōno-no-ura? And it was,
> for the leaves were bright on the yamanashi boughs.[402]

---

[398] The "outer shrine" (*gegū*) of Itsukushima, in present Hatsukaichi-shi. The deity is Itsukishima-hime.

[399] The undersides of chinquapin (*shii*) leaves are white.

[400] The poem plays on *isoji*, "shore road" and "fifty." Actually, Ryōshun is in only his forty-sixth year.

[401] *Man'yōshū* 1099.

[402] The poem draws on *Kokinshū* 1099.

Breakfast was being prepared on the fishing boats closer in, and the waves reflected the rising smoke. I wished that I could show the scene to someone able to appreciate it.

> *nami no ue ni moshio yaku ka to mietsuru wa*
> *ama no obune ni taku hi narikeri*
> People seeming to boil seaweed on the waves
> were really fisherfolk, cooking on their boats.

After that it was all mountain trails. Tsuba, Kurokawa, Koematsu, Yaomatsu—the path ran through mountains immediately above the sea. At Ōtani I saw a mountain stream pouring from a cliff. From that I gathered I was about to cross into Suō. That night I stayed in a mountain village named Tada.[403] The next morning it was a mountain trail again, over Iwakuni-yama. Not a hovel was to be seen. I traveled in these remote mountains under dense forest shade. The crags[404] were indeed high, and the journey was daunting. That evening I saw not a single homeward-bound woodcutter, nor did I hear even a temple bell.

> *tomarubeki yado dani naki o koma nazumu*
> *iwakuniyama ni kyō ya kurasan*
> No sign of shelter here, and my mount falters—
> must I still greet this night on Iwakuni-yama?

> *tachikaeri miru yo mo araba hito naranu*
> *iwakuniyama mo waga tomo ni sen*
> If I return home and rejoin the world,
> I will take with me in memory, as my friends,
> these inhuman crags of Iwakuni-yama.

> *tarachine no oya ni tsugeba ya arashi chō*
> *iwakuniyama mo kyō wa koenu to*
> I would gladly let my father know that today
> I crossed Iwakuni-yama, reputed so wild.

---

[403] Within Iwakuni-shi, Yamaguchi-ken.
[404] Meaning the *iwa* of Iwakuni.

An old poem goes,

> *iwakuniyama o koen hi wa*
> *tamuke yoku seyo araki sono michi*[405]

The day you cross Iwakuni-yama,

make generous offerings: it is rough, that trail!

I must have been thinking of it in that last one.

Much further on I came to a village named Ebisaka and stayed in the temple there. This was on the 22nd.

The next day I came to the Tōshi coast.[406] The Hachiman shrine there faces south below a hill. Far beyond the tidal beach in front of the shrine, the tip of a great rock protrudes from the sea: the Tōshi ["Distant Rock"], apparently. I wanted to call it *hito koso shirane*.[407]

The sun was low that day when I reached the Toda coast. Here another arm of the sea stretches far inland toward the northwest. Small islands (I do not know their names) lie dotted about. One was called Itsukushima.[408] I saw fishing boats hurrying shoreward against the wind. Rain seemed to be threatening, and the clouds were racing overhead.

> *yūshio ni tsurete ya kitsuru itodoshiku*
> *ashihayabune no toda no iriumi*

They must be coming in on the evening tide,

this growing throng of boats speeding into Toda inlet.

On the 24th I reached Kofu in Suō. All along the way the view to the south was hazy, and the mountains[409] resembled an ink painting. The large island below them, Hime-shima, must be in Bungo. In the far

---

[405] *Man'yōshū* 567.

[406] In Tokuyama-shi, Yamaguchi-ken.

[407] "Nobody knows." From *Senzaishū* 760, by Nijōin Sanuki: *waga sode wa/ shiohi ni mienu/ oki no ishi no/ hito koso shirane/ kawaku ma zo naki* ("My sleeves are like the reef at sea, invisible through flood and ebb. Nobody knows it, but they are never dry").

[408] Unknown; perhaps a mistake for Itsutsu-shima, a name that appears on maps to the west of Ōtsushima.

[409] Presumably the Kunisaki peninsula. Hime-shima, below, lies off the northern tip of Kunisaki.

distance, through the haze, I made out Takasaki Castle.[410] I did not fail to recall that that was where *he* lived.

The waves on the sea here were high. I was told that this was where the open ocean begins. Sure enough, the name of the hamlet (*ura*) was Tonomi.[411]

A winding slope leads up from the sea's rocky edge (*isogiwa*). It is called Tachibana-zaka.

> *araiso no michi yori mo nao ashibiki no*
> *yamatachibana no saka zo kurushiki*
> Still harder than the path along the rocky shore
> is the painful slope up Yamatachibana.

Below this pass, to the west, there is an arm of the sea.[412] Mountains surround it east and west, and before it is an island.[413] There are two east-west channels through which boats enter and leave. Out at sea one sees a chain of seven or eight small, thickly wooded islands.

On the rocky coast to the north is a cluster of houses: Kofu. Still further north, facing south from below the higher mountains, is a Tenjin shrine. One can see the access path to it run twenty or more *chō*[414] from the shrine to the sea's edge. Two torii stand along it, and beside it runs a purification stream (*mitarashi-gawa*), crossed by a bridge. To the southwest rises a single, pine-covered hill named Kuwa-no-yama ["Mulberry Hill"]. Below it, an expanse of pine woods runs into the distance. Nearby is a stretch of shore used for salt-making.

> *hana susuki masoo no ito o midasu kana*
> *shizu ga kau ko no kuwa yamakaze*
> How it tosses the waving *susuki* plumes,
> the wind down Mulberry Hill,
> where the peasants feed their silkworms!

---

[410] Takasaki-yama is just west of Ōita-shi. Ryōshun's son, Yoshinori, was in command there.

[411] The name just translated as "open ocean."

[412] Presumably Mitajiri-wan.

[413] Presumably Mukō-jima.

[414] Over 2 km.

I spent the rest of the 9th month at Kofu and set out again late at night on the 7th of the 10th. The path along the shore took me past an endless succession of inexpressibly beautiful islands and bays.

A light haze hung in the air toward Ōsaki and Tajima. The daybreak sky was serene, and the waves made no sound. The cranes called softly among the reeds, their voices announcing dawn.

> *ōsaki no ura fuku kaze no asanagi ni*
> *tajima o wataru tsuru no morokoe*
> During the wind's morning lull on Ōsaki shore,
> cranes cross over, calling, to Tajima.

In the middle distance smoke rose from village houses, while the morning breeze brought the fragrance of plum and cherry blossoms, blooming out of season as though delightfully to conjoin—so I felt— spring and autumn.

While following the shore I received a warning that the tide was coming in. I therefore headed north along the hills, up a gradually rising path, to emerge eventually at a place named Iwabuchi. This was still a part of Natashima, and the beach ran on a long way.[415]

I spent that night at a place called, I believe, Kagawa.[416] Past a bamboo grove I saw a nearby island. A villager told me that its name was Ume-ga-saki ("Plum Blossom Point").

> *tachikaeri haru ya kinuran ume ga saki*
> *chirinishi hana to miyuru nami kana*
> Can spring have come again? At Ume-ga-saki
> the waves might well be fallen petals.

This month seemed to me indeed to be what they call a "little spring." The *yamanashi* and *sumomo* were blooming, too.

On the 8th I left before dawn, in the rain, and started up the mountain. I need hardly describe what that was like. There was not even any earth to walk on, only endless rocks that formed the bed of flowing mountain streams. You could see all the way to the bottom of

---

[415] All these place names are now within Bōfu-shi.
[416] In present Yamaguchi-shi.

the deep rock pools, where the colors of the fallen leaves showed that, in truth, "autumn is past."[417]

This mountain rather resembles Saya-no-nakayama in the east, although it is a somewhat more forbidding, and the path over it is drearier. After spending the day crossing it, I arrived at the village of Asa-no-kōri. Below the ridge where the Itagaki fortress used to be there is a temple where I stayed that night.

The chief image enshrined at the temple here is said to be a copy of the one at Zenkōji in Shinano.

> *ame ni kiru waga minoshiro ni kaenanan*
> *koromo oru chō asa no satobito*
> I would gladly exchange this raincloak of mine
> for the hempen garment they say you weave,
> O villagers of Asa-no-sato.[418]

Dawn came, but it was still raining and blowing. Rain had fallen all night long, mixed with hail. That morning I saw snow on the trees of the mountain I had just crossed, while many of the leaves on those further down, closer to the village, were an intense autumn red. The sight was remarkable.

From there I continued on through the hills to the shore. The name of the place was Habu. Southward, high waves were breaking on the beach, and through gaps in the thick clouds I saw mountains looming not far away. This was no doubt the province of Buzen.

The mountain to the north was thickly wooded with pines, and before it stood a shrine. I learned that it enshrined Hachiman. Before its fence a tidal river ran west to east. There was a bridge over it, then a large torii. Pine groves stood about. The place reminded me of the shore at Sumiyoshi. I was passing this shrine when hail suddenly began falling, borne on a powerful west wind. I had no time even to don my *kasa* hat.[419]

---

[417] From *Kokinshū* 310, by Fujiwara no Okikaze.

[418] A play on *asa*, the place name and "hemp."

[419] Ryōshun seems to be thinking of *Kokinshū* 1091 and the moment during the storm in the "Suma" chapter of *Genji monogatari* when Genji's companions have no time to put up their umbrellas (also *kasa*).

One way or another I managed to get to a stretch of beach called Usuha-gata.[420] The hail let up and turned to snow, which made the sand of the beach look particularly pretty. The cormorants clustered on the rocks nearby lent the scene a special touch.

> *ninu iro mo koto ni zo arikeru shima tsu dori*
> *usuha no kata ni yuki wa furitsutsu*
> The colors contrast starkly: cormorants
> on Usuha strand, under falling snow.

The rising tide kept me from continuing along the shore, so I took a mountain trail again and came out at the village of Kojima. After passing through vast pine woods I reached Kofu in Nagato. At Kitahama ("North Beach") some houses faced southeast. After this village I came to the shrine of Jingū Kōgō.[421] It faces south. Beyond it a mountain ridge, called Mikari-yama, juts toward the northeast.

A prominence named Kushi-zaki projects like a sandbar from the curving recess of this bay, and on it stands a Wakamiya shrine.[422] Over ten *chō* eastward from there, in the sea, two islands face each other. They are presumably the Manju ("Flood Tide Jewel") and Kanju ("Ebb Tide Jewel") of old. Now they seem to be called Oitsu and Heitsu.[423]

I heard that this stretch of coast is known as Dan-no-ura because when Jingū Kōgō set out to conquer that foreign land, she put up an altar (*dan*) at this spot; hence its name. The boulder said to be the one she used is beside the path before the shrine, which apparently stands on the site of the Anato Toyora capital.[424] The Funaki-no-matsu, the wood of which she used to build her ship, is said to be there, too.

A shrine that is Jingū Kōgō stands in the ancient capital of Anato Toyora, in the province of Nagato.[425] This divinity of old made a noble vow to deal with the western barbarians; in awe of which I acknowledged, by offering a few poems, the departure of her forty-

---

[420] A location now within Shimonoseki-shi.

[421] Now known as Imi no Miya. Its deities are Chūai, Jingū Kōgō, and Ōjin.

[422] Toyokoto Jinja. It enshrines Ōjin, Takeuchi no Sukune, and others.

[423] According to *Hachiman gudō kun*.

[424] Near the Imi-no-miya shrine precincts is the site of the Toyora palace built by Chūai when he pacified the Kumaso.

[425] The Imi-no-miya. In medieval Japanese rhetoric, shrine and deity are identical.

eight vessels, while my own warships awaited a favorable wind for Tsukushi and Matsura.

> *nishi no umi ya yasuku wataran chihayaburu*
> *kami no atsumeshi funakazu mo gana*
> How safely I might cross the western ocean,
> if mine were the fleet assembled by the mighty gods!

> *toyokuni no oki tsu shimayama eteshi gana*
> *kokoro no gotoku tama to mirubeku*
> If only those islands off the Toyora Shrine were mine!
> To me they would be my wish-fulfilling jewels.

> *wakazakura hana ni sakaeshi miyako yori*
> *nao kono ura o kami ya shimeken*
> From her capital where young cherry trees bloom,
> the divinity came, it seems, to claim this shore.

I offered four poems to the Ichinomiya Sumiyoshi Myōjin of this province, as I had done at the deity's main shrine.[426]

> *ukikumo no oikaze machite ama no hara*
> *kamiyo ni terase hi no hikari min*
> Drifting clouds await a following breeze, the heavens clear:
> O shine as in the age of the gods,
> that I may behold the brilliance of the sun!

> *sue no yo no mabori mo shirushi chihayaburu*
> *kami no naka ni mo hisa ni henureba*
> His protection in ages to come is certain,
> for among the mighty gods he has so long endured.[427]

> *yawarageru hikari morasu na shiranami no*
> *ahaki no hara o ideshi tsukikage*
> Shine nowhere else your tempered light, O moon
> risen from the billows of Awaki-ga-hara![428]

---

426 Presumably the great Sumiyoshi shrine at Naniwa.
427 "He" and "his" include Jingū Kōgō, who is an element of the composite Sumiyoshi deity.

> *kamigaki no matsu no oiki wa waga kuni ni*
> *yamato kotoba no tane ya nariken*
> The ancient pine within the sacred fence
> may have been the source of our Yamato speech.[429]

I pray, O Deity, that you will consider the spirit of these poems and watch over me from the empyrean. That I, foolish though I am, now serve my lord with undivided loyalty must be due solely to my faith in the bright path that your divinity has traced.

The 13th of the 11th month is Sumiyoshi's day, and I therefore made a pilgrimage to the Ichinomiya shrine. I found it even more impressively holy in feeling than the main one, and more marvelously redolent of hallowed antiquity.

From before the shrine I cast my gaze westward far across the sea. The ships bound for Matsura were heading toward the nearby island of Fukura-jima. I was inspired to address another prayer to the deity and to offer another poem.

> *yume no uchi ni mieken kami no misoginu no*
> *sode no hakaze wa nao zo fukubeki*
> The sleeves of the divine robe once visible in dreams
> wafted forth a breeze that surely still blows.

This is what the poem is about. In the 9th month of this year [Ōan 4, 1371] a monk named Sōkyū[430] boarded a boat to come here, but no favorable wind blew. That night an old man of eighty or so, with white hair and beard, and wearing an *eboshi* and pure raiment (*jōe*), came to him, spread his left sleeve wide, and said, "Let this take you where you wish to go." He waved his sleeve, a favorable wind blew, and Sōkyū dreamed that he reached his goal. He understood that the old man had been the Sumiyoshi deity. At dawn the wind turned fair, Sōkyū sailed,

---

428 Awaki-ga-hara is where Izanagi purified himself after emerging from the underworld.

429 This idea and the mention of Awaki-ga-hara, above, recall *Takasago*, the god play by Zeami.

430 A poet (?-after 1380) close to Ryōshun.

and that day he reached Kudamatsu in Suō. That is what he told me. The story suddenly came to mind[431] and inspired this poem.

A messenger came from Fukura[432] to let me know that my ships would not sail today, either. "I took a small boat over the Ama-no-gawa crossing," he reported. "So," I thought, "there is a crossing called that here, too!" I only wished that it might have been next to Hoshiai-no-hama.[433] The idea inspired three poems:[434]

> *aki ni shimo kagirazaranan ama no gawa*
> *ama no obune wa ima no kayou o*
> Let that crossing be not in autumn alone,
> for fishing boats even now cross Ama-no-gawa.

> *matsurabune haya kogi tsukeyo ama no gawa*
> *mare naru naka no watari nari tomo*
> O Matsura boat, row swiftly over Ama-no-gawa,
> however rare may be the lovers' reunion![435]

They say that the Suwa deity and Tanabata are one, so it seems to me that Suwa and Sumiyoshi protect vessels of war; hence these poems.[436]

I offered these poems on the 18th of the 11th month. The festival of Jingū Kōgō came seven days later. On the day of the sacred offerings, an east wind blew from morning on, and the ships sailed for Matsura. This fair wind seemed the answer to my prayers to the gods, and I made two more poems:

---

[431] It sounds like Genji's journey to Akashi in the "Akashi" chapter.

[432] On Hiko-shima.

[433] Hoshiai-no-hama ("Meeting-of-the-Stars Beach") is an *utamakura* in Ise province. Another Ama-no-gawa, an *utamakura* in Settsu (modern Hirakata-shi) is mentioned in *Ise monogatari* 82. These names are associated with Tanabata.

[434] In the source manuscript the space for the third poem is blank.

[435] Tanabata, but also the legend of the Upper Suwa Shrine, according to which the ice on Lake Suwa melts when the male deity (Hikogami, the Upper Shrine [Kamisha]) crosses to the female deity, the Lower Shrine (Shimosha).

[436] According to *Hachiman gudō kun*, both Suwa and Sumiyoshi protected Jingū Kōgō's ships on her expedition. A note in the source manuscript for *Michiyukiburi* (in connection with the *kyō yori ya nao* poem, above) affirms the unity of Suwa and Tanabata, as do other medieval documents.

> *kami matsuru kyoo zo fukikeru asa kochi no*
> *tayori machitsuru tabi no funade wa*
> At last, this festival day, a morning east wind blows,
> and we sail on the long-awaited voyage.

> *katsu koto wa chisato no hoka ni arawarenu*
> *ura fukukaze no shirube machiete*
> Victory is manifest a thousand leagues away,
> now wind blows down the shore to speed us ahead.

Perhaps my poems truly pleased the deity, because the ships sailed as I had hoped.

However, on the 5th of the 12th month several monks came as messengers from Matsura. I heard them talking among themselves. The ships from here had been so slow to arrive that the Matsura men[437] had banded together and decided on a new course of action. There appeared then off Matsura over forty large ships that they took for the ones from here, and they dispersed without further ado. Meanwhile the unidentified ships simply sailed past and disappeared. The next day, the ships from here arrived. The gods must have decided after all not to force any change to the Matsura battle plan. The passage of those ships off Matsura was undoubtedly devised by the gods themselves.

They say that a poem always moves the gods, who seem to have accepted as an offering even my poor flowers of language. The day when those unknown ships passed Matsura must have been the 18th. Our ships arrived on the 19th.

On the 29th of the 11th month I left Kofu in Nagato and moved to Akama-no-seki. I followed the rocky shore under a hill named Hi-no-yama and then passed along the Hayatomo coast. The hill across the water rises above Moji-no-seki in Buzen. The sea here looks about eight *chō* wide. The rising and falling tides race through it faster than the Uji river rapids.

As far as the Anato Toyora capital is concerned, between present Akama-no-seki and Moji-no-seki there was a single mountain, pierced by a narrow passage, like a hole, through which the flood and ebb tides

---

[437] A league of warriors based at Matsura. They are apparently allied against Ryōshun.

flowed, and with houses clustered along the east-west shore: hence the name Anato ("hole passage"). Since Jingū Kōgō's vessel could not pass through it, this Anato mountain drew back in one night once she was ready to sail, thus forming the present Hayatomo strait. The mountain itself, just as it was, became an island in the sea to the west.

Across from this island is Yanagi-no-ura, apparently once the site of a temporary palace (*sato dairi*); so that the area is also known as Dairi-no-hama.[438] West of Akama-no-seki there is a place called Nabe-no-saki that faces Yanagi-no-ura from the north. Akama-no-seki is near the hills that rise to its north, and a knoll there is dotted with houses. It is known as Kame-yama, and on it stands a shrine to the Otoko-yama deity.[439]

To the east there is a temple generally called Amida-dō.[440] After Emperor Antoku passed away off this shore, Shōshō-no-ama, Lord Tomomori's daughter, stayed behind here to pray for the Heike dead, and it became their ancestral temple. It has a likeness of Emperor Antoku. The principal image enshrined is said to be the Amida from Kiyomori's personal chapel at Fukuhara. The Komatsu Minister's [Shigemori's] sacred image (*honzon*) is there, too. I once dreamed of Emperor Antoku, so I prayed for him there several times. I wonder what bond from past lives there can have been between him and me.

Moji-no-seki is across the water from this temple. Next to it, so I was told, is a temple known as Yamadori-no-o ("Pheasant Ridge"). The name is appealing.

> *umi o sae hedatetekeri na yamadori no*
> *onoe no tera no iriai no koe*
> From the hilltop temple the sunset bell rings,
> while, seas between them, the pheasants rest.[441]

It strikes me now that if this Hiku-shima really pulled away from the Anato passage to form the Hayatomo strait, then its length should

---

[438] Maps still show at the spot an urban district named Dairi Honmachi.

[439] Kame-yama Hachimangū, dedicated to Ōjin, Jingū Kōgō, and Chūai.

[440] Amidaji, now a prominent presence in the area.

[441] Yamadori-no-o could also mean "pheasant tail." The poem exploits a well-established poetic conceit, to the effect that a pheasant pair never sleep together but always keep a ridge between them.

match the strait's width. Under one bygone reign or other the governor of the province measured the length of Hiku-shima with a rope and applied the result to the strait. Apparently the length of the island and the width of the strait matched perfectly. That is extremely interesting. The chief priest of the Kōgō Shrine [Imi-no-miya], an old man, told me about it.

From the 1st to the 15th of the 12th month the divinity of the Ichinomiya[442] is present in this Kōgō Shrine, and sacred rites are performed there. I gather that during that period the local people stay at home, refrain from washing their hands and feet, and abstain from intercourse. The young women serving at the shrine apply no blacking to their teeth, nor do they comb their hair. This is very impressive.

On the last day of the 12th month, when the tide withdraws and leaves the seabed along the Hayatomo coast exposed, the chief priest crosses the sea to a rock where *wakame* seaweed grows, cuts a bundle, and takes it back. Apparently the tide then begins immediately to rise. Now, as always in the past, that *wakame* is offered to the shrine. If I am still here then, I will set down an account of the event for the ages.

Colophons

[1] This is the colophon to the middle fascicle (*chūkan*).

This little work (*sōshi*) enjoyed unexpected success in the capital and Kamakura, and for that I was grateful. In response to its poems the Retired Emperor,[443] princes, ministers, senior nobles, and privy gentlemen, too, added poems of their own. In Kamakura, temple abbots likewise sent poems in Chinese. Consequently I need not apologize for it. At first I wrote it out several times myself, but parts kept going astray. Now I am copying it again, but my writing suffers from the palsy (*chūbu*) that afflicts me, and I am embarrassed that it may be difficult to read.

---

[442] Sumiyoshi Jinja in present Shimonoseki. It enshrines the triple sea deity that under-lies the Sumiyoshi cult.

[443] Go-Kōgon, who died in 1374.

[2] I have copied this work repeatedly, but since all those copies went to others I have copied it yet again. My calligraphy has never been easy to read, and a year or two ago I lost what ability I had. I am therefore afraid that my writing may be particularly difficult to make out.

[3] [Originally] written at Zendōji, on the Takeno estate in Chikugo. Eiwa 4.3.18 [1378]. From notes made on horseback during my journey from the capital to Tsukushi.

Against *Taiheiki:*

NANTAIHEIKI

Imagawa Ryōshun

INTRODUCTION

Overview

The oldest extant copy of Imagawa Ryōshun's *Nantaiheiki* (1402), made by a Mito scholar, dates from Jōkyō (1684-1688). The copyist also gave the work its title, added subsection headings, and provided sometimes helpful glosses. The title refers to the vast chronicle of the fourteenth-century wars. However, Ryōshun's outraged dismissal of *Taiheiki* is only his work's most immediately visible topic, not its purpose.

Nantaiheiki matches no recognized medieval genre such as *kikōbun* or *gunkimono* (travel or battle accounts), and it is difficult. Ryōshun's language is too veiled at times to be readily intelligible to anyone not already familiar with the complex circumstances at issue. This inevitably tentative translation relies on the *Gunsho ruijū* edition;[444] on a modern translation (perforce not necessarily clearer than the original, but accompanied by the genealogical charts gratefully adapted below) published anonymously on the Internet;[445] and on other reading mentioned in the notes. In order to make it more readable and to reduce the number of notes, Ryōshun's titles or bare honorifics have been replaced in nearly every case by names.

Nantaiheiki is a document of exceptional historical value and unusual personal intensity. Ryōshun wrote it to protest his innocence in the turmoil of the 1390s, especially the Ōei Disturbance (*Ōei no ran*). Is he indeed innocent of all charges? Or is *Nantaiheiki*, as Ogawa Takeo argued, an attempt to disguise his leading role?[446] Was Ryōshun, or was he not, implicated in a plot to depose Ashikaga Yoshimitsu in

---

[444] *Gunsho ruijū* 22 (*Kassen no bu*).

[445] http://homepage1.nifty.com/sira/nantaiheiki/index.html

[446] Ogawa Takeo, *Ashikaga Yoshimitsu*, Chūō Kōron Shinsha (Chūkō Shinsho 2179), 2012, p. 193.

favor of Ashikaga Ujimitsu or (after 1398) Mitsukane, the Kanto kubō?[447]

He wrote in the opening lines, "It is incumbent upon a man to know what his forebears were like and what they amounted to in the world." The critical issues behind this sentence are the martial merit of Ryōshun's line (especially his father's) and, above all, the relationship between his line and that of the Ashikaga shoguns. The two are related. No doubt Ryōshun castigates the *Taiheiki* author for having tarnished the honor of the Imagawa by slighting their loyal deeds in the service of the shogun, but such is the trajectory of *Nantaiheiki* that his complaints effectively emphasize his own loyalty. Ryōshun repeatedly reminds the reader, in one way or another, that his loyalty to the shogun has never wavered. This is where his protestations of innocence begin.

The following early passage conveys the sensitivity of the issue even in Ryōshun's youth. It also identifies one source of the tension between him and Yoshimitsu.

> Someone once showed Yoshiakira [Yoshimitsu's predecessor] a family tree that identified my line as senior to the Shogun's. Yoshiakira made no secret of his displeasure. Of course, now that the Shogun governs the realm, everyone in this land of Japan owes him a debt of gratitude, and it is only right that my house in particular should defer to him. Tadayoshi [Takauji's brother] often warned me against aspiring to a standing in keeping with my origins, but urged me instead to assist the realm by cultivating the art of letters and to establish myself thanks to my achievement in that field.

Nothing could draw a sharper line between power (politics, government, war) and mere prestige (poetry). Tadayoshi gladly left a

---

[447] Yoshimochi formally replaced Yoshimitsu as shogun in 1394, but he remained insignificant until Yoshimitsu's death in 1408. Mitsukane was Ujimitsu's son. The title "kubō" could designate the senior Ashikaga in either Kyoto (the shogun) or the Kanto (Kamakura). Takauji used it first, but it came to be used more often for the senior Ashikaga in the Kanto, especially after Motouji's time. The Kanto kubō was distinct from the Kanto (or Kamakura) *kanrei* ("deputy shogun"), an office held by a senior Ashikaga vassal. By the time of *Nantaiheiki*, the title *kanrei* had become hereditary in the Uesugi line of *shitsuji* (chief of staff in Kamakura).

potential Ashikaga rival the "art of letters," which Ryōshun indeed mastered. However, Ryōshun was also an exceptionally able warrior and administrator. As Yoshimitsu's administrator (*tandai*) in Kyushu from 1371 to 1395, he brought the island under Ashikaga control and governed it with outstanding success. In the end, this success contributed to his undoing.

Suspicious and arbitrary, and with pretensions to imperial grandeur, Yoshimitsu came to see Ryōshun as a threat. The political and military developments of the 1390s (see below) then entangled Ryōshun in their complexities. In 1395 Yoshimitsu suddenly recalled him to Kyoto and dismissed him from office. Ryōshun was given no chance to defend himself and, in reward for his service, received just half of the province of Suruga.

Things went from bad to worse when the great daimyo Ōuchi Yoshihiro turned against Yoshimitsu, only to die at Sakai in 1399 (the Ōei Disturbance). Suspecting Ryōshun of complicity in the maneuvering mentioned to depose the shogun (since 1394 Yoshimochi in name, but really still Yoshimitsu) in favor of the Kanto kubō (since 1398 Ashikaga Mitsukane), Yoshimitsu ordered Ryōshun killed, although the order was not carried out. Instead Yoshimitsu summoned him to Kyoto and spared him in recognition of his achievement in Kyushu. However, Ryōshun's career was over and his property gone. He retained only the mastery of letters that Ashikaga Tadayoshi had urged on him his youth.

Near the end of *Nantaiheiki* Ryōshun observes, "A man must give loyal service consonant with his proper station. Service beyond it is sure to cause resentment." That is the theme of the work. Such is the wisdom of age and bitter experience.

Had Ryōshun invited that experience? The movement to depose Yoshimitsu was fueled at once by the ambition of Ashikaga Ujimitsu and his successor Mitsukane, and by widespread dissatisfaction with Yoshimitsu himself. In *Nantaiheiki* Ryōshun makes no secret of sharing that dissatisfaction. He even mentions believing that the realm would be better off without Yoshimitsu. Ogawa Takeo took that as an unintentional but unmistakable acknowledgment of guilt,[448] but one can also take it the other way. Would Ryōshun have so blurted out a truth that he was otherwise exerting all his ingenuity to hide? On the face of it, the passage reads as though the answer were self-evidently no: despite his personal objections to Yoshimitsu's ways, Ryōshun always remained loyal to him and his line. He "stayed completely out of it."

Ogawa's case against Ryōshun, although strong, above all shows only that everyone believed Ryōshun to be involved. In this regard it is worth considering Ryōshun's intended reader. He wrote at the end of *Nantaiheiki*, "I have set this down in order to urge care and caution on my descendants. No one is to see it while I live. Beware! Beware! (*osoroshi osoroshi*)."

"Beware!" indeed. *Nantaiheiki* accuses Yoshimitsu, still alive in 1402, of rank injustice. Ryōshun's anger, tempered in writing by caution and dignity, is what gives so apparently disparate a work a compelling unity. This unity breaks down strangely if his denial of complicity is false. Did he write with such intensity in order to deceive his heirs?

The demonstrable truth will always remain beyond reach. *Nantaiheiki* is either a passionate attempt to "set the record straight" or an eloquently contrived attempt at self-justification. Either way, it conveys a picture of a life lived to the end honorably, through very troubled times, whether in fact or in an old warrior's combative imagination.

The late 1390s: the Ōei Disturbance

Major factors underlying Ryōshun's misfortunes in the last decade of the fourteenth century include the Kanto kubō's designs on the office of shogun; the pride and ambition of the daimyo Ōuchi Yoshihiro; the hostility of such figures as Shiba Yoshiyuki and Ryōshun's nephew Yasunori; and generally rising dissatisfaction over Yoshimitsu's style of government.

---

[448] Ogawa, *Ashikaga Yoshimitsu*, p. 197.

The issue of shogunal succession had arisen already in the early 1350s, in the feud (blandly mentioned in *Nantaiheiki* and summarized in the introduction to *Ojima no kuchizusami*) between Ashikaga Takauji and his brother Tadayoshi. As Kanto deputy shogun (*kanrei*), Takauji's much younger brother Motouji (1340-1367) is not usually thought to have coveted the office of shogun. However, Ryōshun wrote in *Nantaiheiki* that, after the deaths of Takauji and Tadayoshi,

> Yoshiakira may have feared that Kamakura might declare Motouji Shogun on its own. Foreseeing disaster for the realm, he prayed to the gods, and Motouji died before him. That is what I have heard.

Thus in 1367 the gods answered Yoshiakira's prayers with either sickness or poison. Whatever Motouji's personal intentions may have been, his son Ujimitsu definitely maneuvered to replace Yoshimitsu, and Ujimitsu's son Mitsukane (kubō after 1398) inherited his ambition. In the 1390s, rivalry between Kyoto and Kamakura became acute once more, and Yoshimitsu suspected Ryōshun of active involvement in favor of the Kanto. The crisis came in with the Ōei Disturbance (1399).

In Ōan 3 (1370), under the recently installed Yoshimitsu, Hosokawa Yoriyuki (Yoshimitsu's chief of staff [*shitsuji*] or deputy shogun [*kanrei*]) had selected Ryōshun as Kyushu administrator,[449] in effect the shogun's alter ego (*bunshin*) in that turbulent region.[450] Twenty-five years later, in Ōei 2.7 (1395), Yoshimitsu recalled him to Kyoto and, at Shiba Yoshiyuki's urging, replaced him with Yoshiyuki's son-in-law, Shibukawa Mitsuyori. Yoshimitsu may have feared Ryōshun's power, but another factor (apart from Shibukawa's maneuvering) was probably Ōuchi Yoshihiro's desire for the office.

The Ōuchi of Suō, the most powerful daimyo house in western Honshu, supported Yoritomo early and eventually joined the Rokuhara administrator's inner council (*hyōjōshū*).[451] Ōuchi Hiroyo (1325-80)

---

[449] Sakurai Eiji, *Muromachibito no seishin* (Nihon rekishi, vol. 12), Kodansha, 2001, p. 51.

[450] Ryōshun's time in Kyushu is covered in Kawazoe Shōji, *Imagawa Ryōshun*, Yoshikawa Kōbunkan, 1964, pp. 84-114.

[451] This account of Ōuchi Yoshihiro and his rebellion (the Ōei Disturbance) draws on Ogawa, *Ashikaga Yoshimitsu*, pp. 177-187.

turned against the bakufu during the Kannō Anarchy (1350-1352) but submitted to Yoshiakira in Jōji 2 (1363). He then became protector of Nagato as well. In time the Ōuchi also acquired Iwami.

Yoshihiro (1356-99), Hiroyo's eldest son and successor, a brilliant warrior and another devotee of waka and renga, helped Ryōshun to pacify Kyushu. In Kōryaku 2 (1380) he became protector of Buzen in northern Kyushu and, extraordinarily for a daimyo, received the junior fourth rank.

Yoshihiro served Yoshimitsu in Kyoto and commanded troops during the Meitoku Disturbance. It was he who killed Yamana Ujikiyo at Uchino. In reward he received Izumi and Kii. The reconciliation between the Northern and Southern Courts in Meitoku 3 (1393) succeeded largely thanks to his mediation. Yoshimitsu so admired him that in Meitoku 4 he ordered him treated like a man of his own house. When Yoshimitsu (nominally) renounced the world in Ōei 2.7 (1395), Yoshihiro followed suit. Ryōshun was suddenly replaced as Kyushu administrator at about that time. Yoshimitsu is said to have heeded Yoshihiro's denunciation of Ryōshun as being in league with the Kanto. Ryōshun wrote in *Nantaiheiki*, after discussing some sort of difficulty with Ōtomo Chikayo, "Unfortunately, in Kyushu and in this connection as well, for reasons both private and public, it is Ōuchi's schemes that led to my leaving Kyushu."

Thereafter Yoshimitsu, perhaps wary of Yoshihiro's growing power and self-assertiveness, turned against him. When in Ōei 4.3 (1397) the new Kyushu administrator was unable to quell an uprising by Shōni Sadayori and Kikuchi Taketomo, Yoshihiro was ordered to deal with the matter instead. After doing so he did not return to Kyoto. *Ōei ki* (a brief account of the Ōei Disturbance) records talk that Yoshihiro may have heard before leaving the capital, to the effect that the uprising was a trap devised by Yoshimitsu to destroy him. In Sakai, later on, he spoke of having been shown in Kyushu an order in Yoshimitsu's own hand to kill him. His rebellion may have been in part a response to intolerable provocation.

Yoshihiro reached Sakai (in Izumi, one of his provinces) from the west on Ōei 6.10.13 (1399) and fortified himself there. He hoped that Ashikaga Mitsukane, who had recently succeeded to the office of Kanto kubō, would lead an army to Kyoto. Many eastern daimyo, not to mention the remaining Southern Court diehards, would gladly have seen the last of Yoshimitsu. He also appealed to Enryakuji and Kōfukuji.

Yoshimitsu sent an envoy to Sakai to dispel Yoshihiro's suspicion. When the mission failed, he ordered Yoshihiro suppressed. On Ōei 6.11.8 his army camped at Iwashimizu Hachiman. On 11.21 Mitsukane left Kamakura and got as far as Musashi Fuchū, where the Kanto deputy shogun, Uesugi Norisada, stopped him. Mitsukane was unable to raise any significant reinforcements from Shimōsa. Meanwhile, forces from Tanba, Mino, and Ōmi advanced separately and were crushed by Ashikaga allies one by one. Yoshimitsu's army besieged Sakai, and on 12.21 the fortress fell. Hatakeyama Mitsuie took Yoshihiro's head.

According to *Nantaiheiki*, however, Yoshihiro had in mind an alliance against Yoshimitsu well before 1395. Ryōshun reports him as saying:

> Here in the capital I see nothing good in any of the other daimyo. If you and I together were to unite Kyushu and the western provinces, lasting peace would follow. After all, Ōtomo is a Kyushu daimyo. You would have nothing to fear if we were to unite under your leadership.

Yoshihiro even married into the family of Nakaaki, a younger brother of Ryōshun whom Ryōshun had adopted as a son. That, too, suggests a planned Ōuchi-Ōtomo-Imagawa alliance. Ryōshun's refusal to join it (if he did refuse) may have provoked Yoshihiro's hostility, hence Yoshihiro's claim in 1395 that Ryōshun was in league with Mitsukane.[452] Then, in 1399, Ryōshun's nephew Yasuyori made the same accusation on the grounds that Ryōshun's sons had been deliberately slow to reach Sakai.

After Yoshihiro's death, Yoshimitsu suddenly ordered Ryōshun back to Kyushu. Ryōshun ignored him, retired (*inkyo*), and left for Tōtōmi. Sakurai Eiji suggested that he had understood the order to mean exile,[453] but he may only have been trying to stay alive. In *Nantaiheiki* he wrote with bitter irony, "The Shogun should have

---

[452] Sakurai, *Muromachibito no seishin*, p. 56.
[453] Sakurai, *Muromachibito no seishin*, p. 57.

packed me off alone by pirate bark to Kyushu," meaning that Yoshimitsu should have delivered him on the spot to his Kyushu enemies. A few lines later he repeated the same angrily ironic wish that Yoshimitsu had gotten it over with once and for all.

Mitsukane withdrew to Kamakura, while Ryōshun left Tōtōmi and lay low at Fujisawa in Sagami. In Ōei 7.1 (1400) Yoshimitsu ordered the Kanto deputy shogun Uesugi Norisada to have Ryōshun killed. Norisada feared that Ryōshun's presence in Fujisawa might hinder reconciliation between Kyoto and Kamakura and advised him to return to Tōtōmi. Ryōshun did so. Yoshimitsu then summoned him to Kyoto. Ryōshun delayed as long as he could and tried to send his adopted son Nakaaki instead, but in the end he complied (Ōei 7.9.4). Yoshimitsu spared his life, but Yasunori was now protector (*shugo*) of both Suruga and Tōtōmi, and the head of the Imagawa house. Ryōshun's active life was over.[454]

Sakurai Eiji, whose work appeared in 2001, found on the whole little reason to disbelieve Ryōshun's assurances that he had remained loyal to Yoshimitsu throughout, despite his admittedly grave misgivings. However, in 2012 Ogawa Takeo, citing evidence from an unpublished section of *Yoshida-ke tsukinami ki* (a record kept by the father and son Yoshida Kaneteru and Kaneatsu), declared Ryōshun guilty of complicity with Mitsukane.[455] This evidence indeed suggests that Ryōshun may not have been as wholly innocent as he claimed in *Nantaiheiki*. (How could he have been pure as driven snow, under such interminably tangled circumstances?) What it also suggests, however, is that since everyone believed him to be deeply involved, whether he

---

[454] Sakurai, *Muromachibito no seishin*, pp. 58-59. According to Ogawa (*Ashikaga Yoshimitsu*, pp. 183-184), citing *Yoshida-ke tsukinami ki*, in 1400 Yoshimitsu deposed the regent Nijō Morotsugu, the son of Nijō Yoshimoto, and forced Morotsugu's elder brother, the head of Shōgoin, to sever all relations with him. The only reason can have been that Yoshimoto and Morotsugu had been close to Ōuchi Yoshihiro. He also dealt harshly with Setsudō Soboku, the abbot of Myōshinji, because Setsudō had been Yoshihiro's spiritual adviser. The temple property was confiscated, and the grounds were incorporated into Shōren-in. Meanwhile, Morotsugu was reduced to near-starvation.

[455] Ogawa, *Ashikaga Yoshimitsu*, pp. 183-204.

was or not, the threat of Yoshimitsu's wrath may have made this belief particularly attractive.

A retrospective poem

The introduction to *Michiyukiburi* mentions that the major waka poet Shōtetsu (1381-1459) considered Ryōshun his teacher. In *Shōtetsu monogatari* (ca. 1450), Shōtetsu recorded a moment from a poetry contest (*hōhen no kai*) held at some time after the Ōei Disturbance.[456] Those present at such a gathering orally critiqued an anonymously submitted pair of poems, declaring one of them the winner. The set topic (*dai*) on this occasion was *keizetsu koi* ("love after the last parting").

The company considered this difficult poem:

> *kakete uki isomatsu ga ne no adanami wa*
> *waga mi ni kaeru sode no urakaze*

Shōtetsu's account suggests that not everyone present understood it. However, the issue is clearly the anger and regret that linger after the end of a love affair. Perhaps the poem could be half-usefully paraphrased, "The cruelly fickle waves breaking over the roots of the pine on the rocky coast return to my sleeves on the shore wind."

All except Shōtetsu dismissed it out of hand. Ryōshun, weeping, remained silent. "Yes, that's the way it is" (*ge ni sa nite haberi*), he said eventually. That settled it. All agreed that the poem had won. It was Tamemasa's. Need one refrain from imagining that Ryōshun's tears sprang from memories still more deeply painful?

---

[456] Hisamatsu Sen'ichi and Nishio Minoru, eds., *Karon shū, Nōgakuron shū* (Nihon koten bungaku taikei, vol. 65), Iwanami Shoten, 1961, p. 171.

NANTAIHEIKI

PART ONE

1. It behooves a man to know his forebears

Foolish as I am, I seem not to know even my own heart. By that I do not mean that I am unaware of feeling, for example, regret, desire, dislike, pity, and so on. Rather I mean that, properly, I should know what these feelings signify. Similarly, it is incumbent upon a man to know what his forebears were like and what they amounted to in the world. Whatever may be the case for others, I myself know nothing of anyone further back than my father. However, I will relate the scraps that I remember from what my late father [Imagawa Norikuni] happened to tell me about the past. I realize on reflection that my children and grandchildren must know even less about him than I do.

There once lived one Yamana Tokiuji, the father of the Ujikiyo killed during Meitoku [1390-1394] at the battle of Uchino.[457] Tokiuji often told his sons, "I have no doubt that my descendants will be declared enemies of the court. Why? Because I began to make my way in the world only in Kenmu [1334-1336], thanks to the Emperor then reigning. In Genkō [1331-1334] and earlier I was more or less a simple commoner[458] from Yamana in Kōzuke. I experienced the hardship of making a living and learned the insignificance of my origins. I have also known the trials of battle. Therefore I also know what I owe my present lord (*kono miyo*) and where I stand in the world. Even so, though, I realize that I am sometimes tempted to make light of my superiors

---

[457] After Tokiuji's death (1371) Ashikaga Yoshimitsu worked to reduce the power of the Yamana, who were reputed to control a sixth of Japan. This effort eventually provoked the incident known as the Meitoku Disturbance. In 1391 Ujikiyo, Tokiuji's son, advanced on Kyoto but was killed at Uchino by Ōuchi Yoshihiro, in a battle against such great Ashikaga allies as the Ōuchi, the Hosokawa, and the Hatakeyama.

[458] *Tami hyakushō*: less a "peasant" than, at that time, an ordinary, local man who probably had arms and armor.

and to belittle others. My sons, in their time, acknowledge no debt to their sovereign (*kimi*) or to their father.[459] They care only to stand out personally and to rise above their station. They are therefore sure to come under suspicion from on high." His sons heard what he said. Sure enough, they became enemies of the court.[460]

In those days men seem to have grasped the larger picture well. In truth, this man could neither read nor write, but he spoke sense. Yes, I, too, at that age thought little of what my father kept telling me. It annoyed me more than anything else. Looking back, however, I realize that he was right every time. I am old now, and to my sons I am in my second childhood, but they may well reconsider once I am gone. That is why I have written down some of what my father said, omitting whatever I fear having misremembered. I have included only reliable memories or ones for which I have evidence.

2. The Gods in their time had only two children

The gods in their time had only two children, whose generations of descendants became kings (*kokuō*), ministers, or commoners. The lesser among these, useless otherwise, tilled the soil or went into service and came to lack a surname. Since we still know only about my father and nothing about our forebears two or three generations back, my sons could end up no better than men without a surname. That is why I have written down what little I have heard.

3. The descendants of Hachimantarō Yoshiie

"Hachiman-dono" means Lord [Minamoto] Yoshiie, Governor of Mutsu and Chinjufu Shogun. His son, Yoshikuni, was followed by Yoshiyasu, Yoshikane, Yoshiuji, Yasuuji, and so on. Yasuuji was known as Hiraishi-dono; his son, Yoriuji, as Jibu-no-Taifu-dono; and Yoriuji's son, Ietoki, as Iyo-no-kami. Ietoki's son, Sadauji, was referred to as Sanuki-no-nyūdō-dono. His sons were Takauji and Tadayoshi. Despite being

---

[459] It is impossible to be sure whether emperor or shogun is meant by *kono miyo* and *kimi*, or even whether any distinction between the two is intended.
[460] A reference to the Meitoku Disturbance (1391).

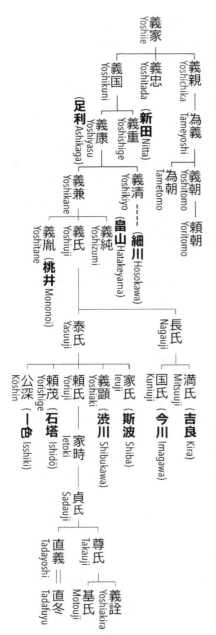

Yasuuji's third son, Yoriuji followed his father as head of the house.[461] The men of Owari, the Shibukawa, and so on, his elder brothers, all became his juniors (*soshi*). [462] The Hosokawa and Hatakeyama lines seem to have parted after Yoshikane.

Yoshikane was over eight feet tall and supremely powerful. He was said really to be a son of Tametomo, [463] although Yoshiyasu had brought him up from infancy. Yoshikane kept this quiet, so that no one knew. He became particularly close to Yoritomo but feigned madness in order to avoid further attention, and he lived his life without incident. He is reported to have declared, "My spirit will possess my descendants for a time and madden them." For that matter, Yoshiie wrote in his testament (*okibumi*): "I shall be reborn seven generations hence and seize the realm." That generation was Ietoki's, who, no doubt realizing that the time was not yet ripe, prayed as follows to Hachiman: "Cut my life short, I beg, and have us seize the realm within three

---

461 Ryōshun is suggesting that (as he states below) his line is senior to the Ashikaga (Yoriuji's).

462 Yasuuji's first son, Ieuji, founded the Shiba line and Yoriaki the Shibukawa. Both were elder brothers of Yoriuji.

463 Whose exploits are narrated in *Hōgen monogatari*.

generations." He then slit his belly.[464] The testament written in his own hand gives further details. My late father and I read it in the presence of both Takauji and Tadayoshi. They said that they owed their conquest of the realm to this prayer. Ambition working over generations had made them masters of the world.

Someone once showed Yoshiakira a family tree that identified my line as senior to the Shogun's.[465] Yoshiakira made no secret of his displeasure. Of course, now that the Shogun governs the realm, all in this land of Japan owe him a debt of gratitude, and it is only right that my house in particular should defer to him. Tadayoshi often warned me against aspiring to a standing in keeping with my origins, but urged me instead to assist the realm by cultivating the art of letters and to establish myself thanks to my achievement in that field. Ashikaga Tadafuyu still held the title of Kunai-no-Daibu when he reported this to Hatakeyama Tadamune, Isshiki Tadauji, and myself, and I imagine that others heard it, too.[466]

4. The Imagawa lineage

As to our ancestors, Nagauji, the son of Yoshiuji, was the first to bear the surname Kira. His son was Kira Mitsuuji, whose younger brother, Kuniuji, first bore the surname Imagawa. Sadayoshi[467] and Motouji, my grandfather,[468] were uncle and nephew. Kira Mitsuyoshi[469] and my late father were second cousins. Sekiguchi, Irino, and Kida were Kuniuji's sons. They were descended from younger brothers of my grandfather. For my father they were the sons of cousins. Only Motouji succeeded to the Imagawa name.

---

[464] This happened when Adachi Yasumori was killed in 1285. Documents describing Ietoki's testament survive at Daigoji.

[465] For a discussion of what makes this true, see Sakurai, *Muromachibito no seishin*, p. 50.

[466] Takauji's son Tadafuyu was adopted by Tadayoshi. The comment on his office suggests that this happened before Tadafuyu turned against the Ashikaga, probably before 1350.

[467] Mitsuuji's eldest son.

[468] Imagawa Kuniuji's eldest son and the father of Norikuni, Ryōshun's father.

[469] Sadayoshi's eldest son.

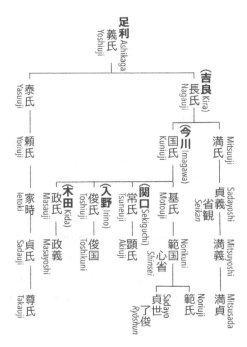

Sekiguchi was an Ogasawara on his mother's side, and he inherited that property. Irino Geishū, who was related on his mother's side to the Ōtawa and Miura people, succeeded to a part of the Irino property and so acquired its name. These are the folk referred to as the Kawabata Imagawa. Motouji's younger sisters all married into the court nobility, and their sons are the Ishikawa Imagawa, also known as the Nagoya. For my father they were brothers, since Motouji had adopted them. During Kenmu he therefore applied to Ashikaga Takauji to make them all one line.

I gather also that the locality of Soga in the province of Ise belongs to a son-in-law of Motouji—a man known as Ishikawa Sanmi, whose father was a son of Hōshi-no-Miya. The father of Isshiki Shōtarō Nyūdō was a yamabushi. He became my father's uncle when Motouji took him as a son-in-law. Isshiki Nyūdō and my father were cousins.

5. Donation of the Imagawa estate to Shōbōin

Yoshiuji had ceded the Imagawa estate to the young Nagauji, to support his clothing needs. However, it was decided that the Imagawa estate came under the control of the heir to the Kira estate. Motouji therefore fell out with the Kira house, and perhaps it was his displeasure that moved my late father in his time to form an alliance with Kira Sadayoshi; whereupon the hostility ceased.

The estate then passed to me, and since Bukkai Zenji of Tōfukuji was my teacher, I donated it in perpetuity to the sub-temple of Shōbōin. The head monk there was an uncle of Takagi Nyūdō, who had

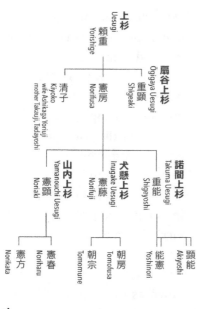

managed the Imagawa estate ever since the Imagawa took possession of it, hence the close bond between us. I therefore donated it in perpetuity, to support prayers for the seven generations of ancestors before me. However, should any descendant of mine value this land from which our name derives, he should apply to the Kubō to exchange it for some other, more advantageous private holding. If the Ashikaga approve, the sub-temple's wishes should prevail. This document can serve to authenticate the arrangement.

6. Miraculous signs regarding Takauji and Tadayoshi

So far I have only mentioned Takauji, but now I will say more about him. Two mountain doves flew down when he received his first bath.[470] One perched on his left shoulder, the other on the dipper handle. Two mountain doves came down when Tadayoshi received *his* first bath. One perched on the dipper handle and one on the rim of the water bucket. In deference to earlier generations these things were not made public. Apparently only senior members of the current generation were informed.

7. Takauji's decision to rebel

A wonder occurred during Genkō [1331-1334], while Takauji was on his way up to the capital.[471] At Yatsuhashi in Mikawa he was almost alone

---

[470] The mountain dove (*yamabato*) was considered a messenger of Hachiman and a symbol of the shogun.

[471] In 1333 Takauji led a Kamakura Bakufu army to attack the Funanoe fortress where Go-Daigo and Nawa Nagatoshi were entrenched, but at Shinomura in Tanba he turned

one evening when a woman with a white robe over her head came to him and said, "Unless disaster intervenes, your descendants will endure for seven generations. Rain and wind will confirm this to you whenever you go into battle." She then vanished like a figure in a dream. Thereafter he resolved to raise vigorous rebellion.

He sent Uesugi Norifusa[472] to announce his decision first to Kira Sadayoshi. Kira replied, "I kept wondering whether you would ever do it! Splendid!" and so on. Then he discussed the matter with others as well. Perhaps Norifusa had been privately urging Takauji to act ever since Takauji set out from the Kanto. Apparently he told only Uesugi of the plan enjoined upon himself and his brother by Iemochi and Sadauji [father and grandfather]. Uesugi gave it his all and died during the Kawara battle. He was the grandfather of Uesugi Tomomune.[473]

8. Taiheiki *is riddled with errors*

Taiheiki claims that because Nagoe Takaie, the commander, had died in the battle for Rokuhara, it is Ashikaga Takauji who surrendered to the deposed Emperor [Go-Daigo]. This is absurd.[474] Deeply committed as he was to Go-Daigo's side, the author must not have known what really happened and resorted to speculation. He was a fool. This passage should be deleted.

Taiheiki is riddled throughout with errors and fabrications. Of old, Echin Shōnin of Hōshōji first presented the work's more than thirty scrolls to Tadayoshi at Tōjiji. Tadayoshi had Gen'e Hōin read it out to him. Its many flaws and errors moved Tadayoshi to say, "As far as I can see, this work contains an extraordinary number of errors. Additions and cuts are required. In the meantime, it cannot be allowed to circulate." The work therefore became unavailable.

In more recent times it has been continued. So many people

---

back and instead took Rokuhara, the Bakufu's Kyoto headquarters. See also *Baishōron*, "Takauji Attacks Rokuhara."

472 An elder brother of Kiyoko, his mother.

473 The Kanto deputy shogun (*kanrei*) when Ryōshun wrote *Nantaiheiki*.

474 No such passage exists in surviving *Taiheiki* texts. All report that Takauji had decided to attack Rokuhara before he ever left Kamakura. Actually, none of the *Taiheiki* passages about which Ryōshun complained survives in that form.

demanded additions that it now contains laudatory mentions of countless figures. Nonetheless, all this added praise amounts to hardly more than a list of names. Many must still be missing.

By now several Shoguns have held sway.[475] I have brought up as I saw fit even events of thirty or forty years ago—ones for which no evidence survives. Alas, I only hope that the work will be denied official recognition as long as old men from that time are still alive.

By and large, *Heike monogatari* is based on the sound *Gotoku ki*,[476] but it is still felt to contain errors. As for *this* work, eighty or ninety percent of it is unquestionbly fiction. In broad outline it is probably accurate enough, but it contains too many falsehoods about one man or another's meritorious deeds.[477] No wonder that Echin, who had witnessed the events of the time, recognized how much of it was wrong as soon as he heard Gen'e Hōin read it aloud at Tadayoshi's residence. I am by no means alone in criticizing it.

9. Taiheiki *omits many who followed Takauji to Kyushu*

The names of many who withdrew to Kyushu with Takauji[478] appear to be missing from *Taiheiki*. The absence of their names does a disservice to their descendants. I should like to see their houses submit written statements on the subject. Such matters merit condemnation. In *Musōki*,[479] Hosokawa Kazuuji mentioned people remarking at the time that *Taiheiki* contains hidden biases. He also observed, apparently, that the names of many who had fought valorously on the way back up from Kyushu to the capital were missing.

---

[475] Ryōshun wrote *Nantaiheiki* under the fourth, Yoshimochi.

[476] The *Gotoku-no-Kanja no ki* attributed in *Tsurezuregusa* 226 to Shinano-no-Zenji Yukinaga as the source of *Heike monogatari*.

[477] Ryōshun's overriding interest lies much less in "history" as now understood than in what was critical to a medieval warrior: the correct recording of individual deeds in war, particularly those of the Imagawa.

[478] On Kenmu 1.27 (1336), Uesugi Norifusa and others died to save Takauji from an attack by Go-Daigo's forces. Takauji managed to return to the capital, thanks to Hosokawa Jōzen and others, but he could not hold it. Some days later he retreated to Hyōgo and from there to Kyushu.

[479] "Record of Dreams," unidentified.

10. Takauji's prayer at Shinomura

Taiheiki notes that when Takauji raised his banner before the Shinomura Hachiman shrine in Tanba, [480] Hikita Myōgen wrote his prayer. When Takauji and Tadayoshi each offered an arrow to the shrine, the two officials (*yakunin*) present were Isshiki [Yoriyuki?] and Imagawa Nakatsukasa-no-taifu. There is a story behind this, and those not orally informed are likely to err. Should *Taiheiki* not mention it? This Nakatsukasa-no-taifu was my elder brother, Noriuji.

11. Taiheiki *should include* rakugaki[481]

There was this *rakugaki*:

> *imagawa ni hosokawa soite idenureba*
> *horiguchi kirete nitta nagaruru*
> When New River [Imagawa] joined Skinny River [Hosokawa],
> the floodgate [Horiguchi] burst, and Nitta [Yoshisada] flowed.[482]

Likewise, *Heike* has:

> *akajirushi shiro tanagoi ni torikaete*
> *kashira ni shi maku konyūdō kana*
> Ah, the little novice, who traded the red badge
> for a white towel wrapped around his head![483]

---

[480] On Genkō 4.27 (1333) Takauji, having decided to attack Rokuhara, offered a *kaburaya* arrow, with a solemn prayer (*ganmon*), at the Shinomura Hachiman Shrine. His younger brother Tadayoshi and the other senior warriors present then offered so many arrows, together with prayers for victory, that they were heaped high before the shrine.

[481] Anonymous, satirical comments scrawled on gates or walls.

[482] This verse seems to refer to an exploit touched on in the *Baishōron* account of "The Battle between Yoshisada and Takauji." Horiguchi Sadamitsu was one of Uesugi Yoshisada's warriors.

[483] The red badge is Taira allegiance and the white towel Genji. This verse seems to allude to Kiso Yoshinaka's chaotic behavior in the capital and Yoshitune's eventual rescue of Cloistered Emperor Go-Shirakawa (*Heike monogatari* [*Kakuichi-bon*], books 8 and 9). However, the verse does not occur in the *Kakuichi-bon*. The *Engyō-bon* includes this version in its counterpart passage: *shiro sabite/ aka tanagoi ni/ torikaete/ kashira ni makeru/ konyūdō kana.*

Amusing items like these being available, it would honor the descendants of the men involved if they were to be written into the text. "Hosokawa" refers to Hosokawa Jōzen.

12. Norikuni dubs his sword Happa-ō

In those days Takauji[484] was camped at Tōji, while the deposed Emperor [Go-Daigo] was on Mount Hiei. Imperial [Go-Daigo] men barred the access points from the four directions, and the Ashikaga force was running out of food. To the east rose Sekizan and Amida-ga-mine; to the south was the Uji road; to the west was Oi-no-yama; and the Nagasaka passage ran to the north. The commanders Takauji sent out were defeated one after another.

My late father started toward Amida-ga-mine. Battles ensued before Suwa and Imahie,[485] and while sweeping the enemy before him he took an arrow in his left shoulder. Two or three days later, Takauji dispatched men to Shinomiya-gawara, and my father was sent forth once more. He removed his left armor sleeve.

First, Niki Yoshinaga set out for Sakaguchi. Then my late father was ordered to Meguri-Jizō, on the road to Miidera. Yoshinaga said, "The battle today will be to the death." "Of course," my father replied. Both fought all day.

When Niki's force withdrew, one Aiso, a vastly powerful Ise man belonging to the Ōsaka force rode up alone behind my father. Such was the intensity of the fight that my father never noticed him. Aiso severed the neckplate of Aki-no-Nyūdō, who fell from his horse. He then cut away the thirty-six battle arrows carried by Noriuji [Ryōshun's elder brother], there beside Aki-no-Nyūdō.

My father turned his mount and attacked with his sword. His helmet shattered, Aiso clung to his horse's neck and brandished his own. He cut both plates of my father's left armguard (*kote*), then

---

[484] After his return to the capital from Kyushu.

[485] Suwa Jinja, in present Shimogyō-ku, was founded in 801 by Tamuramaro, restored by Minamoto no Yoshitsune in 1186, and damaged in the Kenmu wars. Imahie Jinja, in Higashiyama-ku below Amida-ga-mine, was founded in 1160 as the protector deity for Go-Shirakawa's Hōjūji residence.

charged into the enemy before him. The fight stopped. Later on, Aiso showed the helmet and cheek guards (*hatsuburi*) to Tonomura Heizō, an acquaintance of his and a houseman of my father's. "What kind of sword does Imagawa have?" he asked. "I had put this helmet and these cheek plates to the test many a time, but he smashed them and cut my headband (*hachimaki*), and the wound so stunned me that I withdrew." Thereafter my father named the sword Happa-ō, explaining that the incident had involved two *hachi*.[486] The late Noriuji asked for the sword and armguard, which are now heirlooms. The sword was forged by Kuniyoshi.

13. The Hosokawa and the Imagawa disagree

When our side lost the battle of Tagoshi-gawara in Suruga, in Kenmu 2 [1335],[487] Hosokawa Jōzen urged Tadayoshi to die in battle. An aging warrior named Fuchibe said, "I shall die first in battle, before your eyes." He galloped alone into a great host of the enemy and was struck down. We could not follow him. Imagawa Nagoya Saburō was killed in battle at this time.

My late father said, "This is not the time or place to go out and get killed. Instead, we should withdraw, regroup, and win on another day. He took Tadayoshi's mount by the bit and turned it around. The surrounding men all whipped its haunches and sped it on its way. Darkness fell, and my father remained behind alone, but the enemy did not attack. That night he therefore followed his lord to the lodging at Okitsu.

Later, during the withdrawal toward Kyushu, when at Uo-no-midō in Hyōgo all present were ordered to slit their bellies, Hosokawa Jōzen

---

486 The name consists of two characters for "eight" (*hachi*) and the character for "king" (*ō*). Happa-ō is a guess at how it might be voiced. It seems to play on the words for the "bowl" (*hachi*) of the helmet and for the cheek guards (*hatsuburi* or *hatsumuri*).

487 In Kenmu 2 (1335) Takauji captured Kamakura and threatened to turn against Go-Daigo. An army under Nitta Yoshisada then moved to crush him. In response Takauji sent an army under Kō no Moronao to Mikawa. Moronao lost the battle of Yahagi-gawa, and on Kenmu 2.12.2 Takauji's brother then lost badly to Yoshisada at Tagoshi-gawara. According to *Taiheiki*, Yoshisada's archers rained arrows on Tadayoshi's men from behind, under cover of darkness, and the men fled in all directions.

urged Tadayoshi instead to board a boat. My late father urged him to act as ordered.

Thereafter Tadayoshi told these stories often. Both times he thought that he was finished, but the two courses urged on him clashed. "To me," he would say, "any worthy warrior's heart should be the same as any other's, and I still cannot understand this difference of opinion." These incidents are so well known that I think that they should be added to *Taiheiki*. I have noted them here in case they are not.

14. Imagawa Yorikuni's death in battle

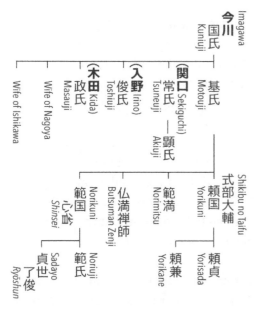

At the time of the conflict provoked by the Kamakura loyalist rebellion (*Nakasendai no ran*, 1335), [488] Imagawa Yorikuni went down as commander along the Coast Road. At Saya-no-nakayama he killed Nagoe. [489] The enemy along the Coast Road held an impregnable position at Yumoto in Sagami. He crossed the hills to the north, with his small band charged straight into their army from above, and dispersed them.

A recent look at this difficult spot showed that it offers no passage to horse or rider. Yorikuni had hurtled down five rocky *chō* steeper than Ichinotani.[490] He had received Matsukaze, his superb, spirited mount, from Nijō-dono. The skin was apparently stripped from the horse's legs and haunches.

---

[488] See *Baishōron*, "The Battle of the Kantō" and "The Kamakura Loyalist Rebellion."

[489] The Hōjō commander.

[490] Yoshitsune's daring ride down the rocky ravine at Ichinotani, in *Heike monogatari* 9.

Now, the Sagami River was running high at the time, and the enemy stood fast. Sasaki Dōyo and his men crossed at the upper and lower fords. Yorikuni's particularly strong middle force crossed at a spot so especially difficult that men and horses alike took arrows in the middle of the river and were killed. Imagawa Saburō [Sekiguchi Akiuji] and one Kawabata were killed together. Yorikuni took twenty arrows. My late father was then with Takauji and did not take part in the battle. Eventually he retrieved Yorikuni's body from the bottom of the river. Perhaps it was excessive cleverness that caused Yorikuni's death at this dangerous spot. His sons Yorisada, Yorikane, and Mitsuyo went into retirement and died.

At the same time Norimitsu[491] was killed at Kotesashi-hara in Musashi. Seriously ill, he apparently had himself lifted onto his horse and fought tied on with leather straps attached to his legs. When one leg was severed he had a houseman named Sakata Saemon take his head. Lacking a successor, he had adopted Yorikane's younger brother Shichirō, and when Shichirō died young the line ended. Butsuman Zenji, abbot of Kenchōji and Engakuji, was the fourth son.[492]

In the days of the Hōjō everyone renounced the world, and in his twenty-third year my late father [born 1297] apparently did so, too. Why? Motouji [Ryōshun's grandfather] always held during his lifetime that, among all the brothers, my late father was the one to succeed to him; or so my grandmother told me. His childhood name was Matsumaru, and he was known as Gorō Norikuni.

[Sekiguchi] Tsunekuni, Toshiuji, and so on were all brothers of Motouji. They are the grandfathers of the present Sekiguchi, Irino, and Kida.

---

491 A son of Motouji.
492 Butsuman Zenji (Daiki Hokkin, 1297-1349), a son of Motouji.

NANTAIHEIKI

PART TWO

15. The battle of Aonogahara[493]

It must have been in Kenmu 4 [1337] or Kōei 1 [1342][494] that the thirty-thousand strong Ōshū army under Akiie, the son of Kitabatake Chikafusa, drove toward the capital. The Utsunomiya men and those of Miura-no-suke joined Momonoi Naotsune to attack them from the rear. My late father, then camped at Mikura-yama in Tōtōmi, hastened to join them, and battles ensued here and there along the Coast Road. From Mikawa, Kira Mitsuyoshi, Kō no Morokane, the Mikawa contingent, and others, more than two thousand in all, rushed to join them and reached Kuroda in Mino. There the protector of the province, Toki Yoritō, came forth from Toki-yama with the announced intention of joining battle at Aonogahara.[495]

Since the next day's battle would be decisive, the men on the Coast Road divided into three sections and took turns drawing lots to decide which should start out first, second, or third. Momonoi and the Utsunomiya contingent drew First; my late father and Miura-no-suke drew Second; and Kira, the Mikawa men, and Kō no Morokane drew

---

[493] In Kenmu 2 (1335) Takauji rebelled against Go-Daigo. Kitabatake Akiie, Go-Daigo's commander in the north, then marched on Kyoto; in alliance with Nitta Yoshisada forced Takauji's retreat to Kyushu; and returned north. In Kenmu 2.8, Akiie and Nitta Yoshioki, summoned back by Go-Daigo, took Kamakura. In Ryakuō 1.1 (1338; Southern Court Engen 3) Akie continued westward together with Prince Muneyoshi (Go-Daigo's son) and Hōjō Tokiyuki. At the battle of Aonogahara (now Sekigahara in present Gifu-ken) he defeated Toki Yoritō, then moved south. Kō no Moronao defeated him at Izumi Sakai in Ryakuō 1.5. According to *Taiheiki*, he died in battle at Abeno while retreating toward Yoshino.

[494] The correct year is Kenmu 4 (1337; Southern Court Engen 2). Akiie died in 1338.

[495] *Taiheiki* 19 incudes an account of the battle ("Aonogahara no ikusa no koto").

Third. The Momonoi men all wore hawk bells. My late father devised a helmet badge (*kasajirushi*),[496] and that night he abruptly decided to put an *akatori*[497] on his horse.

Inagaki Hachirō, Yonekura Hachirōzaemon, Kagazume Matasaburō, Hiraga Gorō and some other young bloods decided that the lottery was all very well, but they preferred to precede the attacking force. Eleven of them therefore charged ahead of Momonoi up a hill known as Akasakaguchi-ameushi-yama. As far as their side could tell, they were enemy men racing up the hill. The first to reach the top, a warrior on an *ashige* horse, was cut down, as were those who followed him. All were killed and tumbled back down the slope.

When their side grasped that these men had been their own, the lead force joined battle. Defeated, the Momonoi and Utsunomiya contingents retreated to Kuise-gawa,[498] south of the Akasaka post station. My late father then replaced them. He killed an enemy named Yamauchi and his men and then, at Nishi-no-nawateguchi, personally shot from their mounts two warriors wearing *horo*.[499]

The enemy still held, however, so he moved down to the outcaste (*hinin*) houses on the Kuise-gawa dike. That night it rained. When the enemy failed to renew the attack, the men around him urged him to join the Kuroda contingent. He declared that he would wait in place for the main army to arrive the next day. Yonekura Hachirōzaemon, who was present despite being wounded, declared, "The best thing to do with such a fool of a commander would be to burn him to death. Set him on fire—the light will attract the Kuroda."

Momonoi said, "In battle, the key to survival is mutual retreat. Fall back a little before an advancing enemy, regroup and move forward again, and the enemy will retreat in turn. Good timing is what secures great fame." As my late father often remarked later on, "Momonoi was one to lose repeatedly in battle against a superior force. No old saw can save a man from his destined fate. The thing is to fight first and retreat only when you can do no more."

---

[496] To distinguish his men from others, especially the enemy.
[497] See note to the next section for a discussion of this word.
[498] The present Ibi-gawa in Gifu-ken.
[499] A sort of cape that protected against enemy arrows.

Now Toki Yoritō advanced and reinforced them by cutting off Kuroji-gawa[500] [between Mino and Ōmi] from the capital side. Our side fought clashes along the Coast Road. After the battle of Aonogahara the Ōshū contingent started along the Ise Road, and fought battles in Nara and at Tennōji. Troops from the capital rushed to engage it on the Kumozu-gawa near Ise, but they lost.

Only Toki Yoritō won glory at Aonogahara. Apparently he was wounded. *Taiheiki* records the battle but unfortunately says nothing about my late father's tremendous efforts there. Perhaps the author never inquired, or we on our side never recorded what had happened. No one in later generations will know of his magnificent achievement. That is a shame. I hope that this account will be added to the work.[501]

16. An oracle at the Fuji Sengen Shrine

The province of Suruga and several tens of domains (*shoryō*) rewarded this rear attack at Aonogahara. I was in my early youth when those involved received them. When I went with my father to salute the Fuji Sengen Shrine, a woman medium (*shinnyo*) delivered an oracle.[502]

"I wanted the nearby province of Tōtōmi for my own *ujiko*,"[503] the divinity said. "I therefore asked before the Akasaka clash, "Do you follow me? (*shireri ya*) Do you follow me?"

My father moved back from where he sat. "What is this about?" he asked. "I do not understand."

The oracle continued, "When you considered that helmet badge I gave you an *akatori*, and that is what won you both victory and this province."

Then my father remembered. "In battle one normally shuns anything to do with women," he reflected. "Where did I get that idea? From the deity, obviously." Fully convinced, he ordered that in the future I and his descendants should always have an *akatori* with us.

---

[500] The border between Mino and Ōmi.
[501] The *Taiheiki* account indeed lacks this material.
[502] The medium speaks as Konohanasakuya-hime, the deity of the Fuji Sengen Shrine. Ryōshun's father, Norikuni, was protector of Tōtōmi at the time.
[503] Roughly, a Shinto "parishioner."

And so, even in Kyushu, I dreamed before every major battle of women riders, as did others; and when I did I always won. That is how the *akatori* became for our house our greatest weapon of war.[504]

17. Sadayo gives up Suruga

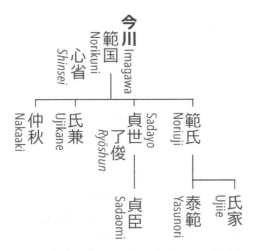

My father meant me to inherit Suruga, but Noriuji [Ryōshun's elder brother] was so eager for it that I repeatedly declined. My father offered it to me again after Noriuji had passed away, but with his permission I passed it to Ujiie [Noriuji's son]. Perhaps out of gratitude Ujiie ceded it before his death without heir to Sadaomi [Ryōshun's son], while Sadaomi was still known as Sonshōmaru. Saddened to think that Noriuji might still be watching from beneath the sod, Sadaomi then recalled Yasunori from Kenchōji, where he was a monk; had him cover his head; and ceded him the province together with his domains. The Deputy Shogun of the time, Hosokawa Yoriyuki, was not alone in calling this gesture unexampled.

The utterly ungrateful Yasunori next coveted Tōtōmi and denounced me to higher authority as entertaining further ambitions. Alas, none of this would have happened if Sadaomi had not recalled

---

[504] Depending on how it is written, *akatori* means either "red bird" or "dirt remover." The "red bird" is a red cloth draped over a woman's saddle to avoid soiling her clothes. The "dirt remover" is at once the Japanese counterpart of a curry comb, used to clean a horse's coat, and a crest ⛩ favored by the Imagawa in the Sengoku period. What Ryōshun's father put on his horse (*niwaka ni tsukerareki*) remains unclear. Why have a "red bird" with him, if in battle a man shuns anything to do with women? However, a "red bird" is what the Fuji deity (female) claims to have given him. What did Ryōshun take into battle in Kyushu? Perhaps in the realm of oracles and dreams all *a-ka-to-ri* objects are the same.

Yasunori to lay life over Suruga. "If you do not accept what heaven gives you...," they say, and rightly. Claiming I had demanded the half of Suruga that I received, Yasunori then angrily required the province of Tōtōmi in compensation. There was no shame in all that, since everyone then knew what was going on. The present Shogun must remember the affair, and I need not enlarge on it.

Being no doubt familiar already with family treachery, my father in his last testament urged obedience. However, the Shogun of the time [Yoshimitsu] remained oblivious, which is probably what allowed this iniquitous relative to succeed. It is a dreadful business.

Earlier, the Shogun had wished Nakaaki[505] to have Tōtōmi, although it is not clear why. Perhaps my leaving Tōtōmi in compliance with his will also had to do with all this.[506]

18. A move to have Sadayo assassinate Kiyouji

My late father gave outstandingly loyal service when Hosokawa Kiyouji came under suspicion, but *Taiheiki* only says that the Shogun [Yoshiakira] repaired to Imagumano.[507] A crisis was looming when my father said privately to the Shogun, "I understand that Sadayo [Ryōshun] is close to Kiyouji. In order to avoid a major incident you might

---

[505] Nakaaki accompanied Ryōshun to Kyushu and helped to lay the groundwork for Ryōshun's success there, in part by marrying into the Ōuchi house.

[506] To summarize the matter of Tōtōmi: Ryōshun followed his father as protector of Tōtōmi in Shitoku 1 (1384). In Kakei 2 (1388), while Kyushu administrator, he ceded it to his younger brother and adopted his son, Nakaaki. In Ōei 2 (1395) Ryōshun was dismissed as administrator and became protector of half of Suruga. However, he came under suspicion in connection with the Ōei Disturbance, and in Ōei 7 (1400) Suruga and Tōtōmi were both awarded to Yasunori.

[507] *Taiheiki* 36 ("Kiyouji hongyaku no koto") relates that slander by Sasaki Dōyo, a rival, led Yoshiakira in Kōan 1 (1361) to suspect Hosokawa Kiyouji (?-1362) of rebellion. Yoshiakira quickly fortified himself at Imagumano, where Ryōshun's older brother Noriuji, among others, rushed to join him. (*Gukanki* for Kōan 1.9.23 says that Go-Kōgon secretly went there as well.) Kiyouji, who according to *Taiheiki* had no such intention, fled to Wakasa and eventually joined the Southern Court. "Repaired to" translates *nyūgyo*, a word applicable in principle only to an emperor or empress. Ryōshun's use of it for Yoshiakira suggests the gradual breakdown of the formal distinction between shogun and emperor in the aftermath of the Kannō Anarchy.

summon him and have him stab Kiyouji to death. That would save you having to kill a large number of men."

I was in Tōtōmi at the time. A courier recalled me to the capital. I had reached the mountains of Mikawa when a second courier informed me that Kiyouji had fled to Wakasa. When I arrived in the capital my father told me what my mission had been. I was appalled. Since the mission had been my father's idea, and the claim of rebellious intent was false, Kiyouji privately summoned Naoyo [Ryōshun's younger brother] in order to protest his innocence. Naoyo was too frightened to go, so Kiyouji told Nobuaki, of the Office of Music (*Gakusho*), that Sadayo should come instead, if currently in the capital. At this my father apparently volunteered his own services. As everyone knew, the Shogun recognized how loyal it was of my father to take his son's place in order to bring this grave matter to an uneventful conclusion. Why, then, does *Taiheiki* say nothing on the subject? Perhaps no one had told the author about it.

At the time, a *rakugaki* appeared:

> *hosokawa ni kagamari orishi ebina koso*
> *imagawa idete koshi wa nobashitare*
> Bent under Skinny River [Hosokawa], Ebina at last
> stood tall once New River [Imagawa] turned up.

It presumably alludes to Kiyouji's hatred of Ebina Bitchū-no-kami, who therefore refused to serve him. It is only a joke, but I have noted it because concerns a matter then current.

19. The question of Kiyouji's ambition

Did Hosokawa Kiyouji really harbor no such ambition? Perhaps someone sought his downfall for having, in an excess of pride, disobeyed his lord. For one thing, he took his sons on pilgrimage to Hachiman, where he wore an *eboshi* at the shrine and styled himself Hachiman Hachirō. [508] For another thing—so the shrine priests reported—the written prayer (*ganmon*) that he lodged at the sanctuary contained a passage about aspiring to take over the realm. My father

---

[508] Hachirō was his own name.

wondered whether this prayer was really in Kiyouji's own writing, and he suspected the paper of being the wrong size.

At the time of the Tōji battle I was ordered into Kiyouji's contingent. I fought under him twice, and he undertook to approach the Shogun on my behalf.[509] Once peace had returned I applied for the then-vacant Kasahara and Hamamatsu estates in Tōtōmi. However, I did not get them. Both went to Kiyouji. Disappointed, I stayed in Tōtōmi and was not in the capital at the time. The Shogun believed me to be intimate with Kiyouji, which is why my father suggested what he did. In this way I gained approval and could succeed to my father after he received leave to retire.

20. Ujimitsu's rebellious intent[510]

Ashikaga Ujimitsu in Kamakura [511] then decided that the current Shogun's [Yoshimitsu's] governance excessively favored certain individuals, and he lamented that the shogunal house would be lost if an exceptionally able man were ever to emerge and seize the realm. He therefore decided to seize the realm himself rather than lose it to someone else. His intent to rebel for the sake of all the people of the realm was so widely known that, even if the Shogun did not, alas, exactly turn over a new leaf and govern entirely according to the principles of benevolence, he at least moderated his recent, evil excesses. With this people should have been content.

Why, then, did Ujimitsu take that position? Considering that the Shogun's good fortune was secure and his authority great, despite constant complaints, who would have wished to side with Ujimitsu as

---

[509] After Tadayoshi's death by poisoning in 1352, his adopted son, Tadafuyu, moved against the capital (and Takauji) together with Yamana Tokiuji, Momonoi Naotsune, and Shiba Takatsune. He occupied it briefly in Bunna 4 [1355], but Takauji repulsed him. The "Tōji battle" narrated in *Gen'ishū* occurred at this time.

[510] See the Introduction for a summary of the complexities and, for Ryōshun, disasters that begin with Yoshimitsu's arbitrary rule and Ujimitsu's ambition to replace him as shogun.

[511] Ujimitsu (kubō 1367-1398) aspired to become shogun himself, and his relationship with Yoshimitsu was extremely tense. His son and successor Mitsukane (kubō 1398-1409) inherited his ambition.

long as the Shogun somewhat modified his manner of governing? Even now, fear inspires many prayers, and there is much talk of suppressing the Kanto. It seems to me, however, foolish as I am, that if the Shogun would drop all such talk and all such prayers, and resolve to set the realm at least to a degree on the right path, Heaven, the Buddhas, and the Gods are sure to be pleased.

Perhaps I might speak of battle. Consider Heaven, Earth, and Man. The benefit (*ri*) of Heaven is to weigh the fortunate character of the year, month, and day, as well as the innate character of the man, and turn them to best advantage. The benefit of Earth involves considering the configuration of a sheltering mountain, of the sea, of some other perilous passage, or of withdrawing into a secure fortress. The benefit of Man is undoubtedly what is right (*kotowari*). They say that the benefits of Heaven and Earth are superfluous when men's hearts join in what is right. In the same way, no evildoer can appear when the hearts of all in Japan are united in gratitude for their lord's blessings. Then all prayers will be answered.

It seems to me that should any evil or injustice arise in the Shogun's desires, and should he wish to redeem them by means of prayer (*kitō*), secret rites (*hihō*) should be effective.

21. Ryōshun dismissed as Kyushu administrator

I had no inordinate ambition whatever when Ōuchi Yoshihiro drove up to Izumi,[512] nor did I receive a single word or written message from Mitsukane.[513] The whole thing must have been Ōuchi's idea. He sent essentially the same directive (*migyōsho*) far and wide, and when I received it I sent it straight on to the Shogun.[514]

---

[512] In Ōei 6.12 (1399) Yoshihiro led an army from Kyushu and Chūgoku to Izumi Sakai.
[513] The Kanto kubō Ashikaga Mitsukane, who had succeeded to his father Ujimitsu in 1398.
[514] Yoshimochi had held the title of shogun since 1386, but Yoshimitsu still wielded the power of the office. Perhaps that is why Ryōshun refers not to a clearly singular shogun (for example, he calls Takauji *Ōgosho*) but to *jōi*, "higher opinion." Below, "Shogun" should be understood as meaning above all Yoshimitsu.

No, my loyalty was in no way divided. However, my sons and housemen in Tōtōmi were slow to reach Sakai, and some therefore accused them of being in league with the Kanto. As a result I heard confidentially that I was under suspicion. The Shogun should have packed me off alone by pirate bark to Kyushu.515 With his conscience pricking, he could availed himself of that way to get rid of me once and for all. The men of Kyushu would have known what to do with me.516 He should have confiscated the directives and orders that I had received, with all their citations of hallowed precedent, and sent me down there alone.

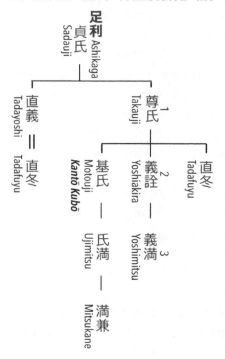

I had received three or four directives merely urging loyalty.517 Increasingly apprehensive about the Shogun's intentions toward me, I decided to retire to my province (*bunkoku*) and entrust my sons' future to him. If Kyoto still refused to spare me, then the Kantō Kubō's [Ujimitsu's] declared intention to take over the realm might insure the future of his house and peace for the people.

Why? When Takauji and Tadayoshi fell out, the people of the realm were unable to prefer one over the other as a transitional successor.518 Each favored the one

---

515 Presumably the fastest conveyance possible. Ryōshun imagines the "pirate bark" belonging to his Kyushu enemies, especially the Ōtomo and the Shimazu.

516 Could this remark possibly have come to Ryōshun's brush if his declared innocence had been (in his mind, at least) a fiction? He wishes that Yoshimitsu had ended his misery immediately.

517 These "directives" are probably from Mitsukane.

518 Until the next generation should come into its own. The introduction to "The Northern Emperors' Journey to Anō, 1352" summarizes the savage quarrel between Takauji and Tadayoshi over succession to the office of shogun. Ryōshun's anodyne remarks about the two, below, illustrate his resolve to speak well of them at all costs.

he pleased. They reflected, "Tadayoshi allows no personal leaning to affect his governance, and that makes him difficult to dismiss. Takauji, as supreme military commander, has no personal bent either, and he, too, is difficult to dismiss."

As the father of Tadafuyu[519] and Yoshiakira, Takauji could dismiss neither; and although Tadayoshi and Takauji were brothers, at the time of the Kamakura loyalist rebellion, at Hakone-yama. Tadayoshi ceded to Takauji both the realm and the headship of the Ashikaga house. Takauji never forgot that. In order to achieve smooth passage of the realm from Tadayoshi to Yoshiakira he said nothing about the deaths of Moronao and Moroyasu at the battle of Ide in Settsu. He said nothing, either, after the battle of Yui-yama, when Uesugi Noriaki retreated from Izu-yama. The two brothers became closer than ever. This sealed the unity of the two brothers.

They may well have discussed the matter in private. As Shogun [Yoshiakira] would not be able to reverse any position he might take and therefore could not in the end keep the realm for long. Never mind a few errors of governance. If the Kanto daimyo were to unite, they would surely protect this land of Japan. Therefore they agreed that the best course would be to place the Kantō Kubō between them and make him the protector of Kyoto. They therefore ceded the Eight Provinces of the Bandō to Motouji and enjoined upon him protection of Yoshiakira and his line.

After the brothers' passing, those hostile to Kyoto secretly and steadfastly pressed their case to the Kanto [Motouji], but in the end Takauji's wishes prevailed. However, as a consequence of what Tadayoshi had said from Kyoto, Yoshiakira may have feared that Kamakura might declare Motouji Shogun on its own. Foreseeing disaster for the realm, he prayed to the gods, and Motouji died before him. That is what I have heard.[520] No one knows the truth of the matter.

---

519 The original has Nakagosho (Takauji being Ōgosho). Tadafuyu seems more likely than the other possibility, Motouji.

520 Motouji (1349-1367) died on Jōji 6.2.27, in his twenty-eighth year. His death is attributed to an epidemic, but Ryōshun may be suggesting that he was poisoned. Yoshiakira (1330-1367) died on Jōji 6.12.7.

In the present instance,[521] I simply resolved after going down to Tōtōmi that, since Takauji had so willed it, his house should retain governance of the realm, and that I would respect its will to govern well. Then, however, just when rumor was insisting that a force was on the way down from Kyoto to suppress me, I heard that, in even the Kanto, Uesugi [Norisada] had strenuously urged reconciliation [on Mitsukane]. In fear of what action Kyoto might take, I therefore retired to Fujisawa, entrusting my sons meanwhile to the good will of Kyoto and Kamakura. Nonetheless, even after reconciliation had been agreed, word had it that I was still egging Kamakura-dono [Mitsukane] on. Kyoto may well have believed it, and Uesugi as well. For better or worse, my fate lay in the hands of the Kanto.

Under the terms of the reconciliation, Kyoto and the Kanto agreed that there would be no change to the distribution of provinces and fiefs, so that I was presumably free to retire where I liked. I let Uesugi know repeatedly that I preferred my province, and indeed I returned there. However, the Kanto only referred the decision to Kyoto, stating that in case of trouble the Kanto was prepared to deal with it. Although dismayed, I was also grateful to receive repeatedly an undertaking from Kyoto, in view of my past loyal service, to spare my life if I would present myself there. I therefore did so.

Reflection suggests that it is rash respect for old ties and obligations that destroyed me and ruined my good name. The consequences exceed grief. It was presumptuous of me ever to go to Kyushu. Why? Because even though the Shogun of the time [Yoshimitsu] showed me rather less warmth and kindness than he did others, I had resolved wholly to forget myself in loyal service to his house; so that when ordered to pacify the western provinces, I simply set out in that spirit to do so. I led several hundred family members and housemen to their deaths, in the end destroyed my reputation, and even lost my lands. No one belonging to my house could have imagined such an outcome.

A man must give loyal service consonant with his proper station. Service beyond it is certain to cause resentment.

---

[521] The possibility that Ashikaga Ujimitsu might succeed in becoming shogun.

22. A visit from Ōuchi Yoshihiro

Some years ago, when Ōtomo [Chikayo] returned to his province,[522] Ōuchi Yoshihiro paid me a quiet visit. He said: "Ōtomo has consolidated his holdings from start to finish thanks to your support, and now that I know all you have done for him, I am deeply disappointed that during this stay to the capital, prompted by the Shogun's displeasure, he should have made no gesture to thank you before leaving again. That was rude and uncouth of him. However, in the present instance, it would be just as well if you were to do him the further kindness of seeing him before he leaves. He will show you more loyalty in the future if I can take you to the harbor of Hyōgo, while he is still there, and effect a reconciliation.

I answered: "I have never felt any antipathy toward Ōtomo. I am here in the capital, by order of the Kantō Kubō [Ujimitsu], because he killed Yoshihiro [Ujisato].[523] Ōtomo insisted that I decide whether or not he should make the trip, and while on the way here I simply sent word back to him that he should. I was questioned when I got here and asked why Ōtomo considered me an enemy, and why he had denounced me. I replied that I had no idea. After Ōtomo's arrival I heard nothing from him. However, I have never addressed [to the Shogun] a single word against him. If he is now talking of wanting to see me because he regrets the error of his ways, I am not against it. However, I have been ordered back down to Kyushu as quickly as possible, and I will be leaving soon. Moreover, on the subject of Ōtomo I have precise instructions. It might displease our lord if I myself were to suggest meeting him. However, I suppose that I might meet him anyway, now that you have already mentioned the idea. Or perhaps I would do better first discreetly to seek higher approval.

Ōuchi answered: "Please keep me out of it. By our lord's command I have twice submitted, in my own writing, an oath never to support

---

[522] Ōtomo Chikayo, the shugo of Bungo, was Yoshihiro's son-in-law.

[523] The "Yoshihiro" of Ōuchi's given name and that of Ujisato's surname differ by one character. Why Ōtomo Chikayo killed Yoshihiro Ujisato, a relative of his, remains unclear.

Ōtomo. It is up to you to propose the idea and to seek private authorization to proceed."

Again, when rumor had it that at any moment I might turn against my lord [Yoshimitsu], Ōuchi came to me and said: "Our lord's actions suggest that the weak, even when guilty of next to nothing, arouse his suspicion and end up disgraced; while everyone knows that he leaves the strong alone despite their opposition. You may feel protected by your loyal service and your standing, but any flaw in your strength could easily mean disgrace. For myself, I have acquired provinces and estates beyond my station, and I mean to ensure that I do not lose them. You, Ōtomo, and I will not suffer, despite our lord's objections, if we unite. He will not move against us. Here in the capital I see nothing good in any of the other daimyo. If you and I together were to unite Kyushu and the western provinces, lasting peace would follow. After all, Ōtomo is a Kyushu daimyo. You would have nothing to fear if we were to unite under your leadership. I therefore propose that I should write out the articles of an oath that binds us and our descendants in firm union. That is why I want to patch things up with Ōtomo.

I answered again: "You and Nakaaki are related by marriage, as everyone knows. Mutual assistance between you requires no solemn pact. Moreover, what you propose would call down suspicion on us both, and a formal alliance between us would slight our lord. Foolish I may be, but that is not something that I could do. For that reason you must not for my sake risk the ruin of your house. Only give the Shogun your full allegiance, and you need fear no loss of provinces and lands. As to Ōtomo, you have already received your instructions, and any attempt at reconciliation on my part would be superfluous. The best thing you could do for him would be to recommend discretion and, for the good of the realm, renunciation of self-interest."

Unfortunately, in Kyushu and in this connection as well, for reasons both private and public, it is Ōuchi's schemes that led to my leaving Kyushu. To put it simply, every one of the Shogun's directives countered the wishes of the men of Kyushu, who therefore suspected me of perfidy and self-interest, and rejected me. I assumed that the Kyushu issue would be settled if I went up to the capital and truthfully answered the Shogun on the matter, but I never had a chance to do so.

Do the Kyushu men still imagine me to have been following my self-interest? Still, the truth always comes out in the end, and surely everyone knows by now that the judgment imposed upon me was wrong.

Furthermore, when Ōuchi revealed his intentions by marching on Izumi, the Shogun immediately remarked to me, "I see now that you were quite right about Ōuchi. I am ashamed of myself." Everyone heard about this.

As far as I can see, I lost my place in the world because I did things that turned out badly for me solely as a result of being old-fashioned. I might have done better to behave, according to circumstance, iniquitously, unjustly, or rudely. The unfilial son; the unjust elder brother; the disloyal, disobedient retainer; the immoral, scurrilous townsman or peasant end up in their time injuring other people. It is the same everywhere.

I have set this down in order to urge care and caution on my descendants. No one is to see it while I still live. Beware! Beware!

> *ko yo mago yo onore sakashi to omou tomo*
> *oya no oroka ni nao ya otoran*
> My sons, my grandsons, you might think yourselves wise,
> but that would make you still more foolish than your father.

Ōei 9.2 [1402]
Tokuō, in his seventy-eighth year

Appended remarks

(1) Zuisenji-dono [Ashikaga Motouji], in Kamakura, has the same name as my grandfather. This has to do with the notion that it is auspicious to give one family member the name of another who promises little (*mutoku no hito*). That may be a good idea. As far as I know, Nitta names match those of ancestors on my side. My father first gave Sadaomi [Ryōshun's eldest son] the name Yoshinori for that reason, and it was unfilial of me, in recent years in Kyushu, to have renamed him Sadaomi.

This year I suffer so from palsy (*chūbu*) that at times I cannot control my wandering brush. My writing is becoming worse and worse. I skip characters or kana. Such are the ravages of age, for which I beg the reader's indulgence.

(2) People attribute my departure from Kyushu to the scheming of two men: Ōuchi [Yoshihiro], who coveted the post of administrator for himself, and Kadenokōji [Shiba Yoshiyuki], who plotted to have it awarded to Shikukawa [Mitsuyori]. It was a clever move, they say, once with great difficulty and at the cost of vast labor I had quelled a powerful enemy, to give the post to a relative by marriage who had contributed nothing to this success.[524] Indeed, the thought of Bitchū makes me ashamed about Shibukawa. I can say no more.

---

[524] Shibukawa Mitsuyori was Shiba Yoshimasa's son-in-law.

CPSIA information can be obtained
at www.ICGtesting.com
Printed in the USA
LVHW010013290722
724659LV00001B/42